BAMIE

BAMIE

Theodore Roosevelt's Remarkable Sister

by
LILIAN RIXEY

DAVID McKAY COMPANY, INC.

New York

BAMIE

LIBRARY OF CONGRESS CATALOG CARD NUMBER: 63-19339

MANUFACTURED IN THE UNITED STATES OF AMERICA

VAN REES PRESS • NEW YORK

Preface

ONCE, speaking only partly in jest, Alice Roosevelt Longworth said of her aunt, Anna Roosevelt Cowles, "If Auntie Bye had been a man, *she* would have been president."

This was praise indeed from the devoted daughter of Theodore Roosevelt, for Alice Longworth never could see anyone but her father in the White House. Stranger still, no one outside the older generation of Roosevelts and their immediate circle seems ever to have heard of Alice Longworth's aunt. The beloved "Auntie Bye" of a dozen Roosevelt nieces and nephews, who called her that because she was always on the go, deserves better of history.

Anna Roosevelt Cowles was the favorite sister of Theodore Roosevelt. He called her "Bamie," a family nickname from the Italian *bambina*. She was also the wife of a high-ranking American naval officer. In the early 1900s, as the President's sister; as "Mrs. Admiral" Cowles, following the custom of an earlier day; and very much as herself, Bamie Roosevelt Cowles set the social tone in Washington, giving that city its first taste of elegant entertaining after the manner of the French salonistes. Her modest house on Washington's N Street, which was within easy walking distance for such an active perambulator as the twenty-sixth president of the United States, was known, for good reason, as "The Little White House." There Theodore Roosevelt held his first

Cabinet meetings, and there, throughout his time in office, he met the people he wished to see informally and unofficially.

History's neglect of Bamie Roosevelt seems odd. Yet, as her old friend, Henry Adams, wrote, "American history mentioned hardly the name of a woman, while English history handled them as timidly as though they were a new and undescribed species." Which was why, no doubt, he preferred his studies in ancient and medieval times, for there, as he observed in *The Education of Henry Adams*, women appeared as they really are, "Always busy in the illusions of heaven or hell—ambition, intrigue, jealousy, magic. . . ."

These elements, particularly the magic of her own unusual charm, are abundantly present in the story of Bamie Roosevelt Cowles. She was ambitious, but only and always for Theodore. There were many, including his own wife, who were jealous of her influence, though Bamie did her best to conceal it. And it took intrigue, of a very high order, to help keep the diplomatic channels open, particularly between England and America, during the days when Theodore Roosevelt led this country into its first overt challenge of Britain's world leadership.

For an extremely successful politician, Theodore Roosevelt was notoriously mercurial in his personal relations and, self-admittedly, no judge of people. He gave his trust and affection instantly and without question. He could, when disappointed or crossed, just as quickly hate with a vengeance. As a close friend of Theodore's warned a new acquaintance, "You must always remember that the President is about six."

In judging people, Bamie and his wife, Edith, were both invaluable to the President. But Bamie, much more than Edith, was wise in the world's ways and at home in the political and social life of two continents, a fact that no doubt sparked some of the undercurrent tension between wife and sister.

Edith was a dignified and decorative First Lady, as well as an exemplary mother, but Bamie was the one who first put Washington on the map, socially speaking. Her influence lasted from 1901, when the Republican Roosevelts first came to power, well through the 1920s, when her niece, Alice, who had become the wife of House Speaker Nicholas Longworth, began to rule the roost. It lasted even down into the 1930s, when the Democratic Roosevelts descended on Washington, for Bamie was also the favorite aunt of Eleanor Roosevelt and Eleanor's adviser on things social and political.

The three most important women in the Roosevelt family—Bamie, Alice, and Eleanor—all had in common a generous share of that remarkable family's outstanding traits. Off stage and on, each of them possessed and exhibited courage, and all three were gallant. On high family occasions, as in times of family crisis, they acted in concert across party lines and often on the world stage with regal grace and dignity. All three had political influence. Alice, following her aunt's example, was a behind-scenes power in the Republican party. Eleanor, unlike her aunt in that respect, achieved high visibility as the Democratic party's elder stateswoman. But first there was Bamie, and indeed it was her early enthusiasm for politics that greatly influenced her brother, Theodore, in his choice of a career, just as it was Bamie's own highly developed political talent, always exercised in his support, that helped make him the president he was.

Speaking of her aunt's influence on her father and taking sober second thought, it seemed to Alice Longworth that "Auntie Bye" was more like Mark Hanna, the Maker of Presidents, than presidential material herself. In either case, Bamie's career speaks for itself in these pages, and her story, supported by an unpublished memoir she left for her son, W. Sheffield Cowles, Jr., and much newly uncovered personal correspondence, is told here for the first time.

"... Busy in the illusions of heaven or hell—
ambition, intrigue, jealousy, magic...."

Henry Adams

Contents

Illustrations

PART I

Early Life of an Unofficial Person

CHAPTER I

Big People

AT the age of ten, Theodore Roosevelt knew that everything concerning himself would someday matter to history. In
order to make the dramatis personae of his story quite clear to
posterity, he then wrote in his diary: "When I put 'We 3' I mean
Ellie Conie and I. When I put 'big people' I mean Papa Mama
and Bamie."

Ellie was young brother Elliott who would become the father
of Eleanor Roosevelt. Conie was younger sister Corinne who
would grow up to be one of New York's most attractive social
leaders. She was also to achieve fame as a minor poet, but
Corinne Roosevelt Robinson would be better known as the
grandmother of two Washington journalists, the Alsop brothers;
as a Republican campaign speaker; and as a perpetuator of her
brother's memory. Bamie defies easy description.

Once Theodore almost succeeded in capturing, in a phrase, his
older sister, Bamie, who was the first Anna Eleanor Roosevelt.
He said she was "a kind of little feminine Atlas with a small
world on her shoulders," and so she seemed to Theodore when
he was a young man, and for many years thereafter. She was
exactly three years and nine months older than he, but from
the first, Bamie belonged with the "big people."

Her nickname, short for *bambina,* had been given her by her
father, but even he could not regard her as an infant for long.

Before she outgrew baby talk, she was independent, determined, and precociously mature. Her father, in his love and concern for his firstborn, had done much to make her that way.

When the Roosevelt family prepared to escape New York's summer heat for the New Jersey shore and Bamie's nurse tried to help her get ready, she would say, "Dora pack Dora trunk. Bamie pack Bamie trunk," and that would be that. The remark became a family classic, one to be quoted whenever it seemed necessary to tell another member of the family, politely but firmly, to mind his own business.

After Ellie was big enough to toddle, Bamie would further lighten Dora's summer chores at the beach by taking full charge of her two young brothers. This was not duty but fun for all. She simply hitched them up in a toy double-harness and encouraged them to play horsie by the hour. The secret of her success with younger males even in those days was that Bamie, reins firmly in hand, enjoyed these barefoot romps on the beach quite as much as Tedie and Ellie did.

The remarkable thing about this behavior was not that an older sister should achieve some ascendancy over such rambunctious young brothers; it was a miracle that Bamie could, by the time she was eight, actually romp and play. None of the family had expected she would ever be able to walk. She had been dropped in her bath as a very small baby, and her spine had been injured. Her first memories, at the age of three, were of being carried, by her father, from the nursery of their home in Manhattan, to lie all day on a sofa on the wisteria-covered back piazza.

She could remember spending her entire time on that sofa, harnessed in some "terrible instrument," and still this had been "a period of great happiness." Each day she would lie there waiting for her father to come home from business. She would listen for "the click in the front door of his key, his quick, light running up the stairs." He would bring ice cream or fruit "or some little thing for me" and would "frequently sit with me until I had my supper." And then, "with his very strong arms," he would "quietly carry me back into the nursery where I slept."

That winter—it was 1858, some months before Theodore was born—her father discovered a young physician, Dr. Charles F. Taylor, who had the revolutionary idea that special exercises could help Bamie. Now limited to her cot in the nursery all day, she would try to move this way and that, as the doctor taught her to do, as Father said she must do, to get well. As she grew stronger, her father brought her a toy iron. "It was a little iron you put something warm into," Bamie recalled, "and I ironed the top of my sheet on the bed all the time, feeling I was greatly helping with family things." Then when she was strong enough to sit up by herself, her father came home with a toy Franklin stove on which he and his daughter cooked make-believe meals. At first, her father had to do most of the pretending. He would stoke the stove with small chips whittled from a piece of kindling and even put a tiny pot of rice on to boil. Of course it never did, Bamie recalled, "But I felt that I had been cooking most industriously."

Long before October, 1858, when Tedie was born, Bamie was up and about, wearing the new, light harness Dr. Taylor had designed for her. She had moved out of the nursery adjoining the piazza on the second floor and to the third floor where all the "big people" lived.

The children of the first Theodore Roosevelt grew up in New York during Civil War times, when the old Van Cortlandt Farm, over which their father had ridden horseback as a young man, was renamed Union Square. They lived in the fashionable part of Manhattan that then extended from Canal Street north to Gramercy Park, a pleasance their Dutch forebears knew as the *Kromer See,* or "crooked lake." By the time Bamie and Theodore were born, the *Kromer See* had been drained for health's sake and to accommodate the march up Manhattan Island of row on row of new town houses. The house of their grandfather, who began in hardware and did even better as a glass importer and investor in city real estate, occupied a full block front on Broadway, between Thirteenth and Fourteenth

Streets. He gave each of his sons, as they married, one of the comfortable new row brownstones within easy, though often muddy, walking distance of his own Broadway mansion. The children's father, Theodore Roosevelt, Sr., and his brother, Robert, had two such houses adjoining each other on East Twentieth Street, just off Fifth Avenue.

Whatever went on in those days behind other formal brownstone fronts curtained in rich, heavy lace, the life of Bamie, Tedie, Ellie, and Conie was anything but stiff and Victorian. Their gaiety and wit came from a Southern mother who had no taste or talent for discipline; their energy and zest, from a father who adored them all. Bamie's recollections of their childhood in the house on Twentieth Street, which always seemed more home than any other, were to remain vivid all her life.

"My father," she remembered proudly, "was far ahead of the people of his period in his ideas concerning the health of his children. He felt that though the climate of New York was severe, still we must have a great deal of life in the open air. The Twentieth Street house was built in the fatal period when all houses of about its size possessed a middle, dark room. He decided that to sleep in such a room was most unhygienic, and had the second story back bedroom made into a piazza, with a railing about nine feet high, and otherwise entirely open on the south. This piazza was fitted with many different athletic paraphernalia, such as parallel bars, swinging bars, ladders, etc. Every day we were allowed to put on our so-called 'piazza clothes' and were turned loose out there for practically the whole morning."

On this verandah, overlooking their backyard and the gardens of their neighbors, Theodore, who was a sickly child plagued with asthma and dyspeptic attacks, gained the physical strength that made a man of him. For Bamie, those mornings on the swinging and parallel bars saved her from being a helpless, distorted cripple. The piazza was so much fun they never thought time spent in this outdoor gymnasium, contrived by an ingenious father for his two eldest who were near-invalids, anything but a

6

special daily treat. Besides, there were always so many exciting things going on in the world immediately surrounding that wonderful back piazza.

"Next door to us," Bamie remembered, "lived our uncle, Mr. Robert Roosevelt, with his wife and family, and they built a similar piazza, which, when they were opened into one another, made a wonderful playground. But unfortunately for our happiness, the aunt next door kept a monkey of violent character. I always thought its temper was ruffled by the fact that she insisted on dressing it perfectly completely as though it were a human being, with finest, most beautiful little shirts and gold studs. It bit us whenever there was a chance, so that the two piazzas were not too often opened.

"One evening I was sent through this back entrance to take a message to my aunt and entered into the nursery and by a small passage to Aunt Lizzie's room. In the small passage the monkey caught me and bit my leg so badly that I bear the marks to this day. It was caught by one of the older cousins and chastised, but my aunt seized it and kept saying, 'poor little Topsy, poor little Topsy,' while I lay on the bed streaked with pain. Fortunately for me, the monkey eluded Aunt Lizzie and went up on top of a wardrobe, where with absolute rage it tore off every garment and flung them on the floor—until it got to its trousers, with which it was totally unable to grapple, as the tail was too long to be pulled through. And I can remember as if it were yesterday lying on the bed and ceasing to feel my wounds while giggling with laughter at the appearance of Topsy dancing up and down trying to get his tail out of his trousers."

Topsy's behavior was, interestingly enough, imitated by brother Tedie, whose first teeth, fortunately for Bamie, were less forbidding than the ones he acquired later. For what reason he could never remember, at the age of four, he bit his sister on the arm, and then, as he tells it in his *Autobiography*, he hid under the kitchen table, dragging with him a huge mess of biscuit dough left momentarily untended by the Irish cook. When his father reached under the table to drag him out, Tedie in a panic

7

hurled the dough at him and dodged for the stairs that led to the third floor where Mama and the other big people lived. Papa caught him halfway up and gave him his first and only thrashing. It was Bamie who rushed downstairs and begged Papa to desist because Tedie's bite had not hurt at all and besides he meant no harm.

It may have been this sort of headlong behavior on Tedie's part that caused their mother to call him her "little berserker," but Bamie seemed always able to cope. Certainly, in retrospect, "the days in Twentieth Street were more delightful than any others," and there "we had a glorious childhood," with much of the excitement furnished by Aunt Lizzie and the animal life with which she surrounded herself in the house next door.

In the third story of Uncle Robert's house, Bamie recalled, "Aunt Lizzie kept a perfect menagerie—guinea pigs, chickens, pigeons, everything under the sun that ought not to have been kept in a house. A little later in our lives she decided to have a cow in the backyard. So the cow, with great effort, was persuaded down the basement steps, through the hall, and out into the yard. There of course it had no sooner arrived than the entire neighborhood rose in arms and had them threatened with legal action unless the cow was at once removed. This proved almost an impossible deed to accomplish, for the frightened creature refused absolutely to enter the house again, and finally it had to have its legs bound partly together and its eyes blindfolded, and then be dragged out."

In addition to Aunt Lizzie's convenient and accessible menagerie, there was also Mr. Robert Goelet's "huge though very melancholy house" with its own "private zoological garden" that bordered the Roosevelt property in the rear and of which the exercise piazza gave an excellent view. "In that enormous garden with its high iron fence," there were "all manner of strange birds, generally with their wings clipped." But "a magpie seemed to have outgrown the clipping and spent a great deal of one winter stealing everything through our third-story back window."

Bamie recalled, "All of this added excitement to our life as children, especially as whenever a spoon or fork was missing it was always supposed that Topsy had stolen it, though later on we discovered that Topsy had been absolutely maligned." There had been a deep snow that stayed on the roof all winter and "it was not until the snow vanished that a watch and all manner of household articles were found that had been carried out by the magpie, which evidently was not strong enough to fly away with them."

Bamie's preoccupation with the birds and animals that came within her ken, her keen observation, and comments on the behavior of the monkey and the magpie, were no doubt heightened because she could not, until Dr. Taylor's treatment began to take effect, range very far herself. Her fascination with these strange creatures, her stories about them, and the way those stories seemed to delight and amuse their father, undoubtedly convinced young Tedie that all big people were interested in nothing so much as animals, of the pet and domestic variety, and in wild specimens as well. Most small boys sooner or later show some curiosity about species other than themselves, but Theodore's was more than casual. He became obsessed with the idea of collecting every kind of animal he came across, and Bamie helped him develop his own small natural history museum.

By the time their little sister, Conie, was able to remember, the Roosevelt family was spending its summers in Riverdale, just over the Harlem River from Manhattan, and there, she recalled, Bamie did everything to help Tedie in his early efforts to become a naturalist. The cook threatened to leave, but Bamie convinced her there was no harm in letting Tedie keep his dead field mice in the icebox. On another occasion, when Tedie advertised in the local paper offering 10 cents for one field mouse and 35 for an entire family, and then was taken off to the Berkshires by his mother for his health, it was Bamie who took delivery of whole families of dead mice offered in quantity and paid for them all out of her own allowance. The family of squirrels he left behind she kept alive by bottle-feeding, and when the turtles in the basement began to multiply, it was Bamie who convinced the laundress they were perfectly harmless and no sufficient cause to give notice.

The Civil War and its repercussions scarcely reached into the nursery on Twentieth Street, but it was a shattering time for all the big people. The Georgia plantation on which the children's mother, Mittie Bulloch Roosevelt, had been reared, before she married Theodore Roosevelt, Sr., at the age of eighteen, was less than twenty miles from Atlanta and right in line with Sherman's march to the sea. "Roswell" was not burned to the ground, but it was looted, and the war left the entire Bulloch family penniless. Mittie's mother and her sister, Annie, had to seek refuge in her home in the hateful North, and, from the time of their arrival, the three Southern ladies immediately closed ranks. Thenceforth, Mittie refused to attend the regular Saturday night dinners and family gatherings held by the elder Roosevelts in the mansion on Broadway.

Tedie, who was too young to understand, marched up and down triumphantly in his little uniform of the New York Zouaves at the news of every Union victory. But Bamie sensed it all. She, too, sided with her father's people, but she had deep sympathy for Aunt Annie, who took on the duties of nursery governess so she might feel less dependent on Northern charity, and Bamie was distressed for her mother. Years later she told White House aide Colonel Archie Butt, who was a Southern gentleman of the old school, how difficult it had been for "my little mother."

"I knew the Roosevelts," Bamie said matter-of-factly, quite forgetting how much part of herself resembled that side of her family, "and I should hate to have married into them at that time unless I had been one with them in thought. They think they are just, but they are hard in a way."

This was true, of course, of her Dutch forebears, but not of Father, who was a gentle man. His wife, Mittie, who had three brothers fighting with the Confederate forces, insisted that it would kill her if her husband fought against her brothers. To save Mittie distress, and also perhaps because he was his Quaker mother's favorite son, the elder Theodore decided not to enlist. Bamie remembered that "always afterward he felt he had done a wrong thing in not having put every other feeling aside to join the absolute fighting forces."

Instead, through his good friend, John Hay, who was President Lincoln's secretary, Father obtained an appointment to the Union army's Allotment Commission. In this job, he visited all the Northern encampments and tried to pledge each soldier to send home a portion of his pay, instead of spending it all with the camp followers and the sutlers. The younger Theodore, who was by nature bellicose, came to be ashamed that Father had not actually fought in the war, even though Theodore Roosevelt, Sr., received an official commendation from President Lincoln himself. His duties often exposed him to front-line fire; he probably saw more action than many Union volunteers; and he had to be away from home for months at a time. His letters to his wife and children show his gentle, tolerant nature.

"I wish we sympathized together on this question of so vital moment to our country," he wrote Mittie from Washington. "But I know you cannot understand my feelings, and of course I do not expect it."

In all his letters home, thereafter, Father rarely mentioned the war or his own rugged experiences, but he usually had a word for the small daughter engaged in her own private battle to become healthy and strong.

"I remember Bamie's morning visits," Father wrote his wife, "but I suppose her time is so much occupied taking care of the rest of the family that she does not miss them. Tell her not to forget the care she promised to take of Tedie during my absence and to see that Elliott does not starve."

Mittie's letters to her husband, in turn, wisely ignored the war but kept him fully informed only about what the children were up to. Tedie, she reported, was miserably jealous because she had taken Ellie into her bed to comfort him when he had night-mares. Bamie's training as a proper young lady was, despite her disability, not being neglected. Mittie had already sent her twice to dancing school.

"The first time," Mittie wrote, "she seemed very tired and uninterested, but I have determined to give her a fair trial. So, on Friday last, when she came home at 12 o'clock, I had her apparatus taken off, and she laid down in bed." That seemed to make Bamie feel better about dancing school, Mittie wrote, "and I can hear her upstairs now singing in the most discordant voice some of her Sunday School hymns."

What Mittie very tactfully omitted from her letters to Father was any account of what she and the other two patriotic Southern ladies in his home were up to. They spent much of their time during his long absences preparing parcels of food, money, and clothing to be sent to their relatives and friends in the South. This was accomplished quite easily by putting all the parcels in a basket and taking Tedie and Bamie "on a picnic" to Central Park. There the parcels were quickly transferred to other rela-tives and friends who seemed to have no trouble running the blockade south.

"One of my most vivid memories," Bamie recalled, "were the days of hushed and thrilling excitement, which only occurred when Father had gone away. Grandmother, Mother, and Aunt Annie would pack a box, while Theodore and I helped, not knowing at all what it was about, except that it was a mystery and that the box was going to run the blockade. Our favorite game for years afterwards, needless to say instigated by Theo-dore, was one of 'running the blockade' over the bridge in Central Park, in which I was the blockade runner, and he was the Government boat that caught me."

One of Mittie's brothers was James Bulloch, the brave Con-federate secret agent who made his way to England where he bought, outfitted, and launched the blockade-running *Alabama*. Another brother served on that disguised Confederate warship until, after many successes, she was sunk in the English Channel

12

by a Union man-o'-war, the *Kearsarge*. Both brothers survived the war, but Jimmie Bulloch was exiled by the victorious Union for life. He made his permanent home in Liverpool, where he had secretly readied the *Alabama*, and there, a few years after the war, the whole Roosevelt family, at Mittie's insistence, paid him a visit. Father agreed to the trip because he wanted his children to have the benefit of a grand tour on the Continent. He was particularly anxious that Bamie, who had so valiantly overcome her physical handicap, should have every advantage, for he had his own ideas about how a proper young lady of her intelligence should be brought up.

By the spring of 1869, when the Roosevelt family went abroad for the first time, Bamie had long since outgrown the home nursery school and the subjects Aunt Annie could teach. She had exhausted her father's library that was tolerably well stocked with history and biography. By the time she was fourteen, she was already receiving with Father when such friends as John Hay, who was now on the *New York Tribune*, and the brilliant young lawyer, Joseph H. Choate, came to call. Bamie amazed and amused Father and his friends with her knowledgeable conversation. Mr. Hay often brought her new books to read that he had enjoyed himself. With such a precocious daughter, Father was determined that she should have the best education the times could offer her, and that meant a year or two abroad.

On this family trip, Mittie had her reunion with her brother in Liverpool and, later on, visited all the fine shops in Paris. Bamie, meanwhile, had the time of her life touring the picture galleries and the museums with Father, even though, as she wrote Aunt Annie, it was "a very long trip for the three little children."

Outside Paris, at Fontainebleau, Father found a finishing school for Bamie that appealed to him very much. It was run by a remarkable Frenchwoman named Mlle Souvestre—one of those rare, gifted teachers who could make history utterly fascinating. Mademoiselle was to unroll before Bamie's enchanted eyes the whole exciting tapestry of world politics with those masters of high strategy—Napoleon, Disraeli, Gladstone, Bismarck, and Machiavelli—posed heroically in the foreground. At Fontainebleau, politics came alive for Bamie as a diplomatic chess game to be played by men of heroic stature, one in which a woman of intelligence and queenly charm could have her part to play, and not as a pawn. Her interest in the world of affairs was to lie fallow for a while for lack of nourishment in her immediate family surroundings, but it would blossom in time, through Theodore, into the central passion of her life. Mlle Souvestre planted the seed.

CHAPTER II

"O, Energy, Thy Name Is Bamie!"

IT was the custom of Mlle Souvestre, who permitted the daughters of a few wealthy British and Americans of good family to attend her establishment at Fontainebleau, to advise her young charges to lie down after midday dinner and fix their minds for a full hour on a single thought. Later in the day, her young ladies were invited to take tea with Mademoiselle in her own apartments. Each, appropriately dressed in her best tea gown, with boned, choker collar of lace and net, was expected, at Mademoiselle's afternoons, to discourse on that single thought and its development in French.

Vague or random thoughts were not welcome at the tea table of Mlle Souvestre. A regal little woman with a beautiful head too big for her body, she was the daughter of a *philosophe* of some distinction who had been an intimate of the artist Pierre Puvis de Chavannes. Mademoiselle had inherited her father's intellect, along with some rather startling Puvis de Chavannes' nudes that decorated the walls of her sitting room. Though these paintings overpowered some of her pupils, Mademoiselle managed to draw out even the most self-conscious and tongue-tied. But her large brown eyes would snap if she were offered as conversation the simple parroting of classroom facts learned earlier in the day. An accomplished young lady was expected to converse as Mademoiselle herself did—a formidable task, for her

15

well-stocked mind ranged easily over all that was best of the eighteenth and nineteenth centuries. She steeped, to the extent that they could take it, each of her charges in world history, high diplomacy, art, music, and literature. As for religion, Mademoiselle was a product of the Age of Enlightenment and an agnostic, but she required her pupils to brew their own cup of intellectual tea.

Of all the young ladies gathered around Mademoiselle's tea table at Fontainebleau during the bright winter afternoons before the Prussians took Paris—for the first time, in 1871— none pleased her more than Anna Roosevelt, the sixteen-year-old daughter of a New York glass importer. Mademoiselle could tell immediately that here was an original.

The girl was not beautiful, and her figure, which required a special, light corset, left something to be desired, but she carried herself well. Mademoiselle took inventory. Good skin, yes, but olive in tone. Long black hair with a burnish of *noir doré*. That was good. And the nose, though far from classic, was fetchingly retroussé. What was it that made her so utterly charming and appealing? But, of course, it was the eyes, and they were incredible—of a deep, penetrating blue and heavy lidded. When they fastened with interest on anyone, they were alive not only with curiosity but with warmth and understanding.

America was indeed a remarkable melting pot, Mlle Souvestre observed, if it could produce from stolid Dutch parental stock crossed with English blood—which had been warmed by the Georgia sun for several generations—such an engaging young lady as Anna Roosevelt. Mademoiselle was delighted to find her an extremely apt pupil, particularly in political science, for that happened to be Mademoiselle's own speciality. She put her young American charge, who naturally became one of her pets, through a course of study that prepared her to take her place, if need be, beside such great salonistes as Mme Roland and Mme du Deffand.

When Bamie came home from Fontainebleau, she seemed to all the family to have become, almost overnight, a very sophisticated young lady indeed. She had gone off to Mlle Souvestre's a rather undisciplined, bossy little body, somewhat spoiled by an indulgent father, full of very definite opinions she never hesitated to express without fear of challenge in the tolerant circle of her immediate family, and a burning desire to learn everything there was to know at once. One of the first things she learned at Fontainebleau, and this intrigued her immensely, was that learning all about everything was going to be a fascinating lifetime process. She felt herself very fortunate to have someone like dear Mlle Souvestre to help her begin. It was not that Bamie learned humility at Fontainebleau, for that was not in her nature, but Mlle Souvestre, by her very example, showed Bamie the exciting dimensions of the world she could live in if she chose, even as that excellent schoolmistress managed to soften some of the harsher outlines in Bamie's character and teach her the value of listening intelligently to what others had to say.

Bamie also came home very stylish in the gowns made for her in Paris while she was at Mlle Souvestre's; she was half a head taller in her new French-heeled shoes and with her dark, wavy hair piled in a high chignon; and her manner was almost demure, deceptively so, for Bamie had lost not one iota of her unbounded energy or her instinct to dominate.

Brother Tedie, Bamie discovered on her return, was also growing up fast, physically. He was going on fourteen and was already being tutored for Harvard. Yet his most ardent interest continued to be the animals and birds around him, of a much larger size, however, than the magpie, the field mice, and the live turtles that had once fascinated Bamie as well as Theodore. Now Theodore, with the shotgun his father had given him, went after crows, owls, and woodchucks, and these he preferred dead and stuffed to alive. With the help of a taxidermist in the neighborhood he had learned to stuff the specimens he shot, and these, much to his mother's disgust, were threatening to fill the Twentieth Street house to overflowing. But Bamie and Father argued that Theodore should not be discouraged in his taxidermy efforts for he had his heart set on becoming a naturalist, and this might break his spirit. Mittie Bulloch Roosevelt did not have the heart herself, or the energy, to put her foot down. Perhaps she concluded in her easy Southern way that shooting and stuffing dead animals was, at least, a relatively harmless occupation for a boy as high strung and aggressive as Theodore had turned out to be.

As they grew up, all the children—Theodore, Elliott, Corinne, and Bamie not excepted—were proving too much for Mittie Bulloch Roosevelt, who retained much of her native Georgia indolence along with her saving sense of humor. The proverbial Roosevelt energy, displayed by each of her children in his or her own way, seemed to increase with the years, even as Mittie, whose health was never robust, wilted into gradual, though decorative, decline. The combined hustle and bustle on Twentieth Street—to which Father contributed at least his share, in person and by frequently inviting his friends and associates home for luncheon or dinner—unnerved Mittie so that she could often find peace and quiet only by retreating, with a cold pack for a sick headache, to her room upstairs. There, after she had discovered how successful this device could be, she was mercifully permitted to recline undisturbed for hours.

Mittie had already managed to establish this restful pattern of temporary escape from her family even before Bamie went off to Mlle Souvestre's. Now, on her elder daughter's return, Mittie encouraged Bamie, much to her daughter's delight, to take over many of the chores of housekeeping and entertaining that Mittie herself was only too glad to relinquish.

Bamie would have another year before her debut, but she was much too impatient with social protocol to wait for that. Very much her father's daughter, she went with him everywhere and adored every minute.

"From the beginning," Bamie recalled, "Father had brought to the house the people who were most delightful to know, people interested in political and civic matters. He was one of the original founders of the Metropolitan Museum of Art and the Museum of Natural History, and very philanthropic. Every Saturday, he took off from his business to devote to other matters.

"Generally these Saturdays commenced by a ride on horseback in the Park, followed instantly before I had time to fairly get into my clothes, by a visit of inspection to both the Art Museum and the Museum of Natural History, and then to some one of the Children's Aid Society schools. We would get home for lunch very late, and as a rule would find whoever was most interesting of the moment in New York, lunching with us. By the time that was over, we either drove in the Park or visited a hospital. At all events those wintry days, when 5 o'clock came, I was a complete wreck. Mother always used to say it was a case of 'butchered to make a Roman holiday,' that by Saturday evening I was dead, owing to Father's lovely afternoon. Still it was marvelously instructive."

Mittie was no doubt relieved that she did not have to accompany her husband on this strenuous round of good works, just as she had been happy to share with her daughter the responsibility of running such a hectic household. Life was a bit easier now for Bamie's lovely, languid mother, but still Mittie found it difficult to be on time for any engagement. A great beauty in her day, with a passion for lovely things and personal adornment, Mittie enjoyed taking hours and infinite pains on her costumes for all occasions.

"I remember darling little Mother's exquisite beauty," Bamie recalled. Attending a wedding at the old Jay home in Westchester, Mittie wore "an enormous crinoline and a perfectly exquisite white muslin dress over a pink silk lining with all the little ruffles at the bottom edged with real lace." Her cloak and her ivory-handled parasol were of pink silk, muslin, and lace, to match the dress exactly. "She wore a bonnet tied under her chin with great pink ribbons. On the brim was a great big rose with perfectly realistic little green dragon flies. She was considered one of the beauties at the wedding."

19

With such a mother to live up to, Bamie may well have dreaded her own official entry into New York society. She did have one qualm, but that was when the doctor gave her spectacles for her beautiful but slightly myopic eyes, and Father said jokingly, *he* would never bring out a daughter who wore glasses. Bamie threw the spectacles away, never to wear them again, and, as events turned out, she made not one debut but three, the first in Vienna. After that, Philadelphia and New York were relatively easy.

Father decided the winter of 1872 that they should all make another extended trip abroad. The following year he planned to install his family in a larger house, moving with the rest of social New York farther out Fifth Avenue, to No. 6 West Fifty-seventh Street. It would take a full year to remodel and furnish this elegant new home, and he felt the whole family could spend this year of waiting more pleasantly in travel.

The second grand tour began with a trip up the Nile in a dahabeah and here, Theodore, the boy naturalist, was much in his element. During these winter months, he was growing fast, and he was a sight to behold.

"He outgrew all his clothes," Bamie recalled, "and of course there was no replacing them on the Nile. He would put on a pair of spectacles and swing his gun over his shoulder and start out on whatever small donkey was provided at every place we stopped. Then he would ruthlessly lope after whatever object he had in view, the donkey almost invariably crowding between any other two who might be riding together."

Frequently the disturbed twosome would be Bamie and Augustus Jay, or Bamie and Nathaniel Thayer, two of the four young men from Harvard who joined forces with the Roosevelt family and tracked up the Nile with them in another dahabeah. Bamie found them both most attractive, though she modestly said, "Mother was much more the object of their attention than I was." Still, when sister Conie wrote her best chum, Edith Carow—who was also Tedie's childhood sweetheart—all about their trip up the Nile, Bamie added a footnote saying, "I wish you knew Mr. Thayer and Mr. Jay. They are so *very, very* nice." And it was Bamie, rather than Mittie, who went on the moonlight rides to the Temple of Amon at Karnak and the tombs of the Pharaohs. Certainly Gussie Jay, if not the other three young Harvard men, had Bamie in mind when the quartet on the neighboring dahabeah serenaded with such lively contemporary ditties as "She's Naughty but So Nice," and "Clochette, Clochette, She Was a Sad Coquette."

At eighteen, Bamie was of course more big sister than coquette. Even better than the moonlight rides, she enjoyed the two hours she spent each morning giving lessons to her brothers and sister, taking particular pride in Theodore's progress.

"Really this course of governessing," she recalled, "taught me more than I ever learned before, though I cannot say as much for my pupils. I had to learn everything I taught them in advance, and of course Theodore knew a great deal more than I did on almost all the subjects I taught." Remembering those days on the romantic Nile teaching geography, spelling, and simple arithmetic, which had not been stressed by Mlle Souvestre, Bamie was to say rather wistfully, "I do not think I ever quite let myself be young."

From the Nile, they went through the Holy Land on horseback, camping out along the way. Then came Constantinople, the Black Sea, the Danube, Budapest, and Vienna. "At this point," Bamie recalled, "I grew up incontinently and without any intention. We were asked to some very delightful houses, and I was hastily put into debutante clothes and produced."

With what good effect, sister Conie hastened to inform her little friend, Edith Carow, back in New York. "Bamie," Conie wrote ecstatically of a night at the opera when Adelina Patti sang, "wore a *long trained* blue silk, her *first* train, beautifully trimmed and fitting her splendidly," and over that "an Oriental bernoose."

Bamie thought Viennese society "gay and enchanting for the older people—not so alluring for the young. I remember very well my first ball and my horror at being put into what was called the 'countessen's room' which meant where all the young girls were left between dances. Instead of having partners who continued with them and chatted, our partners merely came and took us out and brought us back. O, but I was glad to go home, and hoped not to see such an entertainment again."

The rest of the year abroad, the family were scattered about the Continent. The younger members were sent to live with a family in Dresden so they could learn German. Bamie and her mother went to London and Paris to buy furnishings for the new home and then on to Carlsbad and Franzensbad where Mittie tried the cures. "Father went home to the United States," Bamie wrote, and "somehow the summer was rather an anticlimax to the winter."

Of their purchases in London and Paris, Bamie often spoke rather amusedly. "Darling little Mother," she would say, "bought bolts and bolts of claret-colored cloth in London for the servants' livery to store against the day when these garments would wear out. Alas, in time, all those bolts of lovely woollen made a feast for the moths. Of course, everything that Mother bought was perfectly beautiful, but her exquisite taste proved rather fatal to the family fortunes. We had no letter of credit left long before we were ready to go home so that it was rather a hard day for Father when we landed."

Father may have had a difficult time the winter of 1873, not so much from Mittie's extended letter of credit as from the money panic of that year. Moreover, as Bamie recalled, the architect for the West Fifty-seventh Street house "made the most curious mistake, which delayed us a good deal in getting settled. In some mysterious manner, his plans and their fulfill-ment were quite different. The staircase from the first floor to the second missed its connection by about three feet, which was rather painful, necessitating a complete remaking of the staircase, which, as it was all hand carved, took time. Also he had given the wrong measurements for most of the carpets, and the beauti-ful Persian rugs for the halls were all about two feet too broad. So instead of being in one piece, they had to be carefully clipped off and the borders sewn again. This, and the fact that the gas fixtures were late in being completed, made my Father eventually decide it would be best I should make my debut in Philadelphia."

She went to stay with a gay, youngish couple, Mr. and Mrs. J. Dundas Lippincott, who were "Father's friends and halfway between him and myself in age." Her first ball, not counting the ones in Vienna, was an Assembly held in the foyer of the Academy in Philadelphia.

"It was the fashion," Bamie recalled, "to send girls innumerable bouquets for their first ball, a perfectly idiotic fashion. Still I was immensely pleased with the fact that the two chairs next mine in the cotillion were entirely filled with my bouquets, sent by old friends of my father's, as I had very few of my own in Philadelphia." She was also pleased with her Philadelphia escort, Coleman Drayton, "the most priceless treasure amongst the young men of the day."

By the end of January, 1874, the house on Fifty-seventh Street was presentable enough for Bamie's debut in New York, and this time her beau of the moment was Jack Kingsford, "who had no end of 'go' and made our part of the cotillion very gay." Still, she always remembered that winter "with mingled feelings of pleasure and disappointment. On account of my darling little mother's having been a Southerner, I had been brought up in a singularly isolated way in New York and had practically no intimate friends. Not knowing many young people made it very hard, and Father himself was so very young that it was with great difficulty I could ever get him home from a dance. He was so popular that I felt like a wallflower, which was anything but satisfactory to a debutante's mind. By the next year, however, I made my friends, and from then on thoroughly enjoyed what I had of life in New York."

From that time on, Bamie never seemed to lack friends. Once launched, she enjoyed company perhaps even more than Father did. She was busy with dinners, balls, weddings, receptions, the opera, the art galleries, and concerts, meanwhile taking on some

23

of the good works—a club for newsboys and a hospital for crippled children—that had always occupied her father. In an early letter from college, Theodore once greeted her with the salutation, "O, Energy, thy name is Bamie!" and he tried to describe, with a touch of his usual hyperbole, "an ordinary programme" for one of Bamie's days:

A.M. 7:45 Prayers
      8:00 Breakfast
      8:30 Write between two and three hundred invitations
     10:00 Visit patients at St. Luke's
     11:30 Sewing Class

P.M. 1:00 Lunch (from seven to ten minutes)
      1:30 Mrs. Alexander's prayer meeting
      3:00 Call on sixteen intimate friends
      5:00 Drive with Father
      6:00 Dress for Swell Dinner
      7:30 S. D. (swell dinner)
     11:00 Ball
      (??) Bedtime
           when?

Such a tightly packed day was no burden to Bamie, for she, as well as Theodore, took delight in following their father's advice, which was, "Whatever you do, enjoy it."

Now young Theodore, well prepped by a private tutor and tuned to a fine physical pitch by his own strenuous efforts to become a taxidermist, naturalist, gymnast, amateur boxer, mountaineer, hunter, and all-round woodsman, was thoroughly enjoying his first year at Harvard.

Neither Bamie nor Theodore could at first believe it when the elder Theodore could no longer follow his own advice. Father's health began unaccountably to fail in the late 1870s, before he reached fifty. He was already far from well when he became involved in his first and only political battle, one in which Bamie was at his side and his elder son away at college, quite unaware either of his illness or the political difficulties in which he had become involved.

In 1877, President Rutherford B. Hayes, responding to pressure for reform after the scandalous Grant Administration, decided it would be politic to appoint an incorruptible citizen with the public spirit of Theodore Roosevelt, Sr., to the office of Collector of Customs of the Port of New York. The elder Theodore had not sought the post, but he was willing to take it because he had been one of the very earliest advocates of civil service reform.

Unfortunately, this excellent appointment by President Hayes met with violent opposition. The Republican political machine in New York was determined not to let such a prize as the collectorship fall into the hands of a reformer. Unused to practical politics, Theodore Roosevelt, Sr., already a sick man with an undiagnosed cancerous condition, was deeply hurt by the antagonism his appointment aroused. Led by Senator Roscoe Conkling of New York, the machine attacked Hayes and Roosevelt in the New York and Washington press, and, with the usual delaying tactics, managed to block confirmation of the Roosevelt appointment in the United States Senate.

Bamie could only stand by and suffer with her father as he agonized silently under the double affliction of unwelcome notoriety and painful illness. She probably did not share his ultraconservative view, which was that, since he did not yet hold office, the battle was not his to join but rather one between the President and a faction of his party. At his request and for his health's sake, Bamie protected her ailing father from the reporters who besieged their home. Whatever her own feelings in the matter, she said "No" for him, politely, firmly, and repeatedly, when they urged that he speak up and wage public counterattack on the corrupt Republican political machine in New York. Bamie's instinct may well have been to agree with the reporters, but Father, even when in the best of health, hated the idea of engaging in rough-and-tumble, intraparty strife.

Though Bamie bowed, under the circumstances, to her father's decision to remain as aloof as he could in the midst of this factional fight in the Republican party, she would never forget the political defeat he suffered in the late 1870s and the part it played in his last illness. Nor would she have been one of Mlle Souvestre's best pupils had she not absorbed, among other things, that remarkable Frenchwoman's firm conviction that, in the light of history as she read and taught it, a woman could, acting with finesse and diplomacy, play a considerable role behind the scenes in any sort of battle.

But strategic retreat seemed in order to Bamie that summer of 1877. She was convinced that her father's illness was aggravated, if not actually caused by, the public political opposition to his appointment. Thinking a change of scene would alleviate his increasing despondency, she took him to Bar Harbor for a visit with her good Boston friends, the Minots and the Welds. These two families were among the Bostonians who had made Theodore's first year at Harvard so pleasant, for as he had written Bamie exuberantly, "It's a great thing to have a popular sister. All your friends have been very polite to me."

It was partly her desire not to spoil his fun at Cambridge and in Boston and partly her wish that he concentrate on his studies that first rather difficult year at Harvard, that kept Bamie, at the onset of their father's illness, from confiding in Theodore. She knew how he idolized their father, and, as always where her favorite brother was concerned, she was given to mothering him over much. Bamie had even gone up to Cambridge before Theodore's freshman year to choose his rooms for him. Since the only rooms available in Harvard Yard were on the ground floor and their dampness might conceivably bring on one of the asthma attacks he had largely outgrown, Bamie had selected for him a pleasant, sunny, second-floor room in a private house two blocks south of Harvard Square and furnished it with cosy things from his own bedroom to make him feel at home in his new surroundings.

Kept almost in the dark by Bamie, and by "darling little Motherling" as well, during this trying family period, Theodore in his letters home and in his diary dwelt almost exclusively on his own activities. He seemed a very callow young Harvard man indeed and a rather unconcerned son, but that was no doubt because, in sparing him any distress, Bamie had kept him in total ignorance of their father's illness and his political difficulties. The fight over the collectorship, therefore, touched Theodore very lightly at first. He was not even sure what the presidential appointment was for. "Tell Father," he wrote Bamie in the autumn of 1877, "I am watching the 'controllership' movements with the greatest interest." This was, nevertheless, the first expression of interest in things political ever made by the young man who then intended, with his father's blessing, to lead the quiet life of a natural scientist and literary man on graduating from Harvard. In November, Theodore was still taking a fairly detached view. He wrote Bamie thanking her for sending him a copy of the *Scotch Naturalist* and commenting, "At present it looks as if Father would not get the collectorship: I am glad on his account but sorry for New York."

Early in December, however, when the battle over the New York Collectorship reached the floor of the United States Senate and spilled over into national headlines, the young Harvard man's interest became so deeply aroused that he could hardly concentrate on his studies. Nothing seemed more unfair than that Senator Conkling, his father's political enemy—who would be his, too, for life—should by coincidence, perhaps even by evil design, be chairman of the very committee charged with reviewing his father's appointment. Now thoroughly angry, but as helpless as Bamie, Theodore read in the papers how Senator Conkling took advantage of the absence of committee members favorable to his father and had the committee recommend to the Senate that the appointment not be confirmed, and then how

Conkling harangued the Senate, damning Theodore Roosevelt, Sr., as an amateur in politics and an ineffectual do-gooder.

When Senator Conkling finally mustered enough votes to defeat the appointment of Theodore Roosevelt, Sr., on the floor of the Senate, young Theodore wrote bitterly to his father, "I am very much afraid that Conkling has won the day." Within the week, Theodore heard from Bamie that their father was not at all well. This time he wrote, "I am very uneasy about Father. Does the doctor think it anything serious?"

Bamie surely must have dreaded the impending Christmas holidays in 1877. The doctors had undoubtedly told her by now that her beloved father was dying of an inoperable intestinal malignancy. Perhaps no one but Bamie, who was in constant attendance on her father, actually knew how seriously ill he was or how gallant was the front he put up for his wife and children during the family gathering that Christmas on West Fifty-seventh Street. After Theodore had been home for a few days, it seemed to him that Father, though tired, was much better, and, on his return to college after the holidays, his letters and his diary were as full of such jolly activities as dinners, dances, and sleighing parties as ever.

The elder Theodore died early in February and the shock to his son at Harvard, who did not manage to make train connections from Cambridge in time to reach home before his death, was overpowering. From this point on, Theodore's letters home to "darling little Motherling" and to Bamie, Ellie, and Conie took on a much more manly tone.

Soon after his father's death, now back at Harvard in the midst of his sophomore year, he wrote Bamie, "My own sweet sister, you will have to give me a great deal of advice and assistance, now that our dear father is gone, for in many ways you are more like him than any of the rest of the family. . . ."

During his last two years at Harvard, Theodore stood much in need of advice. He lost interest in making a career of natural science after his father's death, yet he had no clear idea what he should do. At Bamie's suggestion, on one of his holidays in New

28

York, he went to see their father's friend, Joseph H. Choate. This was the brilliant Harvard Law School graduate who remembered Bamie from the Twentieth Street days when her precocious conversation had entertained all Father's friends. Bamie had followed Mr. Choate's career with interest, and she was well aware that he had become one of the powerful Committee of Seventy, the group of important business and professional men who had originally joined forces, in 1871, to rid New York City of the notorious Tweed Ring. It occurred to Bamie that, if Boss Tweed could be eliminated, the same treatment could, with the proper organization and leadership, be administered to Senator Conkling and the Republican machine that had caused her father such anguish in his last illness. Perhaps Mr. Choate's very considerable success as a corporation lawyer and his membership on the committee that had unseated Boss Tweed would be an inspiration to Theodore.

By the time senior year at Harvard came round, Theodore thought he might go in for the law. That was encouraging. He also took part in a college debate on "Machine Politics," and, just before graduating, he told a classmate, rather vaguely, that he hoped to do "something to help the cause of better government." But when he graduated from Harvard, Theodore did not immediately exhibit a burning desire to follow in his father's footsteps as a civic reformer or to emulate Mr. Choate, for a very good reason. Theodore had fallen in love.

CHAPTER III

Theodore's Career Begins

IN 1880, his last year at Harvard, marriage, not politics, was much on Theodore's mind. He became engaged, in January, to Alice Hathaway Lee, the pretty, eighteen-year-old daughter of the George Cabot Lees of Boston and Chestnut Hill. Mr. Lee, true to family tradition and his affiliation with the conservative banking house of Lee Higginson and Company, insisted that the young couple had best wait a year or so before marrying or at least until Theodore had established himself in a career.

Theodore had no intention of waiting. The date he had personally set for his wedding was October 27, the year of his graduation. That happened to be his twenty-second birthday, and he enlisted Bamie's support in bringing it off. Theodore was certainly of age, though just barely, and he had inherited from his father, as had each of the other Roosevelt children, about $125,000. Wisely invested, Theodore argued, this would temporarily provide a modest, if not princely, income for him and his young bride, whatever career he chose.

During the usual exchange of visits between Chestnut Hill and Manhattan, the Lees became extremely fond of all the Roosevelts. They were no doubt as disturbed by the extravagance of Theodore's younger brother, Elliott, who was busily spending his inheritance on big-game safaris to Texas, India, and Tibet, as they were charmed by Mittie, Corinne, and Bamie, who impressed them most of all.

By the first of March, Theodore had Alice Lee's secret promise that she would marry him that autumn, but, as he wrote Bamie, "I have not approached Mr. and Mrs. Lee on the subject yet." He thought there would be a "battle royal, in which I shall probably get worsted." He added that he was finding it "awfully hard to study" and said, "I most sincerely wish I had you here to assist me."

Bamie immediately wrote the Lees that, if they would permit the marriage to take place in the autumn, she and Mittie would both welcome having the young people live with them their first winter in New York. As he wrote to his younger sister, Corinne, a week later, this helped Theodore carry the day. "Indeed," Theodore said, "I don't think Mr. Lee would have consented to our marriage so soon on other terms. I think Bamie's words had a good deal of weight with Mrs. Lee."

Alice Lee and Theodore were married at the Unitarian Church in Brookline on his birthday, and they spent their honeymoon at "Tranquillity," the summer home rented by the Roosevelts at Oyster Bay. Here, too, Bamie smoothed the way for the young couple by tending to all the housekeeping chores in advance.

"I have been living in a dream of delight," Theodore wrote his mother from Oyster Bay. "The house is just perfection; Kate cooks deliciously, and Mary Ann is exactly *the* servant for us; and Davis does his part beautifully, too. . . . We breakfast at ten, dine at two, and take tea at seven; thanks to Bamie's thoughtfulness, Alice does not have to order any meals. . . . The pretty darling sends her love to you, Bysie, Pussie, and Nell." *

At the end of two weeks, the young couple moved into town, occupying their own private quarters on the third floor at 6 West Fifty-seventh Street, though they shared their meals and their social activities with the rest of the family. Bamie was for them all, as Theodore delighted to put it, "the Driving Wheel of

* Bysie was another pet name for Bamie; Pussie was Corinne; and Nell, Elliott.

Destiny and the Superintendent-in-Chief of the Workings of Providence." It also pleased him to remind Bamie that matrimony had conferred on him and his young bride the right to "matronize," or chaperon, not only his younger sister, Corinne, but twenty-five-year-old Bamie as well at all the parties they attended that winter, Alice Lee's first, in New York.

Society was beginning to pall on Bamie, if not on the rest of the family. She had, as Theodore put it, "the usual miscellaneous crowd of adorers around her," even in her late twenties, and this was unusual in the 1880s. Yet Bamie seemed incapable of settling her affections on any one person outside the immediate family circle in which she was so obviously "the Driving Wheel of Destiny."

In the tradition of the times, the Hyde Park cousins of the New York Roosevelts offered two likely matrimonial prospects —Bamie's fourth cousin, the middle-aged widower, James Roosevelt, and Cousin James's son, J. Roosevelt Roosevelt, who was more nearly her contemporary. But Bamie was not in love with "Rosy" Roosevelt, who beaued her about on her frequent visits to Hyde Park, and he later married her friend, Helen Astor. And Bamie was too intractable, too independent and full of life, to consent to an arranged marriage with Rosy's father, the then Squire of Hyde Park, a man old enough to be her own father. Cousin James subsequently married Sara Delano, and one might say that Bamie thus lost the historical opportunity of becoming the mother of a president.

None of the others in Bamie's "potpourri of admirers," again quoting Theodore, fared any better. Once Theodore asked Bamie whether in her dreams her rejected suitors did not form "a spectral procession of reproachful shadows stretching from Gussie of Egypt and Johnnie of Oyster Bay through Samuel the Uncertain of Utterance and Willie with the Immaculate Part down to Widow Miller's military lover and the dimpled Leslie?" And another time he quizzed Bamie with, "By the way, *did* Rowe propose? And if not, pray *how* did you stop him?"

Bamie turned all such questions in great good humor, saying

she intended to keep stirring her "potpourri," by including not just the usual sort of people they all knew but by adding more and more interesting people who did things. And now, during the winter of 1880–81, she had long serious talks with Theodore about the career he should follow. He was certainly busy enough, studying law at Columbia and reading law in the office of Uncle Robert Roosevelt, as well as completing his *Naval War of 1812* that he had started at Harvard. Even so, Theodore had to acknowledge that he and his wife were a most "irresponsible couple," and he promised to make up his mind, after they had had a summer abroad, whether "to go into politics and literature" or "to follow law or business."

Already Theodore had made the move that was to help make up his mind for him. In the autumn of 1880, either shortly before or after his marriage, he had joined the Twenty-first District Republican Association and attended meetings regularly in the clubroom at Morton Hall on Fifth Avenue, only a few blocks from home. In this activity, Bamie was undoubtedly the only member of the entire Roosevelt family circle who gave him any encouragement. His uncles and some of the family's friends told him no gentleman would associate with the saloonkeepers, bricklayers, and other such folk who made up the membership of the city's political clubs. But Theodore insisted, and Bamie openly agreed with him, that it was his plain duty, as his father's son, to take his place in the community. To be effective, he was convinced that he should join his local political club, or as he put it years later in his *Autobiography*, "It merely meant that the people I knew did not belong to the governing class, and that the other people did—and that I intended to be one of the governing class...."

Before leaving for Europe with Alice Lee in the spring of 1881, Theodore had already become embroiled in the intraparty fight at the club that was to catapult him at the age of twenty-three into the New York State Legislature. From the beginning, Theodore's purpose, which was civic betterment, was exactly the same as his father's had been, only his methods were different.

At Morton Hall, he began to work for city charter reform and for a nonpartisan street-cleaning bill, and he soon joined forces, as his father probably never would have done, with a young Irish politician named Joseph Murray who was astute enough to sense a reform wave in the offing not only in his district but throughout the state.

On his return from Europe, Theodore went back to his law studies but, on learning that the street-cleaning bill had been defeated in Albany and that William Trimble, the incumbent assemblyman from his own district, had voted against it, he wrote in his diary, "Am going to try to kill our last year's legislator." The vehemence of this entry is partly explained by the fact that Trimble was known to be a Conkling man and, as such, anathema to all Roosevelts.

What Theodore probably did not know when he marched over to Morton Hall one night early in October of 1881 was that his new friend, Joe Murray, now had control of the Twenty-first District and was just as anxious as Theodore to kill off Trimble. Theodore told Murray he had come to protest Trimble's renomination and was utterly astounded when Murray offered to back him for assemblyman instead.

"No," Theodore told Murray, "I would not dream of such a thing. It would look as though I had had selfish motives in coming around to oppose this man."

"Well," said Murray, "get me a desirable candidate."

"Oh," said Theodore, firmly convinced that his friend was guying him, "you won't have any trouble."

Three weeks later there was probably no one more amazed than Theodore Roosevelt when he received the nomination for assemblyman after a one-sentence speech of endorsement before the district convention by his friend, Joe Murray.

Once he was nominated, everyone in his district seemed to become intrigued with the idea of sending one of the Fifth Avenue set to the legislature. Joe Murray's men, among them the bricklayers and the saloonkeepers, worked for Theodore. So, too, did the football and baseball squads at Columbia and all the

34

professors and students at the law school. He also had the endorsement of his father's friends—among them, Joseph H. Choate, Elihu Root, and Chauncey Depew—and the support of the civic reformers. On election eve, Carl Schurz wrote an editorial endorsing him in the crusading *New York Post:*

Mr. Roosevelt has hereditary claims to the confidence and hopefulness of the voters of this city, for his father was in his day one of the most useful and public-spirited men in the community and the son has the good opinion of everybody who knows him.

This was one of the most cherished clippings to be pasted in the scrapbook that Bamie had started for her brother. It was followed by the news story reporting Theodore Roosevelt, Jr.'s victory in the Twenty-first District by nearly twice the usual Republican margin.

When Theodore went up to Albany in January of 1882, his unbounding confidence in himself was very much enhanced by the presence of his young wife. Alice Lee stayed with him that first winter in a rooming house at 15 Washington Avenue, but every Friday they managed to escape Albany and the dull society offered in that grubby town and take the train to New York. There, Bamie had already begun to turn the family home into a rendezvous for civic reformers, artists, writers, journalists, politicians, in fact any and everyone whom it would be stimulating and helpful for Theodore to know. As his own acquaintance widened, Theodore would often write Bamie in advance and tell her whom he would like to see in New York over the weekend, at tea, dinner, and even breakfast. This was a practice Theodore followed all during his political career, and he told Bamie in the very beginning, with a trace of youthful snobbery, that he hoped for nothing less than "a salon wherein we are to gather society men who take part in politics, literature, and art and politicians, authors, and artists whose bringing up and personal habits do not disqualify them for society."

The effect of this weekend exposure on the eager young legislator was nothing short of astounding. The change that took place in Assemblyman Roosevelt, between his first appearance at Albany and the end of the session of 1882, was duly noted, without specifying the cause, by a fellow-assemblyman named Isaac Hunt, who also lived at the boardinghouse on Washington Avenue in Albany.

Isaac Hunt was a tall, lanky country lawyer of thirty-two from Upper New York State who bought his first Prince Albert coat to attend his own first session of the legislature. Decked out in his elegant new finery and feeling mighty swell, he went to the Republican caucus and there encountered another young man, just twenty-three, resplendent in silk topper and full evening dress. This city slicker, moreover, wore a pince-nez and English side-whiskers, or "dundrearys." He kept popping up every two minutes to interrupt the meeting by asking the chairman a lot of questions.

After the meeting, the country lawyer was not a little embarrassed to find himself singled out by the brash young dude who, with a smile full of teeth, introduced himself as Theodore Roosevelt, Jr., of the Twenty-first District in Manhattan and promptly subjected Hunt to searching questions.

"You are from the country," young Roosevelt said. "I want to ask you how you manage caucuses like this in the country."

Despite this tactless penetration of the rural gentleman's disguise, Theodore soon found a firm friend in Isaac Hunt, who turned out to be just as anxious as he was to combat corruption in the political machines of both parties. Of his friend, the city slicker, Hunt said many years later:

"I think he grew faster than anybody I ever knew. When he would go away Friday afternoon—I lived right there in the same house with him—he would go down to New York and Monday, when he got back to Albany, he would throw out new things he had never had before, just like a child that you see grow. . . . He increased in stature, in strength, mentally all the time. In those days, when he first started in there, I thought I knew more than he did, but before we got through he grew right away from me."

CHAPTER IV

Quick Success with Home-bred Strategy

THEODORE'S first term as an assemblyman in the
New York State Legislature was as exciting for Bamie as if she
had been in Albany herself. Though Mittie might complain that
politics, politics, all the time, gave her a headache, Bamie, Corinne, and Alice Lee encouraged Theodore to linger at the dining table and reenact, with his considerable gift for mimicry,
each week's happenings in the legislature.

One of Theodore's best performances was his story about how
he and Mike Costello, a young Democratic assemblyman with a
leaning toward reform, had tried to defeat "perhaps the most
openly crooked measure" ever pushed at Albany.

This particular bill had originally gone through the Assembly
as an innocuous tax measure. It came back from the Senate with
everything stricken out after the enabling clause and a single
amendment inserted in its place. The amendment gave the Manhattan Elevated Railway Company a reduction in taxes from
6 to 4 percent. This steal had been maneuvered through the
Senate by Roscoe Conkling, then lawyer and lobbyist for Jay
Gould, who owned a good tenth of all the railroad mileage in
the United States as well as the Manhattan Elevated.

Theodore would describe for his admiring audience of family
and friends how he had been temporarily absent from the
Assembly when this scandalous bill was reintroduced. With

gestures, he would reenact his astonishment when he returned to the floor and found his friend, Mike, in a violent struggle with the Sergeant at Arms who was trying to evict him bodily from the Assembly. Then Theodore would rise from the table to demonstrate how he had charged down the aisle to the Speaker's dais, his slight, nervous frame dancing about the dining room as a lightweight boxer might, his voice raised in a bellow of indignation. In this fashion, he had continued his friend's one-man filibuster against the bill in spite of the pounding of the Speaker's gavel. One moment Theodore would be banging the table with his fist in imitation of the Speaker's gavel, and the next he would be Mike struggling with the Sergeant at Arms.

It was a famous victory for two legislative neophytes. It did not matter that the Speaker pro tem had taken advantage of the uproar caused by Mike and Theodore to announce that, in the confusion—and who could deny it—the bill had been passed. All the New York press reported the young reformers' disorderly conduct on the Assembly floor, and all, except the *World*, which was then Jay Gould's paper, endorsed it. And this public airing of the bill for the relief of the Manhattan Elevated prompted the Governor to veto it.

During his three terms in Albany, Theodore was not always to meet with success in the attacks he launched on this corrupt combination of business and politics. He learned that it often existed in much more subtle form than he had at first supposed when he went, hammer and tongs, after a State Supreme Court justice whose name had been linked with Gould and Conkling.

Around the dining table at 6 West Fifty-seventh Street during the winter of 1882, someone remembered a story in the *Times* that had accused Judge Theodore Westbrook of favoring Jay Gould when the Manhattan Elevated had been in receivership. The story may have been recalled by Theodore, who was an omnivorous reader of all the newspapers, or by Bamie, who made it a practice to save newspaper clippings and bring them to her brother's attention. No one could remember seeing that story challenged or denied, and that in itself was suspicious. This inspired Theodore to march down to the offices of the *Times* and ask City Editor Henry Loewenthal if he might see the documents in support of the article. He studied these for a while and then prevailed on Mr. Loewenthal to go home with him. There and then Theodore's strategy and his next reform move was planned. He decided to go after the Gould-Conkling ring with the new evidence at hand.

On March 29, 1882, Theodore Roosevelt rose in seat forty on the floor of the Assembly, leaned far forward over his desk, and pointing his finger directly at the Chair shouted his characteristic "Mr. Spee-kar, Mr. *Spee*-kar." He offered a resolution that brought utter and complete silence. It empowered the Judiciary Committee to investigate the conduct in office of Judge Theodore Westbrook of the New York Supreme Court.

Theodore charged that the Judge had taken part in a campaign to depress the stock of the Manhattan Elevated Railway Company and that this had made it possible for Jay Gould to buy control and defraud innocent stockholders. The Judge had prevented sale of Manhattan Elevated securities, Theodore said, while it was in receivership and then had declared the company to be solvent as soon as Jay Gould had acquired control. On one occasion, the Judge had even held court in Jay Gould's office.

In a series of intricate maneuvers, which showed he was fast learning parliamentary strategy, Theodore forced his resolution to a favorable roll-call vote of 104 to 6, and once again he had the support of the entire New York press, with the exception of Jay Gould's *World*. He was, then, shocked almost beyond words when, invited to luncheon about this time by one of his father's friends, he was told that he, Theodore, had made his "reform play" and that, for his own good, he should now subside. There was no such thing as a political "ring," his father's friend told him bluntly. There were certain powerful businessmen, not just old Jay Gould, and certain politicians, lawyers, and even judges in alliance with them. In this alliance, all their acts were not necessarily illegal, and these powerful men would be after his political scalp if he did not cease and desist in his childish reform efforts. Theodore was told quite frankly that, if he persisted, he would lose the backing of all the best elements in society, and this would work to his disadvantage in his future career.

At that luncheon, Theodore realized how very subtle corrupting influences could be. He told Bamie of this startling conversation with their father's friend, but he never publicly identified the man. Nor did the warning have anything but a saddening effect. Theodore returned to the attack with a much clearer idea of the forces he would have to fight.

For seven weeks, the Judiciary Committee held hearings in New York City and at Albany. It was no surprise when the committee, in its majority report, said that, though Judge Westbrook had been a little indiscreet, he did not merit impeachment. A minority report, supporting Theodore's charges, said that he did.

When these two reports were brought to the floor of the Assembly, Theodore attacked again, this time in the first full-length speech of his career that gave a foretaste of the great emotional orator he was to become. His voice breaking with intensity, he reviewed the evidence presented at the committee hearings and demanded that the minority report impeaching Judge Westbrook be adopted.

"The Judge," Theodore told the silent Assembly, "writes to Jay Gould's counsel and tells him that he intends to save the Manhattan. He suggests that it might be a good financial operation for Mr. Gould to go into Manhattan stock, and says that he (the Judge) will go 'to the very verge of judicial discretion' to conserve Mr. Gould's interests. As Gould did not then have Manhattan stock, this letter was simply an invitation to him to buy it and an assurance to him that the Judge would protect him in it. He further writes that he has not told any human being, except Gould's lawyers, what his decision was going to be; when to them he absolutely writes what motions they shall make in the suits he intends to decide in their favor."

Then Theodore spoke his own indictment:

There cannot be the slightest question that Judge Westbrook ought to be impeached. . . . To you, members of the Legislature of the greatest commonwealth in this great Federal Union, I say you cannot by your votes clear the Judge. He stands condemned by his own acts in the eyes of all honest people. All you can do is to shame yourselves and give him a brief extension of his dishonored career. You cannot cleanse the leper. Beware lest you taint yourselves with his leprosy.

The text of Theodore's speech was reported in full by the papers and duly pasted in the scrapbooks at home. It did not so much matter to his career that the majority report against impeachment was finally adopted, 77 to 35, for it was now widely acknowledged that Theodore Roosevelt, Jr., had, as his friend, Isaac Hunt, said, "won his spurs." The words, "You cannot cleanse the leper," were on everyone's lips.

CHAPTER V

"An Exceedingly Verdant Young Man"

THE winter of 1882–83 Theodore and Alice rented a small house on West Forty-fifth Street, and there the young assemblyman was idyllically happy. These long winter weekends down from Albany were, as he wrote in his diary, like a dream:

"Back again in my own lovely little house with the sweetest and prettiest of all little wives—my own sunny darling. I can imagine nothing more happy in life than an evening spent in my own cosy little sitting room, before a bright fire of soft coals, my books all around me, and playing backgammon with my own dainty mistress."

Going into the second winter of his marriage, Theodore's dreamlike existence at home was unfortunately matched by a tendency to political behavior at Albany that was equally divorced from reality. He had been reelected by an even greater Republican majority than he had scored for his first term, and that in the face of a Democratic landslide. He had been his party's candidate for speaker and, though defeated by a Democrat, that had made him, at the age of twenty-four, minority leader in the Assembly. These early successes undoubtedly went to his head. His conduct in office the year he spent away from Bamie and the family on Fifty-seventh Street made him for a time the laughingstock of all serious politicians and cost him, temporarily, the support of most of the New York press.

Quite on his own, without Bamie's tactful advice and guidance, Theodore in the legislature of 1883 showed himself to be a model of inconsistency. First he was for the five-cent fare, and then he voted just as vociferously against it. When the Assembly refused to seat a friend whose election had been contested, Theodore publicly offered, in a fit of pique, to resign from the Committee on Privileges and Elections. He introduced and seriously pressed for the passage of a bill that required that anyone inflicting pain on a minor should be punished at the whipping post.

Even more than his actions, Theodore's language reached the height of intemperance. He went out of his way to antagonize everybody. "Jay Gould and all of Jay Gould's associates" were "part of that most dangerous of all dangerous classes, the wealthy criminal classes." The Democratic party was the party of "Sodom and Gomorrah." "The Aldermen of New York City" were "a public laughingstock." One colleague was characterized on the floor of the Assembly as "a confirmed dodger" and another as "the highly improbable, perfectly futile, altogether unnecessary, and totally impossible statesman from Ulster." Often William O'Neill, one of Theodore's faithful supporters, would grab him by the coattails and try to haul him back into seat forty. "What do you want to do that for, you damn fool?" Billy O'Neill would growl. "You'll ruin yourself and everybody else."

Now the clippings pasted in the scrapbooks at home began to reflect a different public sentiment toward the young legislator. The *New York Herald* felt that young Roosevelt "has little tact and says and does many things that a calmer judgment would disapprove." The *Lyons Republic* said that he was "not a good party leader." He was "not quite enough of a partisan and a little too much of the gentleman." The *Boston Evening Star* called him "a bogus reformer." The *New York Times* quoted a Democratic leader who described him as "an exceedingly verdant young man" who "paraded a great deal of nonsense." The *New York Observer* said that "young Mr. Roosevelt has been very silly and sullen and naughty." And Jay Gould's *New York*

World, of course, had a field day, during which it delivered the unkindest cut of all. The *World* said that Theodore Roosevelt, Jr., had brought "discredit upon a name made honorable by the private virtues and public services of his father."

Theodore's diaries, which usually glossed over or ignored unpleasant news, took no note of these increasingly unfriendly notices in the press, but when the 1883 legislature adjourned in May, he was no longer in the bouncing physical shape he had enjoyed the year before. His asthma had returned and so, too, had the dyspeptic attacks that had plagued him as a youth. Ever resourceful, Theodore decided in the spring of 1883 that the best cure for these ailments would be a hunting trip. He promptly made plans for a buffalo hunt in western Dakota early in the autumn in order to get himself in condition for his third winter in Albany. Meanwhile, with Alice Lee, he went to the Catskills for a few weeks for his health, and then, together, they spent most of the summer with Bamie and the rest of the family at "Tranquillity" in Oyster Bay.

This summer was one of the happiest the family ever spent together. First, Elliott became engaged in July to Anna Rebecca Hall and seemed finally about to settle down. Then there was the glad news that Alice Lee was pregnant, to which Theodore reacted with characteristic enthusiasm. It was agreed that it would be much more sensible, under the circumstances, and pleasanter for all, if Theodore and Alice Lee would give up the Forty-fifth Street house, subletting it to Elliott and Anna, and come back to live with Bamie and the family the following winter.

Now that he was an expectant father, Theodore aggressively took on the role of *pater familias.* He decided that, instead of renting "Tranquillity," he would buy land of his own at Oyster Bay and build a home there for Alice Lee and all the children they would have. He would buy enough land so that Bamie could purchase part of it and have a summer home of her own adjoining his. Bamie's investment could not be as large because her entire $125,000 inheritance, under the terms of their father's will, was tied up in trust, with their uncle, James West Roosevelt, head of Roosevelt & Son, as controlling trustee. Theodore and Elliott could draw up to $45,000 on their share of the estate, without asking "Uncle Jim's" approval.

Bamie was not sure they could afford this investment. By the terms of Father's will, they all had to keep up the Fifty-seventh Street house for their mother, and this was proving an expensive establishment to run. But Theodore and Alice Lee were already studying plans to build, on the sixty acres they would purchase at Oyster Bay, a $22,000 house, stable, and lodge, and they had already named it "Leeholm," so Bamie agreed to go along.

All the young Roosevelts, not excepting Bamie, seemed to have inherited their mother's cavalier attitude toward money, and, had they not been able to rely from time to time on the sound business sense of Douglas Robinson who married Corinne, they would probably never have managed.

Late in August, Bamie went off to Nova Scotia with her friends, the Lippincotts, to seek brief relief from family chores. Before leaving early in September on his buffalo hunt, with which neither impending fatherhood nor the purchase of a sizable property at Oyster Bay was allowed to interfere, Theodore wrote Bamie how he had been handling matters in her absence. The land survey was almost completed, and he was having her property "mapped out, with monuments, making it continous and adjacent to mine." Then he reported the somewhat casual way he had purchased their property:

"I paid ten thousand down, and gave a mortgage for the remaining twenty thousand at five per cent interest. Your land cost about $7,500; of this you will need to pay $2,500 down while the remaining five thousand you can either pay down at once, thus clearing your property of all encumbrance forthwith, or else keep it as a mortgage, paying 5 per cent interest a year, and the principal whenever you feel inclined, or have saved enough. These details can be arranged in October—but as regards the $2,500, you had best write at once to Uncle Jim, and tell him

45

to turn it over to me, as I have already paid the ten thousand, and will need the money as soon as is convenient. . . ."

In his next letter to Bamie in Nova Scotia, Theodore wrote anxiously, "Neither Uncle Jim nor any of his family except Emlen when I told him about it, have spoken a word, good, bad, or indifferent, to me about the place."

Still this did not change Theodore's plans. He went off on schedule to hunt buffalo. On her return, Bamie must have convinced Uncle Jim, perhaps with Douglas Robinson's help, of the soundness of their Oyster Bay investment. This was before Theodore, that autumn out in the cattle country, made another investment, all on his own, without benefit of consultation with Uncle Jim, Douglas, Bamie, or even Alice Lee.

CHAPTER VI

Theodore's Career Almost Ends

THOUGH he adored his young wife, whom he left temporarily with her parents in Chestnut Hill, Theodore was always to think of western Dakota as the place where "the romance of my life began." When he stepped from the train at Medora and looked around him, he fell in love for the second time—with the dark, sharp-rising buttes, the rolling plains of rich buffalo grass on the banks of the Little Missouri River, and even with the ranchers and the tough, ignorant cowboys who, in turn, regarded him, but only at first, with the suspicion and scorn reserved for all Eastern dudes.

From these rough men, whose respect and affection Theodore was determined to win, he heard tales of the immense profits to be made in the newly opened, grazing land of Montana and the Dakotas. He was impressed with the stories of Bad Lands ranchers who, by running their herds on the lush public grazing land, had doubled their initial investment even as they earned 10, 20, and even 30 percent a year on the sale of their fat cattle.

In less than two weeks' hunting along the Little Missouri, Theodore had made up his mind. Here was the perfect life for a man of his restless energy. For several months each year, he would be a rancher himself in this wonderful hunting country. The investment was sure to augment considerably his present modest income. Moreover, ranching and hunting would fortify him physically for life back in the effete East, and it would not interfere at all, he felt, with family life or with his political career.

Theodore had met and liked instantly two former Canadian lumberjacks who had a cabin just south of Medora. He made an overnight decision in the midst of his hunting trip and the next day turned over a check for $14,000 for the purchase of cattle to these two men, Sylvane Ferris and William Merrifield, who agreed to go shares with him. They called their joint venture the Maltese Cross Ranch. There was talk, also, of Theodore's putting up another $30,000 for cattle in the next few years, if all went well. After that transaction, Theodore went out and shot his first buffalo, surprising his guide, Joe Ferris, by dancing an Indian war dance around the carcass and handing the brother of his new ranching partner a one-hundred-dollar bill as bonus.

Theodore came home from the Bad Lands, to Alice Lee and the family on West Fifty-seventh Street, bronzed and healthy from his weeks in the saddle. In the light of his successful Western trip, the unfortunate figure he had cut at Albany during his second term had, in his own eyes, faded into the distance. He was now—as cattle rancher, prospective father, and owner of a sixty-acre property on Oyster Bay—feeling very much his own man, and with better reason. With all his early enthusiasm renewed, he threw himself first into his election to a third term at Albany and then, with even more vigor, into a battle in earnest for the speakership. He was in line for it, as minority leader of the year before, for now once again Republicans would be in power in the Assembly.

In the autumn of 1883, Theodore stumped the state, on foot, by buggy and train, urging fellow Republican assemblymen to vote for him at the party caucus. His sincerity, his man-to-man approach, which had in it now less of the superior dude and something of the Western rancher's down-to-earth directness, won new friends over and old friends back to his side.

On the eve of the party caucus held just after Christmas,

Theodore appeared to have a clear majority for the speakership, and then the machine, with big-business support, stepped in against him. Here was one more lesson for Theodore, who sat there in caucus and heard his supporters, under this combined pressure, desert him and vote on the first ballot, one by one, for the machine candidate. This was a sharp blow to Theodore's pride and prestige, but he surprised the entire caucus, by proposing, like any party regular, that the machine candidate's election to the speakership be made unanimous. Theodore never again underestimated the power of the machine and of its allies in big business. Where downright evil was involved, he attacked as before, but for most of his career, he was to decide it was best to vote regular. He was to say, in later years, that he had, following his defeat for the speakership, "to pick myself up after learning by bitter experience the lesson that I was not all-important and that I had to take account of many different elements in life."

Theodore did not brood over this defeat. He welcomed his appointment as chairman of the powerful Committee on Cities and began immediately to hold hearings on corruption in New York City, spending Friday through Monday of each week in Manhattan and Tuesday, Wednesday, and Thursday in Albany. He found endless evidence of wrongdoing, and he was in Albany pushing through eighteen bills he had personally drafted to correct it when he received Bamie's telegram on the morning of Wednesday, February 13, informing him that he and Alice Lee now had a baby girl, born the evening before. Happy and exultant, Theodore was nevertheless planning to stay on briefly at Albany and shepherd through to passage the most important of his bills when he received a second telegram that sent him running to catch the train for New York. He arrived home in a heavy, gloomy fog, just before midnight.

With Bamie at her bedside, Mittie Bulloch Roosevelt lay dying of typhoid fever in the ground-floor bedroom where her husband had passed away six years before, almost to the day. In the third-floor bedroom, Alice Lee, attended by Corinne, lay unconscious and dying of Bright's disease. Theodore's healthy little new-born daughter was in the care of a wet nurse hired by Bamie at the home of Aunt Annie Gracie, who lived nearby, and her father would not see her for many sad hours. Three hours after her elder son arrived from Albany, Mittie Roosevelt died. The following afternoon, at two o'clock, Alice Lee, who never regained consciousness, also died, in Theodore's arms.

For a very few days, through the joint funeral services on Saturday at the Presbyterian Church at Fifty-fifth Street and Fifth Avenue, Theodore seemed to a family intimate to be "in a dazed, stunned state. He does not know what he says or does," in fact, "the whole family are utterly demoralized." But, not for long. Bamie saw to it that life went on, for small Alice and for all their sakes. Theodore was back in Albany in seat forty on the floor of the Assembly on the fourth morning after the double funeral. The hours and the effort he put in there for the rest of the term made this year, Theodore's last in the Assembly, the best and most constructive of his legislative career.

And yet, as Theodore wrote in his diary, "the light has gone out of my life." He was restless, plagued with insomnia, and grimly determined "to try to so live as not to dishonor the memory of those I loved who have gone before me." He wrote Bamie from Albany, "We are now holding evening sessions and I am glad we are, for an evening in an Albany hotel leaves much to be desired; indeed the more we work the better I like it."

As the National Republican Convention of 1884 approached, Theodore, though only twenty-five, was now recognized, throughout the state and New England, as one of the party's outstanding leaders. He had lost his zest for politics, but he was expected to play his part on the national scene, and, in this further involvement that helped divert his thoughts from his personal tragedy, Bamie encouraged him. Bamie herself was busier than she had ever been in her life. The year 1884, she recalled, was "a perfect nightmare." Uncle Jim sold the house on Fifty-seventh Street a week after the funeral, and hers was the task of "dividing everything that had always meant home

Bamie spent the summer supervising the work at "Leeholm" out at Oyster Bay. Two young, "very devoted cousins"—John Elliott and Frank Roosevelt (not F. D. R., but another relative) —"came to stay with me, and always said that no one made them work so hard. John, being an engineer, had to lay out the road up to the house—we had none at the time—and Frank, being an electrician, said I forced him to live permanently in the cellar, owing to the fact that we had forgotten to put any bells except the frontdoor bell in the house. He also had to regulate the clocks. I can see him now going from one room to another and listening to each clock, as he had such a well-trained ear that he could always detect the slightest inequality in the ticking of the pendulum."

Bamie, who would always have devoted, helpful young men around her, had a reason for spurring on Cousins Frank and John. She wanted "Leeholm" to be ready just as soon as possible, for she hoped that would bring Theodore back East.

From the letters that came to Bamie from Dakota during the early summer of 1884—and he wrote her regularly, almost every Sunday, throughout his life—it seemed that Theodore, though not quite twenty-six, sought refuge in the tall grass of the Western plains, as if he were some ancient, wounded animal. Without Cabot Lodge to stimulate his interest in politics, Theodore continued to brood over the double tragedy of the winter before. He had no heart for politics, or indeed for anything or anyone back home. He sent "best love" and "many kisses" to his small "Mousiekins," left in Bamie's care. He urged his sister to keep after the architects at "Leeholm." They would spend their summers together there in future, and Bamie would rear "Baby Lee."

But Theodore was obviously living only from sunup to sundown as he sat his Western saddle and rode the range after cattle and wild game. His past seemed too painful, his future too empty, to contemplate. Reading between the lines, Bamie sensed his utter dejection, but even she could only guess its depths. For many weeks, in camp at night, Theodore's rough but sympathetic companions tried unsuccessfully to cheer him. One of them, who reminded him that he must live for the sake of his small daughter back East, never forgot his sad reply, "Her aunt can take care of her better than I can. She would be just as well off without me."

Sometime during the summer of 1884, between June and October, Theodore rather abruptly changed his mind about making his Western ranch a permanent retreat. He did not, as his earliest letters from the Bad Lands indicated he might, withdraw altogether from politics. He went on his hunting trip to Wyoming, but he was back East in time to campaign, in New York, for the national ticket headed by Blaine and, in Massachusetts, for Congressman Henry Cabot Lodge. And he stayed on in New York with Bamie at 422 Madison Avenue through Election Day in November, when, as predicted, Blaine went down in defeat, dragging Lodge, among others, with him.

This reversal in Theodore's plans was brought about by a number of things—time's healing effect, his invigorating outdoor life, the heady excitement of stalking big game, and the strong pull of the news conveyed in Bamie's own regular letters to him —chatty letters about how she was fixing up his study and bedroom in her town house in New York, about the cunning behavior of Baby Lee, about how well things were progressing at Oyster Bay and of the summer fun they would all have there together, and a steady flow of clippings from the papers on all the important political news of the day, with her own shrewd comments on events. Their new friend, Cabot, who promised to bring his wife, Nannie, to them for a visit next winter, now seemed to stand alone. He was being snubbed by the Boston friends who had become political Mugwumps rather than support Blaine of Maine. There was news, too, of mutual friends in New York who were also going over to Cleveland and the Mugwumps. Bamie wrote that some of them even thought Theodore would join their ranks and bolt the Republican party. These friends told Bamie, and they told him directly, too, in the letters she forwarded to his ranch, that he should be man enough at least to speak up and say publicly and unequivocally exactly where he stood.

Such news, waiting for Theodore at the end of a long day herding cattle or a week's hunting trip, had the effect of a match applied to a tired, slow-burning fuse. Here was a challenge no man of Theodore's temper and caliber could long withstand. What bothered him most was the lone position of their friend, Cabot Lodge, to whom he had paid a brief visit at Nahant on a trip east in July to see his publisher and his dead wife's parents at Chestnut Hill. And yet, well into that summer, Theodore was still hoping to stay out of the fall campaign. He wrote Lodge in mid-August from the Bad Lands, "We can take part in no bolt; but I do not think we need take any *active* part in the campaign." This was scant comfort for Lodge, and scarcely practical, since he was to run for reelection to Congress on the regular Republican ticket. But to his Boston friend, Theodore now repeated what he had written Bamie earlier, "Indeed I may be in Dakota on Election Day."

The change in Theodore's plans undoubtedly came about during the month he was hunting elk and bear in the Big Horn Mountains. Bamie could detect, in the letter he wrote her from Fort McKinney in Wyoming late in September, the very day he came down out of the mountains, an entirely different tone. He had just killed three grizzly bears and six elk. He now had "a dozen good heads," and Bamie was delighted to note that he intended them for the hall of "the house on the hill" at Oyster Bay. He had had "good sport" and "enough excitement and fatigue to prevent over much thought" so that he had "at last been able to sleep well at night."

Bamie was also much interested to read that "after I had begun bear killing, other sport seemed tame" and that Theodore now felt that "unless I was bear hunting all the time I am afraid I should soon get as restless with this life as with the life at home." The best news of all was that he was starting at once for his ranch on the Little Missouri. He would reach there in a fortnight "and a week afterwards will be on my way home." What he would do there, Theodore did not say. He was sorry, so he wrote even then, that "my political career should be over," but he asked if he would be in time to register for voting, and he cautioned Bamie that their Mugwump friends "had best not express their discontent to my face unless they wish to hear very plain English." This was enough to convince her that Theodore was happily almost ready to be his old combative political self again.

Theodore arrived at Bamie's house on Thursday, October 9, in tip-top shape, his face a reddish brown from the Western sun. He found the desk in his new study stacked high with mail from Mugwumps and party regulars and the front door besieged, as the Roosevelt home had once been long before in his father's time, by reporters anxious for political news. He was delighted to renew his short acquaintance with the small daughter who was thriving under Bamie's care. He had long political discussions with the sister who had already concluded, as Lodge wrote her in one of his early letters, that "Theodore would not be happy out of public affairs." In Theodore's study, they discussed their father's earlier decision to let matters take their course and play no active part in an intraparty fight. But their father had been a dying man, and Theodore, fresh from the West, was in his robust prime.

By Saturday evening, two days after his arrival, Theodore had made up his mind. He agreed to an interview in his study with a reporter from the *New York Sun*.

"When I started out to my ranch two months ago," Theodore told the reporter, who shared a sherry with him, "I had no intention of taking any part whatever in the presidential canvass." But he had, all this while, been "revolving the matter" in his mind, and he had now decided "it is altogether contrary to my character to occupy a neutral position in so important and exciting a struggle." Besides, Theodore told the man from the *Sun*, it was his "natural desire to occupy a position of some kind," and he had consequently made up his mind that it was clearly his duty to "support the ticket." He would, on Saturday evening next, tell an audience of Young Republicans in Brooklyn "the full reasons why I would advise all independent Republicans to support the Republican ticket."

In the campaign of 1884, in which he himself was running for no office, Theodore made seven speeches in all, three of them in Massachusetts for Lodge. Though Lodge lost in his Congressional District—by 300 Mugwump votes—he never forgot that Theodore, and Bamie, too, were among the few friends who stood by him at a critical early period in his political career.

On the stump, Theodore showed himself to be adept at de-emphasizing the role of the "Plumed Knight." He admitted frankly he had been against Blaine at Chicago, but he felt sure that the candidate could be made to live up to the "party's ideals." Instead of defending Blaine, he damned all Democrats, for they belonged to "the party that tried to destroy the Union, that supported slavery, that favored greenbackism." His most slashing attacks were reserved for the Mugwumps, who, throughout the campaign, accused Lodge and Roosevelt of being turncoat reformers. He and Lodge, Theodore countered, had worked for reform within the party. They had often defied the machine and accomplished what the Mugwumps only talked of doing. And he likened all Mugwumps to ornamental "poodles." They were "possessed of none of the robuster virtues that would enable them to come out and do the right."

Long after the election of 1884, Theodore continued to disavow publicly any interest in politics for himself, even though he had astutely drawn bead that year on the Republican party's chief enemy. Curiously enough, just as a marginal Mugwump vote did for Lodge, temporarily, in Massachusetts, so on the national scene where New York's electoral votes were crucial, a few hundred Mugwump votes swung Cleveland, over Blaine, into the White House. It was all "simply cruel," Theodore wrote Lodge from Bamie's, "and I do not dare to trust myself at present to speak to an independent on the subject." Lodge himself would "come back in time," but, as for Theodore, again he did not believe that he would "ever be likely to come back into political life."

Theodore did not hold public office again until more than four years had passed, but he was never really out of politics from 1884 on. Bamie, Lodge, and Theodore, himself, ever seeking new outlets for revived and restless energies, saw to that. In the years ahead, all three were to meet with some opposition to his choice of politics as a career from an unexpected quarter. His second wife, Edith Carow, would often fail to see how Theodore could possibly expect to support a growing family properly on the meager rewards of public office.

After the Democratic victory in 1884, Theodore spent a great deal of time out West where he added the Elkhorn Ranch, farther down the Little Missouri River, to his Maltese Cross herd. At Oyster Bay, where he moved with Bamie and Baby Lee for their first summer, in June of 1885, and stayed on through the fall for fox hunting with the Meadowbrook Hunt, he spent much of his time writing magazine articles on political affairs and completing his *Hunting Trips of a Ranchman*. He liked, then, to call himself just a "rancher" or "a literary fellow," but he never lost touch with what was going on politically in his city and state. He seems always to have been present, during these years, at political gatherings of any importance. At one such meeting, he told a reporter, who found him sitting modestly in the rear of the hall, "I am only a private in this battle—but I am ready to be commanded for any movement."

During this period, just as Oyster Bay was Bamie's summer home, so 422 Madison Avenue was home for Theodore. Indeed, even after his second marriage, Bamie's town house served not only as Theodore's headquarters whenever he was in the city but as his permanent and official address for voting purposes. Bamie spoke of this rather unusual arrangement, years later, in words that imply more than they explain.

"I always insisted," Bamie said, "that we did not live together, that we only visited one another, realizing beforehand that that would be a much easier relationship to break than had we made a mutual home. And this proved the case when he married his second wife."

Theodore met Edith Carow—again—on the stairway of Bamie's town house in October of 1885. He was just twenty-seven and Edith, who had been his sister Corinne's closest chum on Twentieth Street, had also been his childhood sweetheart.

Now Edith and her sister were living, in somewhat straitened circumstances, with their widowed mother, not far from Bamie's house on Madison Avenue. From time to time, since Corinne was now a young matron living in Orange, New Jersey, Edith would drop in at Bamie's for what she called a "talkee-talkee" about old times.

At this surprise meeting on the stairway, Theodore, dramatically, had his arm in a sling. Always prone to accidents when restless or unsettled, he had just had a bad fall out with the Meadowbrook Hunt. Both were embarrassed, partly because both undoubtedly knew that he had told Bamie always to warn him in advance whenever she was expecting a visit from Edith. Very properly in the tradition of the times, Theodore thought it best to avoid anyone who might be attractive to him, so soon after his wife's death.

At the meeting on the stairs, Edith must have wondered. Had Theodore ignored Bamie's warning this time? Or had Bamie failed to warn him? No one would ever know, but Bamie may have worried that Theodore might, though alcohol was never his problem, go the footless way of brother Elliott and the rest of the hard-riding, hard-drinking Hempstead, Long Island, crowd who were then the moving spirits in the Meadowbrook Hunt. Certainly Bamie had, by this time, come to the conclusion that Theodore would be much better off married.

In any event, Theodore fell in love once more during that brief encounter at Bamie's. In the next few weeks, he struggled manfully with himself—one fox-hunting friend, who was a guest at Oyster Bay, said Theodore spent half the night pacing his room, muttering angrily to himself, "I have no constancy—*no* constancy."

On November 17, Theodore succumbed. He became secretly engaged to Edith, so secretly that his diaries during that winter referred to her only as "E." Bamie and Corinne were told, but no one else was to know. In the spring, Theodore departed for the West and Edith for Europe, with her mother and sister. They wanted to wait the proper period of respectful mourning for his first wife.

Before his second marriage in London more than a year later, Theodore busied himself chiefly with ranching and writing. During the summer of 1886, he wrote a life of Thomas Hart Benton almost while in the saddle. Lodge had convinced a friend who was the Boston editor of the American Statesmen series that Theodore was just the man to do that great Western senator. He later got Theodore the biography of Gouverneur Morris to do over his editor friend's objection that Morris did not really belong in the Statesmen series. In typical Lodge fashion, Cabot won the editor over with, "But Theodore needs the money, you see." One reason why Lodge furthered Theodore's biographical writings may have been that he did not altogether approve of all the magazine articles Theodore was turning out about his life on the plains. But then, neither did Bamie. During that summer while Bamie was visiting the Lodges at Nahant, she and Cabot discussed one of Theodore's Western stories—about how he had stalked and captured three dangerous horse thieves. Both managed to convince him, by letter, that, although all the facts were undoubtedly true, he had perhaps put too much "I" in the article for magazine publication.

Also during the summer and fall of 1886, Theodore made several attempts to begin his political career again. While he was in the West, he was voted in as head of New York's Twenty-first District Republican Association, but he did not think it right to accept the post when he was at such a distance.

"You were very sweet to send me the newspaper cuttings," he wrote Bamie. "I was greatly amused to find I had unknowingly won a political victory, but I would much rather not have been made President of the Association. If I am going to do anything at all I like to give my time to it."

The next opportunity that turned up was an invitation to Theodore from the nonpartisan Mayor of New York City to come home and be president of the local Board of Health. Theodore seriously considered this offer for a while. He would soon be twenty-eight, and a married man again, and he could scarcely expect a woman of Edith's gentle breeding to share his life on the range. He wrote Lodge, "As my chance of doing anything in the future worth doing seems to grow continually smaller, I intend to grasp at every opportunity that turns up." Soon he was writing Bamie that their friend in Boston considered matters of city sanitation "infra dig" for a Roosevelt, with which no doubt Bamie agreed.

The last political offer Theodore received before he sailed for England to meet Edith, was, though more acceptable, rather a hollow honor, as everyone involved was well aware. He was asked by Elihu Root, whose friendship with the Roosevelt family dated from the elder Theodore's time, to make himself available as the regular Republican candidate that fall for mayor of New York City. He would run in that campaign against the Single-Taxer Henry George, whom all good property owners greatly feared, as well as against Abram S. Hewitt, a Democrat who nonetheless had the respect of all good men in the Republican party. No one, including Theodore, Lodge, and Bamie, seriously thought he had a chance of winning. But he had said he was "only a private" who stood "ready to be commanded for any movement" and the party managers took him at his word. Theodore accepted the nomination and campaigned to win, even as he made plans to sail for London immediately after Election Day. Since he did not want his supporters to know he expected defeat, he booked passage as "Mr. Merrifield" traveling with his sister, "Miss Merrifield," for Bamie had decided to go with him.

In a letter to Nannie Lodge on Election Day, just before they sailed, Bamie wrote:

61

"Theodore is radiantly happy and we sail on Saturday for England. Edith will be in London & they are to be married there early in December.... Theodore has against my will insisted on my keeping Baby, in fact for the present at least we will go on just as we are; all this sounds so crude in writing & it would have been a great thing to me could I but have talked over all these plans with you.... Edith we have known intimately always. She is very bright & attractive & I believe absolutely devoted to Theodore so I think their future looks most promising.... Today is of course politically one of intense excitement to me personally & apparently to New York generally. Theodore, Douglas and a number of men have been in to lunch & tonight I shall simply haunt the streets. Mr. Lodge will I suppose telegraph at once when he knows his own fate. We talk of him continually—How I wish Theodore & Mr. Lodge could ever be together during these kind of days.... I really need to hear from you. With my love to you & almost the same to Mr. Lodge."

Cabot Lodge was returned to Congress by his Massachusetts district but the Republicans of New York City dared not risk letting a Single-Taxer squeak in on a three-way split. Most of them voted for the Democrat, and Theodore ran a poor third. Before sailing, Theodore wrote Cabot, "At least I have a better Party standing than ever before." Men like Root, who were the real party managers in New York, had learned that the young maverick of legislative days could accept party discipline and act as if he were a regular himself—on occasion.

CHAPTER VIII

A Foggy Day in London

THEODORE and Edith were married in London on December 2, 1886. His best man was Cecil Spring-Rice, an engaging young British diplomat and big-game hunter whom he and Bamie had met for the first time on the boat going over. The camaraderie of all three was instant and enduring. So enchanted was Spring-Rice with Bamie and "the Boss Republican young man of New York," as he called Theodore, that he could scarcely do enough for them when they arrived in London. During their brief stay at Brown's Hotel before the wedding, Spring-Rice introduced them to all his most interesting diplomatic and literary friends. Theodore wrote Cabot Lodge that, though he had not bothered to bring along any letters of introduction, he had been put down at the best clubs and had had a good day out with the Essex hounds where, of course, "there was not any of our high jumping or breakneck galloping." To Corinne, who was taking care of small Alice in their absence, Theodore wrote that Bamie "has had a glorious time. She has ... afternoon teas with as many incongruous men in attendance as at New York."

On this trip to London, decided on by Bamie at the last moment because she felt some member of the family should be with Theodore and Edith when they married so far from home, she met, through Spring-Rice, the whole attractive Ferguson clan whose family seat was at Raith near Kirkcaldy in the

Highlands north of the Firth of Forth. The eldest son in this delightful Scottish family, presided over by a widowed mother with considerable talent as an amateur artist, was Spring-Rice's best friend, Sir Ronald Ferguson, and Sir Ronald, who was then parliamentary secretary to Gladstone's witty foreign minister, Lord Rosebery, was one of the most promising younger men in the Liberal party. There were also Valerie and Edith Ferguson, who were in their twenties, and two extremely handsome younger sons, Robert and Hector. All Fergusons tended to fall in love with Bamie on first acquaintance, and while Theodore was testing the hedges of England and enjoying the exclusively male society of London's clubs, Sir Ronald and his sisters prevailed on her to come to Raith for her first visit to the lovely country place beyond Edinburgh that was to become her second home whenever she was abroad. From the first, the Fergusons adopted Bamie as one of their own, and she responded to their affectionate Scottish hospitality as if she had been born into the clan.

Bamie's particular favorite among the "Fergies," as she and Theodore both soon began to call them, was the middle brother, Robert H. Munro Ferguson, a tall and dourly handsome young man of eighteen, quick-witted and rather mature for his years, whose extraordinary charm lay in the way his long, sad face would light up instantly at the prospect of fun and adventure, particularly if this were proposed by Bamie or Theodore, whom he came to regard in later years with something akin to hero worship. For Bamie, in spite of the fourteen years' difference in their ages, he developed an attachment that lasted all his life and was nothing short of adoration.

Just as Spring-Rice had fallen under the spell of Theodore and Bamie, putting in for an immediate diplomatic transfer to the United States, so, too, did Bob Fergie, after making Bamie's acquaintance at Raith and meeting Theodore later in London, set his heart on trying his luck in America. With the complete approval of Sir Ronald and his mother and sisters, he would later go to the United States, first to help Theodore out on his ranch and then to be helped, by Bamie, to an excellent position with the

Astor Estate. In time, handsome young "Fergie," as everyone called him, would become a sort of permanent fixture, despite the disparity in their ages, in Bamie's social entourage, and this, all the Roosevelts said, no one but Bamie could ever have managed without scandal. For there certainly was, between Fergie and Bamie, an attachment that could only be described in the Edwardian term "affinity," and curiously enough in those days the age difference did not matter so much and certainly not on the Continent. And, as Bamie managed it, although Fergie was almost a perennial house guest or household familiar wherever her home, in London, New York, or Washington, the affinity that existed between them was never touched by one breath of scandal. All her friends and relations simply took Fergie's perpetual presence in Bamie's ménage, into which he fitted perfectly as a sort of gentleman major domo, as a matter of course. Only Edith Carow Roosevelt would persist in regarding the personable young bachelor so much at home in Bamie's various establishments as "rather eccentric." But then Edith always possessed, and expressed, her own independent opinion, and this trait became apparent quite early, even as early as that December day in London in 1886 when she married Theodore.

Bamie unreservedly approved of that marriage, of course, even as she had encouraged their romance from its start on the stairway. But already she was beginning to sense in Edith, who was a very mature twenty-five at the time of her marriage, a firm, if not stubborn, mind of her own. There were small signs, only a flicker perhaps here and there, that Edith might resent the close tie between brother and sister. They were ebullient, warm, and demonstrative, while Edith, as Fergie so perceptively put it, "don't encourage much intimacy." On the eve of the wedding, when Edith came over from the Continent with her mother and sister to meet Theodore in London, it was already apparent to Bamie, who could not always check her tendency to dominate, that Edith might very well become jealous of any influence over Theodore except her own. It was no wonder then that Bamie, so soon to be alone in London as later in New York, should gravitate, during those few weeks abroad at the time of Theodore's wedding, into the center of the whole attractive Ferguson clan. Moreover, in handsome Fergie, she acquired a most amusing young admirer, wise beyond his years, even as she seemed on the verge of losing her irreplaceable Theodore.

At the wedding in St. George's, Hanover Square, Bamie was Edith's attendant. Recalling the occasion later, Bamie usually dwelt with some amusement on the behavior of her brother and his best man, Cecil Spring-Rice.

"Dear Springy was so delightful and like himself when I went to put on Edith's veil," Bamie would say. "I warned Theodore to start immediately for the church as it was a foggy day, and they were intensely occupied in a discussion over the population of an island in the South Pacific."

This intense discussion on the demography of the South Pacific continued in the hansom cab, as Edith and Bamie followed in another. At some point en route to Hanover Square, Springy insisted on an unscheduled stop. He was seen to dash from Theodore's cab, and the occupants of both hansoms soon lost sight of each other in foggy London. Springy, who was quite dégagé in matters of dress, had decided at the last minute to purchase a pair of bright orange gloves for the groom. Wearing these horrors, undoubtedly a shocking sight in Edith's conservative eyes, Theodore managed to reach the church in time for the ceremony. At its conclusion, bride and groom signed the St. George's registry, Theodore adding his occupation, with a flourish, as "Rancher." Then he and Edith, who was relieved to have done with such hectic nonsense, started immediately for their honeymoon on the Continent.

At Dover, Theodore posted a letter to Bamie in London before she sailed for home, where for a few months more she would care for the child who had now become almost her own.

"You dearest sister," Theodore wrote, "I cannot say how much I appreciated your coming over; it has been everything to Edith and myself; I am so very glad you came over as you did; and you have been too sweet for anything during the past fortnight."

Then touching on a matter much on all their minds, he added, "Remember to give my letter, with a thousand kisses, to Baby Lee."

Baby Lee, who was just going on three years old, with her long flaxen curls and big, appraising, bright blue eyes so much like Bamie's, made all the difference to her that Christmas of 1886, the first Theodore had ever spent away from home. Even when he was out in the Bad Lands, he had always come back for the holidays. Now, as the winter weeks went by, even though Theodore's letters came as frequently and regularly as before—from Paris, Florence, Rome—Bamie had time to realize how much of a change his second marriage would make in her life. One thing she hoped, perhaps foolishly, would not change. It had been Theodore's suggestion that Bamie continue to bring up his daughter by his first wife. This might be better for Alice, less awkward for Theodore and Edith, and, most of all, as Bamie was beginning to realize, a Godsend to her. It would give point and focus to her life.

As Theodore and Edith progressed from place to place on the Continent, his letters soon began to show an impatience with travel. He spent many hours, with Edith's help, brooding over the state of his finances. News from the Bad Lands warned him it would be a terrible winter for cattle. In a letter from Florence, Bamie was shocked to read that he and Edith were even considering the sale of the house at Oyster Bay, the summer home now rechristened "Sagamore Hill" that Bamie had built and loved almost as her own. But Theodore promised her, "I do love Sagamore Hill: I will not give it up if I can help." Later, he wrote, "My financial affairs for the past year make such a bad showing that Edith and I think seriously of closing Sagamore Hill and going to the ranch for a year or two." Bamie could not quite see Edith roughing it in this fashion, but here, nevertheless, was a very real threat to the political career Bamie wished for him. It was doubly distressing to read that he did not "much care whether I change my residence from New York or not" for "I have not the slightest belief in my having any political future."

Certainly Theodore had expressed these doubts before, but now it was perfectly plain they had been buttressed by Edith's instinctive dislike of life in the public eye. With such discreet sentiments Bamie could readily sympathize, but she was determined from the first not to let them interfere, if she could help it, with her brother's happiness that now, it seemed to her, depended so entirely on his following a political career.

In dealing with this particular facet of their intertwined lives, Bamie thought it best to wait, until perhaps Edith could be made to see how important such a career was to Theodore's well-being, and until, on their return from abroad, she might further enlist Cabot Lodge's support. On the much more personal matter of the child, however, the lonely winter days prompted Bamie to the tactical error of reminding Theodore in a letter of his proposal that Alice stay on with her. They had said they wanted to economize; they might even go to the Western ranch, and that would be no place for a child of three. Bamie then received a rebuff from Edith that, though indirect and only the first of many, she never forgot. She heard from Theodore, undoubtedly mighty uncomfortable at being caught in this fashion between two equally determined women, early in January of 1887.

"I hardly know what to say about Baby Lee," Theodore wrote from Rome, "Edith feels more strongly about her than I could have imagined possible. However, we can decide it all when we meet. Give my best love to the darling; and many kisses."

Bamie's reaction to this initial defeat was characteristic. She spent the rest of the winter moving into a new house farther out on Madison Avenue. She imported an English butler and maid, Chamberlain and Mary, and settled in at No. 689 in comfortable style. If she was going to be quite alone, then she would make the best of it, for Bamie never lacked company.

Cabot Lodge came on from Boston and Springy, now attached to the British legation in Washington, came up in mid-March to stay with Bamie and greet the returning honeymoon couple, who would spend the early spring with Bamie before going out to Sagamore Hill—which was not to be jettisoned after all. Alice, carrying a huge bunch of red roses, met her new mother for the first time on the stairway at No. 689. Neither then nor at any time in her whole life, Alice was to recall years later, did she ever hear her mother's name spoken by Edith or her father.

The spring of 1887 was a difficult time for Bamie, and no doubt quite as awkward for Edith, who was already expecting her own first child in September. Everyone seemed to go off in all directions. Theodore, Bamie was happy to see, still showed some interest in how the Republican party would fare in the next national elections. He took Springy and Cabot out to Ophir Hall for a luncheon with the *New York Tribune*'s Whitelaw Reid, already a power in the party as well as the husband of Bamie's best friend, Elisabeth Mills Reid. Then Theodore headed for the Bad Lands to inspect the winter's damage, and Edith departed shortly thereafter for a visit with relatives, leaving Alice, for a few weeks still, in Bamie's charge.

Theodore found things much worse than he had expected out in Dakota. He wrote Bamie from his Elkhorn Ranch:

"I am bluer than indigo about the cattle; it is even worse than I feared; I wish I was sure I would lose no more than half the money I invested out here. I am planning how to get out of it." Then he added, "I have thought very often and very lovingly of you, my darling sister, since [I] left you alone in New York— that is, as much alone as it is ever possible for you to be. Give many kisses to Sweet Baby Lee."

When Theodore and Edith returned to Bamie's early in May they were now both anxious to settle down at Sagamore Hill, at least for the summer and fall. It was decided that, since Edith was expecting, Alice might best, that summer, make the first of many annual visits to her Lee grandparents in Chestnut Hill. Edith and Theodore also decided, and Bamie could only agree, that after her Chestnut Hill visit, Alice would not come back to her aunt but would go directly out to Oyster Bay to make her home with them. Bamie wrote Grandmother Lee to come for Alice the middle of May and then, unable to face the child's actual departure, went off herself, on an extended tour of the Civil War battlefields, leaving Edith in charge at No. 689.

On her trip through the South, she heard, of course, from Theodore—how he envied her her tour through such historic country, and he reported, most lovingly, that Alice looked "just like a little white penguin when she said good-bye" the day Grandmother Lee took her away.

One letter from Theodore that Bamie received at this time reposed for years in her desk torn quite in half. It told her how he and Edith had moved into Sagamore Hill, and "We have been working for the past week with a zeal and energy that would have done your heart good to see." This part of the letter would have caused Bamie, still on tour of the Southern battlefields with congenial friends, scarcely more than a pang or two. She was usually generous, a stranger to self-pity, and a realist. Had she not chosen to absent herself, she could have been at Oyster Bay, too, helping them get settled. It was doubtless the rest of the letter that caused her to rip it in half.

Now in her early thirties, Bamie was beginning to round out a bit, not too much for the times, of course, but her figure had definitely developed stylish matronly lines. Edith, even after she had had a number of "bunnies," remained for all her life slender and willowy. This particular letter from Theodore, late in May, 1887, informed Bamie of the unfortunate state in which he had found their joint stables at Oyster Bay. He was "sorry to say that your saddle horse is as lame as ever," and he wished, with much affection and brotherly lack of tact, that "Caution were big enough for you to ride; but I am afraid she is much too light." Theodore certainly did not remember, though Bamie undoubtedly did the instant she read those lines, what he had written her from abroad about that same little mare, Caution, when he had been so worried about finances. Then Theodore had said he might have to sell the entire stable at Oyster Bay, including his own beloved horse, Sagamore, and even Bamie's carriage horses —if indeed he had actually bought them as Bamie said he had. (This sort of thing Theodore could never keep straight.) But,

70

Theodore had written, he would not, under any circumstances, sell Caution because "Edith thinks she would like to ride her very much."

When Bamie returned from the battlefields, she knew it would be much wiser for her to keep her distance from Oyster Bay for a while. She went out to Sagamore Hill with Springy when he came up from Washington for a visit, but she felt restless and stayed only a few days. Sagamore Hill did not seem the same without little Alice. Later, when Sir Ronald Ferguson came over on his first trip to America, she again went to Sagamore Hill, with him and with Springy, but this visit was even more brief. The truth was that she and Edith found it difficult to ignore their lack of congeniality. They were so successful in concealing it from those around them, if not from each other, that Sir Ronald went home marveling at the jolly good times his friend, Springy, was having with all the happy Roosevelts.

Theodore, unhappy man, was not fooled for a moment. When Bamie begged off from paying more frequent visits to Sagamore Hill that summer—because she was too busy in town or promised elsewhere—he grew increasingly uncomfortable. And, of course, it was through Theodore that Bamie received once again, in the autumn of 1887, what seemed to her a major rebuff from Edith.

Early in August, hoping to lure Bamie back to Oyster Bay for a long visit, Theodore wrote her how delighted they were to have Alice home from Chestnut Hill. He reenacted in his letter the following little scene between Alice and her stepmother: "Small straw-colored Parent (to blue-eyed offspring) 'Well, what do you want to say to Auntie Bye?'... Offspring (with seraphic smile) 'A Kiss!' " Then Theodore added, "We miss you dreadfully."

It was a temptation to run out to Sagamore Hill, if only for the day, but Bamie continued to keep her distance. Perhaps because she, too, missed Alice and Theodore just as "dreadfully," she was oversensitive; she could not help noticing the absence of any personally extended invitation from Edith in Theodore's use of the editorial "We."

71

At the end of August, Bamie was still away, this time visiting the Lodges at Nahant in Massachusetts, and there the good political talks with Cabot made her long to see her brother and tell him the high hopes she and Cabot had for his future. It was disappointing, in a way, that Theodore's regular letters to her now dwelt on family news rather than politics, and once again he urged that, on her return from Nahant, she come for a long visit because "we miss you dreadfully."

If Edith had echoed this sentiment even in a handwritten footnote, as she sometimes did in later years, Bamie would have gone to Sagamore immediately. Instead, it was not until early in September, when Edith's child was almost due, that Bamie decided she was probably being utterly ridiculous to stand on ceremony and wait for her to extend the invitation. The more she thought about it, the more it seemed to her that, with the baby coming, Edith might really need her at Sagamore Hill, particularly since Edith's own mother and sister were abroad. Family nursing cares had always devolved on Bamie; it seemed only natural, then, to offer to be with Edith and to keep house for her, if she wished, during her confinement at Sagamore Hill. Bamie wrote Theodore she would indeed like very much to come to Oyster Bay if she could be of real assistance in this way to Edith.

This suggestion was obviously not at all welcome to the new mistress of Sagamore Hill. No doubt Edith's reserve and disinclination for "much intimacy" was heightened by the anxiety of expecting her firstborn. Besides, she had already arranged to have in attendance her childhood nurse, Mame, and Mame would stay on to be her own child's nurse. It was not Edith, however, who explained this situation to Bamie, as anyone might expect, but Theodore, poor man, who wrote his sister as tactfully as he could.

"Just a line to say how very, very much we appreciate your proposal, you blessed blue-eyed Rogue (?); you always were true as steel in any tight place. [But] Mame is devoted; you know how much she is to Edith; I do not think there is need of any one else...."

Beyond this there was no word from Edith on the subject, and Bamie could only conclude her presence was not wanted at all. She felt a fool for having offered, and the damage to her pride would take years to undo. It seemed to Bamie, and to Corinne, too, when they discussed it, as they often did, that they would have to tread very lightly in all their dealings with Edith. The sisters concluded that the new Mrs. Theodore Roosevelt, whom they had known all their lives, was likely to misconstrue the interest they naturally took in everything Theodore did and consider it an attempt to exert undue influence. And, as Corinne said, both of them knew only too well that if Edith were to become really annoyed with them, loyal Theodore would, of course, in the end have to side with his wife. Perhaps they might never even be permitted to see him again! After such discussions, Corinne and Bamie were determined never to give Edith the slightest excuse for feeling that they were interfering in any way.

For a time, Bamie almost succeeded in divorcing herself entirely from Theodore's and Edith's affairs. These were the years when Bamie was very much "Auntie Bye" to the growing crop of nieces and nephews. She would stop in for a few days' visit, then off she would go again in no time. She was restless, trying not to live through others and doing so in spite of herself.

First, she took care of Elliott and his family while that attractive but self-destructive brother was slowly but surely drinking himself to death. Winters she traveled extensively on the Continent with her Philadelphia friends, the Lippincotts. Summers she spent up in the Adirondacks with Cousin Rosy Roosevelt and his family, or with the Whitelaw Reids in their elaborate "camp" on the Upper St. Regis, or out at "Westbrook" on Long Island with the Bayard Cuttings. She even became one of the Lady Managers of the Chicago world's fair of 1893 to keep herself busy and away from Sagamore Hill. Often, wherever she went, handsome young Fergie was in faithful attendance. Still,

73

this period of her life was so empty of real interest to her, in later years, that she telescoped it all in her memoir in a few brief lines.

"For many years," Bamie recalled, "my career was that of an odd-job man. There were always children arriving in the world or ill, and I was always at one house or the other; very busy with their families, with no time to even remotely think of getting married, so that I always said it took the solitude of a London season to give me time to become engaged."

CHAPTER IX

"Dear Cabot"—"Dear Bamie"

BAMIE'S multifarious family duties or, as she put it, her career as "odd-job man," took her to London in the early 1890s. She went with the idea of staying only a month or so, but as things turned out her visit lasted three years, punctuated by quick trips home in summer or fall, chiefly to see how Theodore was getting on. By this time, Cabot Lodge, using his influence in Washington, had gotten Theodore his first important public office, an appointment from President Harrison to be one of three Federal Civil Service commissioners.

Theodore was supremely happy as a member of Washington officialdom during his early years as a commissioner, and Edith, who now had three children of her own with a fourth on the way, seemed more or less content. Both continually urged Bamie to visit them in their small rented house on Jefferson Place, Theodore writing that Edith was sure his dressing room could easily be converted into a perfectly adequate guest bedroom for her.

Shortly before Christmas in 1893, Bamie was planning one of her political dinners in New York, at No. 689 Madison Avenue, especially for Theodore—who frequently came up from Washington to renew contacts, at her house, with various and sundry leaders in his home state—when she received a distressing cable from London. The cable was from their Hyde Park cousin,

James Roosevelt Roosevelt, older half brother of F.D.R. It informed her that his wife, Helen Astor Roosevelt, had died very suddenly. "Poor Rosy" was left a widower, with a girl of twelve and a boy of fourteen, just as he was taking over his duties as first secretary of the American Embassy in London. Bamie, who had been one of Helen's bridesmaids, cabled Rosy instantly, "Would it help if I came over to be with you for a while?" The result was that this particular dinner of Bamie's went off quite successfully, so Theodore reported, with her faithful couple, Chamberlain and Mary, doing the honors, even though Bamie herself was on the high seas on her way to Cousin Rosy.

"You are an angel, as usual," Nannie Lodge in Washington wrote Bamie after she arrived in London, "to go & take care of all the poor forlorn things of the world," but, "for us, it is a great blow. We had counted so much upon having you here for a long visit."

Nannie Lodge, as well as Cabot, had conspired mightily to get Theodore to Washington. Even before Cabot's successful attempt in 1889, Nannie had tried to convince the then secretary of state, who was none other than Blaine of Maine, the "Plumed Knight," that Theodore would make him an ideal assistant secretary. But that gallant gentleman, who loved to oblige such attractive dinner partners as Nannie, said his summer sleep at Augusta or Bar Harbor would be much disturbed if someone as aggressive and belligerent as Theodore were running the State Department in his absence.

Now that Cabot had managed to get Theodore his commissionership, the Lodges were disappointed that Bamie, too, was not to be on the Washington scene. They had recently moved into a big, comfortable brick house on Massachusetts Avenue and had looked forward to having Bamie with them often, for they loved going to her at No. 689. As Cabot, that usually sardonic and reserved Bostonian, wrote Bamie after one of their New York visits, "I cannot tell you how much I have enjoyed these last days with you all—You are so like my own that it is difficult to say how much pleasure you have given me because I take it all as a matter of course." To which Bamie responded, much more typically for her: "Please never feel it in your mind to thank us for a visit here & only remember that there is nothing can give me the same gratification as feeling you are happy with us. You & Nannie have filled a place not only in Theodore's life but in mine also that you can never realize & which is an unceasing source of real happiness."

When she was in London during the winter of 1893–94, far from Theodore and the Lodges, Bamie, at first, felt terribly homesick. In her memoir, she recalled arriving "about the middle of December quite early on a terrible dreary afternoon, to realize that the sun preferred setting by half past two up in the very top of the sky, as I discovered it continued this habit for the winter —and there I found my poor little dark-eyed Helen badly wanting some one to help her, but Cousin Rosy also being in no condition for me to take her from him, so that very unexpectedly I remained there until September, 1894."

During her first winter in London, with Cousin Rosy of course in deep mourning and very little entertaining to be done in the house on Upper Belgrave Street, Bamie wrote Cabot, "We are so very quiet here in the midst of the fashionable whirl. It would be difficult for you to realize it as possible. We literally never go out in the evening; but the lunches I find fortunately more agreeable than the dinners & for them I am always free. I probably would have felt very lonely as far as friends were concerned this winter had it not been for Mrs. Dugdale and the Fergusons. . . . You cannot imagine how I missed Theodore, Nannie, & you this winter. I feel cut off from so much. . . . Do, Mr. Pinkie,* just write me soon if only a line & tell me how Theodore's cough & throat are. It makes me anxious the way they continue. . . ."

When spring finally came to London in 1894, and the days of strictest mourning on Upper Belgrave Street had passed, Bamie was free to indulge her gregarious nature. Now, as she wrote Cabot, "All the inhabitants of the United States seem to be com-

* Nannie Lodge's pet name for her husband.

ing over," and "the Hays are in town for a long stay." She had just come from a tea given them by the American ambassador and his wife, Mr. and Mrs. Thomas F. Bayard. "Mrs. Hay looked extremely handsome in black velvet & jet with a fine piece of Venetian lace in the bodice," while her daughter, Helen, was "fascinating in white & silver." Then, as Bamie wrote, "After viewing our national representatives, I went to Lady Helen Ferguson for a real Drawing Room tea, which was amusing, Lady Dufferin & several of the others wearing gorgeous jewels & orders; little Lady Terence, very French dolly, pretty & without air. From there, thanks to these long days, Rosy & I were able to go to the Royal Academy, it being the Private View day, which of course meant a packed crowd of the most marvelous looking beings & but a poor sight of the pictures."

All Bamie's letters from London during her three years there were treasured by the Lodges and shared, as they arrived, with Theodore, Edith, and their children. Bamie also wrote Theodore long gossipy letters from London, and these, too, were shared with the Lodges. Unfortunately these letters do not survive, for Edith eventually destroyed all such family documents, including Theodore's letters to her.

One of the long, chatty letters that Bamie sent Theodore described, quite hilariously, the august occasion when Bamie was presented at Court. This letter inspired her young niece and nephew, Alice and Ted, Jr., as well as the Roosevelts' good friend, Cecil Spring-Rice, who was still in Washington at the British Embassy, to record this event for posterity. These drawings eventually found a proper home in the collection of family letters at Theodore Roosevelt's Birthplace. They record an event on which Bamie's memoir throws further light.

"In the spring," Bamie wrote, "much to the amusement of everybody, our Ambassador, dear Mr. Bayard, suddenly firmly decided that I was to be presented at Court, which was entirely against the rules, not even an unmarried sister of an Ambassador being allowed officially, but Mr. Bayard's very lovely, handsome appearance and perfectly deaf ear mastered the situation. As one of the officials told me, late in the afternoon after Mr. Bayard's request had been made and not been accepted, owing to the fact that Mr. Bayard had not heard, it had been agreed to, owing to his firmness, that I was to be presented, but on no ground whatever. It was really a great deal better, though they might not have recognized the fact, and all during the season I went to whatever entertainment seemed worthwhile. . . ."

Ambassador Bayard's insistence on Bamie's being presented at Court stemmed from the fact that Mrs. Bayard, who was a rather shy hostess, had come to rely more and more on Bamie to arrange and supervise all social functions at the Embassy. Consequently, Bamie became a sort of unofficial person attached to the Embassy, and, with the help of Commander William S. Cowles, the naval attaché, who was a gallant old beau about town, she did all the real entertaining of distinguished visitors for the Bayards.

Throughout her years in London, Bamie kept up a steady interchange of correspondence with Cabot and Nannie. Cabot sent her copies of his speeches to read and newspaper clippings on how they had been received. He also kept her posted on all the important news in Washington and everything that Theodore was doing. In April of 1894, shortly after Bamie had been presented at Court, he wrote that he and Nannie were in New York at the Waldorf, for a rest and a change.

"Mr. Pinkie" said, "We are enjoying both, but although this is a simple pleasant tavern it is not 689—It is more expensive to begin with. This brings me to a very serious matter which Theodore & I discussed & considered the other day—We have decided that you have been of use to the Hon. Sec. of Embassy about as long as he deserves & that, as Theodore beautifully put it, it is high time you came back to be in a position to be of use to us— Now that you have seen the Queen & made it all right with her it seems as if your line of duty was quite clear & led in the direction of Theodore & myself.

"Theodore, as you know," Cabot continued, "has been living up to the highest duty of American citizenship by having a son born to him. Mother & child were blooming when we left Washington. The house, however, seemed a little crowded. We offered to take part of the family but Edith would not let any of them go. Upon this new & innocent infant Theodore proposes to bestow the resounding, noble, revolutionary & highly patriotic American name of Archibald Bulloch. I am to be his godfather or one of them—But I dislike responsibility for the name & predict to Theodore that the child will be known as 'Bull' Roosevelt. . . . We miss you very much but if you are enjoying life stay by all means although we hope that enjoyment may soon pall & that you may come back."

Such letters as these from "Mr. Pinkie" drew Bamie home just as soon as she could leave Cousin Rosy and his daughter, Helen, after settling them in their summer home outside London. Early in September of 1894, she managed a steamer home; then Bamie went straight to Sagamore Hill, and there she found a most disturbing state of affairs. Immediately she wrote Cabot, who was spending the summer at Nahant, to tell him all about it.

Theodore had, quite on his own, while out at his ranch that summer, turned down a serious offer to run for mayor of New York City on the Republican ticket. Having done this, he was now "restless & unhappy at having to refuse" and had returned to his duties in Washington thinking this had been "his one great chance & that he had thrown it away." It was "frightful" to Bamie "for him to take the view that his whole future is ended in consequence of this decision." She urged Cabot to write Theodore assuring him that he would have many more chances and to cheer him up.

Bamie also found Edith and the children "looking sadly white & worn on my arrival from England," so she took them all on a two-week vacation to the Vermont hills to restore their health and, incidentally, to find out from Edith more about the offer that had come Theodore's way.

"This little change to the high air," Bamie reported to Cabot from Bennington, "has done wonders for them. If only Edith,

80

poor little woman, could be free from care for a while. I always, as you know, realize how heavily the responsibilities weigh on her." And yet, Bamie was horrified to learn that Edith had not encouraged Theodore to accept the mayoral offer. Edith had, instead, withdrawn into one of her reserved and disapproving silences that often, Bamie knew, had more of a disturbing effect on Theodore than anything she said. Bamie reported to Cabot that Edith had "literally said nothing to dissuade him" from refusing the offer even when it was made a second time on his return from the ranch that summer to Sagamore Hill.

After the two weeks in Vermont, Edith and the children went back refreshed to Sagamore Hill, and Bamie to No. 689 where she immediately set about learning more of the offer. First, she heard from their sister, Corinne, that she had urged Theodore to accept and that Corinne's husband, Douglas, would have been willing to help raise the necessary funds for his mayoral campaign. Corinne also reported that Edith's attitude had been that they simply could not afford to take the chance. What if Theodore resigned his commissionership in order to run and then lost the election?

To Bamie such timid reasoning was no reason at all. She was convinced that Theodore was destined to go far in politics, but only if he actually ran for office. She recalled his amazing successes as a young legislator, his incredible personal magnetism as a stump-speaker and vote-getter, and, even more important, how Theodore himself blossomed in the very thick of political battle. He could not forever expect appointive plums from other victorious party leaders, and they, in turn, needed to learn how effective Theodore could be on the ticket. It seemed to Bamie that ever since his second marriage, Theodore had been unnecessarily torn between his promising political career and his duty, as he saw it under Edith's influence, to support his growing family.

The next thing Bamie learned in town that September made her even more sorry that she had been unable to return sooner, as Cabot had urged her to do that spring. If only she had been in New York when the offer had come a second time. She found it had been made not only by the Good Government people, or the "Goo-Goos" as Theodore called them, but that it had the backing of a number of important Republican leaders, including some of the Committee of Seventy.

On top of that, Cabot reported that he had just received a "very gloomy letter" from Theodore. It was "much worse than I imagined possible," Cabot wrote. "He is morbid even—Time will help him out all right & I think I can cheer him when we meet—There is certainly nothing else to be done—He makes the cause of his refusal very plain but takes the whole blame on himself." Then Cabot confirmed what Bamie had heard from Corinne: "He gave as his reason that he could not afford to give money, that Edith strongly opposed it & that he felt he ought to decline."

With this new information, Bamie sat down and wrote a letter to Edith at Sagamore Hill that probably scorched the paper it was written on. That letter no longer exists, but Edith's answering letter, one of the few she ever wrote that showed deep feeling, was a measure of the impatience and wrath that had been expressed in Bamie's. It also gave indication that Bamie, when aroused, could be every bit as "hard" as any member of the older Roosevelt generation.

"Dearest Bamie," Edith wrote, ". . . I cannot begin to describe how terribly I feel at having failed him at such an important time. It is just as I said to you he never should have married me, and then would have been free to take his own course quite unbiased—

"I never realized for a minute how he felt over this, or that the mayoralty stood for so much to him, and I did not know either just in what way the nomination was offered; in fact, I do not know now for I did not like to ask too much.

"I am too thankful that he is away now for I am utterly unnerved and a prey to the deepest despair. . . . If I knew what I do now I should have thrown all my influence in the scale with Corinne's and helped instead of hindering him.

"You say that I dislike to give my opinion. This is a lesson that will last my life, never to give it for it is utterly worthless when given.... It has helped to spoil some years of a life which I would have given my own for. I shall be myself again by Saturday when the darling gets back.

"Much love—E."

There was little more to be said on the subject of the rejected mayoral offer. As Cabot had written, "Time will help him out.... There is certainly nothing else to be done." But Theodore did not come home to Sagamore Hill that October weekend. He wrote he could not get away from his pressing Washington duties, so Bamie went out instead and reported from there to Cabot:

"Your letter to Theodore, though he wrote when he enclosed it to E 'of course Cabot does not mean all he says' has made *every* difference to him & in the tone of his letters—No one can be more unhappy than I am if he has lost the great opportunity of his life & I am afraid to think of all he has gone through taking it as he has done.... I have come down here for these few days but as I feared Theodore did not reach home. So this time I miss him. Still I wished to come as Edith is very lonely & minds the solitude more than formerly."

Thanksgiving out at Sagamore Hill that year was a rather subdued time for all the Roosevelts. Early in November, the reform candidate for mayor won the election, and this was sad proof that, if Theodore had run, his fine record as civil service commissioner would have brought him in the winner. Edith and the children went back with Theodore to Washington, and Bamie, after a visit with the Lodges, returned to 689 Madison Avenue. There she was bombarded with cables from Rosy begging her to return to London. His daughter was not well, and he said he would have to resign as secretary at the Embassy if she did not come back. Feeling she could do nothing that winter to help Theodore, Bamie sailed for London soon after Christmas, writing Cabot as she left, "For heaven's sake, if by any chance any question is ever impending such as [the mayoral offer] has been, write me on the subject so I can hear something definite."

CHAPTER X

Unofficial Person in London

HER second winter abroad Bamie felt very much at home in the London that sparkled into being even before the old Queen's death, during the days when the fun-loving Prince of Wales had already begun to set the pace for Edwardian England. Americans were just beginning to be taken up by the British aristocracy, and titles by the dozens were allying themselves with the well-endowed daughters of the Four Hundred. Bamie, who knew her way in that giddy, gilded world, became one of the most popular hostesses in this first international set.

Her sure progress as a London hostess had its origins in the afternoon tea parties of Mlle Souvestre at Fontainebleau, for there she had been prepared for anything she might meet in England or on the Continent. Her position as Rosy's official hostess and, at the Bayards' insistence, her role as unofficial Embassy hostess, gave her the opportunity to use these latent talents. Her friendship with the Fergusons opened up to her political and social circles not usually frequented by other Embassy people, and her own personality consolidated her position.

Bamie was nearing forty, but her direct, deep-set eyes still held their electric blue. Their limpid, almost hypnotic depths tolerantly bathed the reflections of even the biggest bores in an ambience of interest, which was decidedly an asset in an unofficial person. Not that she was ever hypocritical. She truly found all manner and sorts of people fascinating. And these veiled blue eyes searched and seemed to find something to interest her in everyone, for, in the phrase of the day, Bamie knew how "to draw people out," chiefly because she liked them.

Her figure, though stoutish, had improved with years of discipline, going back to the days on the outdoor piazza, until now she sat a horse like a duchess, and, in the elegant gowns of the day, on the ballroom floor Bamie only seemed to be bending toward her partners. As the London season of 1895 wore on, it soon became apparent that the most persistent of Miss Roosevelt's partners was the Embassy's naval attaché, Commander Cowles, and together they cut a particularly fine figure in the waltz.

Bamie did not really make up her mind to marry Will Cowles until the summer of 1895. In the spring, Cabot had written her that New York City's new reform mayor had offered Theodore the job of police commissioner. Cabot thought that, after six years as civil service commissioner in Washington, Theodore would further his career by the change. Bamie had agreed because she felt "he needed to be once more in touch with his own surroundings" in New York. She had written Theodore and Edith offering them, at a nominal rental, her house on Madison Avenue. It was a bit small for their large family, but at least the arrangement gave the new police commissioner a pied-à-terre in the city.

When the Lodges came over that summer to see the glory of Chartres and Mont-Saint-Michel through the sensitive old eyes of their traveling companion, Henry Adams, they fully expected that Bamie would be returning, for her annual visit to New York, on the same boat with them. Bamie met them in Paris as planned, but there she announced to Cabot and Nannie that she had decided to marry Commander Cowles and stay on in London for at least another season. She told Cabot that she was finding London more agreeable than New York. Besides, No. 689 was so small; it would be much better for Theodore and Edith to have it to themselves. To this Cabot took sudden and violent objection. Why on earth, he asked Bamie, half-serious, half-joking, should she marry when she knew she had Theodore—and him—to look after. Just as suddenly, first noting the flush on Bamie's face and then catching his wife's eye, Cabot dropped the subject. Next day he presented Bamie with an engagement present—a sapphire-studded brooch she always treasured. The Lodges left on the boat train, without Bamie, and Nannie wrote, "I did hate to steam away that day and leave you on the platform.... It seems incredible to think you are really married, dear girl.... I am depending on some kind friend to tell me all about the wedding."

Bamie's marriage in London, in November of 1895, startled all her family and friends, for they had long since put her down, despite her great charm, as an Old Maid. So far as they knew, suddenly, while taking care of Cousin Rosy, who was something of a hypochondriac, the dashing Old Maid had married the naval attaché at the American Embassy. "I am so glad it wasn't an Englishman!" Theodore wrote, "I should have hated that. And I am glad it *was* a naval officer. I have a very strong feeling for the navy.... By the way, tell me his exact rank; is he a captain or a commander?"

Commander Will Cowles, whom Bamie fondly called her "Mr. Bearo," was a genial, hearty old beau nine years her senior. Though rather portly, he cut quite a dashing figure himself with his fore-and-aft hat, his gold epaulets and sword sash, and his great walrus mustaches. Even Theodore never looked quite so resplendent as the naval attaché in his full-dress blues. Theodore and Edith, which was even more remarkable, would soon welcome Will Cowles, with open arms, into the bosom of the family.

Bamie and Will had a quiet church wedding near Cousin Rosy's on Upper Belgrave Street and then went off to the Continent on their honeymoon. As Bamie recalled it, "Everything to do with that wedding was perfectly ridiculous. It bored Cousin Rosy so terribly to have me marry, that he left town for ten days.... Rosy wanted very much for us to live with him on our return from the Continent, where we had a brief trip," but Will "perfectly firmly said we could live as near as we wanted, but not in the house."

On their wedding trip, they went first to Bonn for a few days, then to the French coast, and afterward to Paris. There her sister, Corinne, and Douglas, were the first of the family to meet Bamie's husband. On arriving at the Robinsons' hotel, where the Cowleses had also arranged accommodations, Bamie was amused at the next development in their honeymoon trip. She found that "Corinne could not resist the good opportunity for sight-seeing and had decided, as I had arrived, to leave her children with us while she went to visit the châteaux of the Loire." To Bamie "there was something so funny about this that we could hardly bear it. I can see Will now trying to read the Blue Fairy Book aloud to the children when they came in to call at all hours of the day, as they did."

On the trip cross-Channel back to London, there were further complications. These were caused by Congressman W. Bourke Cockran of New York, who was traveling abroad "in the most fantastically deep mourning for his first wife." Congressman Cockran decided the Cowleses needed not only a respite from the Robinson children but from "our solitude à deux," "so he arrived on the scene to create a diversion by insisting on joining us for the remainder of the time." On the Channel crossing, Mr. Cockran invited Bamie, "very nobly, to share his wonderful and elaborate cabin for the trip. Fortunately I had one of my own. Although the trip was only two hours long, I never came so near permanently parting with Will as I did at that time, as he insisted on coming in at intervals of five minutes looking splendidly well, and saying, 'Now if you would just come on deck, you would be perfectly well.' I knew quite positively that my only chance was to keep my eyes shut tight and not see everything breaking about me."

After the Channel crossing, the Cowleses thought they had seen the last of Congressman Cockran, "but in some perfectly complicated manner he with all our things, and we with all of his things, got on two trains and went to different stations in

London. So when we arrived there we still apparently belonged to each other.... We found our little house in West Eaton Place, with the admirable butler Frazer taking charge, and Mr. Cockran arrived at odd intervals for the next ten days, I think perfectly indignant because he was not invited to join us permanently."

Bamie had scarcely had time to unpack all the new gowns she had bought at Worth's in Paris when she received a long letter from Cabot. This letter presented her with one of the most difficult decisions of her life.

Cabot Lodge had promised to write Bamie just as soon as he returned how Theodore was getting on in his new job as New York's police commissioner, and his news was not sanguine.

"He looks very well," Cabot wrote, withholding some of his concern, "but yet I am anxious about him, not from physical but from mental signs. He seems overstrained & overwrought—That wonderful spring and interest in all sorts of things is much lowered. He is not depressed but he is fearfully overworked & insists on writing history & doing all sorts of things he has no need to do. He has that morbid idée fixe that he cannot leave his work for a moment else the world should stop."

This was frightening enough even though Senator Lodge had not written his worst fears for his friend's state of health because he had not wanted to alarm Bamie unnecessarily. While Cabot had been abroad, Dr. W. Sturgis Bigelow, the distinguished Boston Orientalist, who was also a most perceptive physician, had seen Theodore several times and was much disturbed by their friend's condition. He told Cabot quite bluntly, on his return, that unless Theodore were "*shifted*, somehow, to an *easier place*," it would be "only a question of time when he has a breakdown, and when he does it will be a bad one. . . ." This news Cabot Lodge did not impart in his letter to Theodore's sister so soon after her wedding; he was sure that Theodore's sturdy physique —and what he could do for his friend—would pull him through. Meanwhile Cabot promised Bamie he would keep her posted and told her not to worry.

It was, of course, impossible for Bamie to follow this advice. No one knew better than she Theodore's problems and his emotional ups and downs. It was perfectly plain from his regular weekly letters to her that he was taking the political frustrations of his new job as police commissioner much too seriously. He was also driving himself to write on the side in order to make up to Edith and his growing family for the losses he had sustained on his cattle out West. And, Bamie suspected, Theodore was so burdened with family cares and duties, that he was not getting proper exercise or the relaxation and sheer fun out of life he needed to keep him on an even keel.

Her immediate instinct on reading the first part of Cabot's letter was to leave her bridegroom of a few weeks behind in London and take the next steamer home. But she had several second thoughts on that course of action. Edith would surely feel she was interfering if she arrived in New York on such an impromptu visit. Theodore and Edith might be offended, too, if she stayed anywhere but at No. 689 Madison Avenue, and that small town house was already overcrowded. It also ocurred to Bamie that, unless her brother were desperately ill, her place was undoubtedly with Will, of whom she had become more than fond. She knew now that she had really made her choice, long before Cabot's letter arrived, during the summer before when she had announced her engagement to the Lodges in Paris, perhaps even before that when she had returned to England the last time, after the debacle of the mayoral offer. Now that Bamie was Mrs. Will Cowles, a degree of understanding had no doubt joined caution in her attitude toward a sister-in-law who was overzealous in defending her proprietary rights.

Next Bamie addressed herself to the other news in Cabot's letter, and this clinched her decision to stay out the season in London, for it gave her the opportunity she had longed for all her life—to play the kind of behind-scenes role in great events for which the inspiration of dear Mlle Souvestre and her own continuing interest in world affairs had so well prepared her.

In his letter, Cabot told Bamie that, on his return to the United

States, he had found feeling "running very high" over "the Venezuelan crisis." He believed there was real danger of war between England and the United States, and Cabot was in a position to know for he was now serving his first term in the Senate and had become a member of that body's important Foreign Relations Committee. Bamie had not realized the situation was that serious, for the London newspapers had carried no such reports. She did know there was resentment in political circles that President Cleveland had warned Britain publicly in his message to Congress of December, 1895, that it must respect the Monroe Doctrine and keep hands off Venezuela.

Now, in Cabot's opinion, "A spark would kindle a blaze." He wished "England could be made to understand the feeling here.... The situation," he assured Bamie, "is very grave," and he urged her to "try to make some of the people you see, who are sensible, understand it, for we don't want war."

To Bamie, Cabot's request had the force of a command. This was not just another intimate letter from "Mr. Pinkie." It was an order from an influential member of the United States Senate's Foreign Relations Committee to an unofficial attaché of the American Embassy. Bamie did not doubt for one moment that she could be effective in presenting the American case in the proper British circles; it delighted her that Senator Lodge, whose statesmanship she admired, would entrust her with such an assignment.

Knowing the Ambassador so well, Bamie suspected that that courtly old gentleman had grown much too deaf to hear what British officials were saying and that he, having become so thoroughly British himself, may have failed to put the crisis with the bluntness his government had instructed him to use. She consulted with Cousin Rosy and discovered that this was indeed the case. Then she began her own private campaign to enlighten Britain's political leaders.

Her course of action was clear. This was her first London season in her own home, and she promptly went over her engagement calendar—tea with the old Queen at Windsor; the Duchess of Sutherland's ball; the Duchess of Marlborough's supper party for the Prince of Wales. Good, but not good enough. She must reach all the political leaders, many of whom she already knew. She went over the lists for her Tuesday afternoons and for her series of intimate luncheons and dinners, augmenting them with the bright young men from the Foreign Office whom she knew through Sir Ronald Ferguson; with supporters of Lord Salisbury, the prime minister; and even with members of the Opposition. Now—at her teas and at her table, made so attractive to Londoners by her good French chef, and the excellent wines that pleased Commander Cowles, as well as the lively conversation one was sure to find at No. 3 West Eaton Place—she could report the real news from America and underline the significance of American sentiment.

Before the season was over and in the midst of Bamie's one-woman campaign to explain the American position on Venezuela, she received good news from the faithful correspondent who kept close and loving watch over Theodore for her in New York, just as Cabot did from Washington.

This friend, of course, was Fergie, who was now working for the Astor Estate, which permitted him to divide his time between London and New York. Fergie's letter about Theodore was reassuring, though Bamie had to allow for his usual tendency to treat serious matters lightly. She, too, shrugged at life, but not when it touched Theodore.

It was true, Fergie wrote, that Theodore had talked wildly of throwing over his job as police commissioner, even if that meant the ruin of his political chances forever. He had even threatened to retire, in his middle thirties, to Sagamore Hill and there "become a literary hermit for the rest of his days." But, said Fergie, "I don't think somehow that the seclusion will suit our Ted's temperament," which exactly matched Bamie's own instincts about her brother.

Then, in his letter, Fergie had a bit of fun with Bamie, even as he relieved her worst fears, by referring to a raid into New York City's worst tenderloin district on which he had accompanied the Police Commissioner. On this exciting expedition, Fergie wrote, "our Ted" had seemed more his old self. And, undoubtedly reporting Theodore's personal reaction to the Venezuelan crisis, Fergie further comforted Bamie by observing, "A great & glorious war, for which he yearns, might give effective outlet to his more natural & active inclinations."

In closing, Fergie, British patriot, made this wistful and perceptive comment:

> I wish Theodore could have a spell abroad to study foreign politics a bit. They are bound to come, more than one expects almost, upon the stage of American policy. . . . I don't think people here have anything like an adequate idea of their complicating influences—of the trouble that is ahead in turn for the U.S.A. just as much as for decaying European monarchies.

Bamie agreed completely with her young friend's keen insights about Theodore and America's future involvement. She thoroughly understood the underlying patterns of European politics and greatly admired the way British diplomacy, backed by the British fleet, had managed always to hold the balance of power. She had been reading only recently, and so had Theodore, a new book written by their friend, the American admiral, Alfred Thayer Mahan, and this pioneer study of the effects of sea power on world history had fascinated them both.

Fergie's letter convinced Bamie that Theodore's health was not immediately threatened. She could really settle down now, with her mind quite free, to the business of entertaining. She was not at all surprised to find that many of the leading English politicians with whom she conversed that winter had no idea what the long-forgotten Monroe Doctrine was all about. Neither had most Americans. The English were, however, quite prepared to understand it in terms of power politics. As Fergie had written, "*We'll* get a definition of the Monroe Doctrine for Europeans to go on," reminding her that Spanish and German influence in the Western Hemisphere was no more palatable to England than it was to the United States.

The English resented, however, "the rude way" President Cleveland had made public his demand for arbitration of the Venezuelan question—by a message to Congress rather than in quiet negotiations with the British Foreign Office. But how else, Bamie would ask, put European powers on notice? Ah well, quite irregular, just the same. Only what one might expect from her inexperienced fellow-countrymen.

Despite the damage done to British prestige, the Foreign Office swallowed its pride and did not respond to Cleveland's virtual ultimatum. The London newspapers made the best of the situation by adopting this official line, carried in the *Annual Register*—Americans had "given themselves up to a delirium of jingoism, and had that feeling continued and been reciprocated by the English press and the English people, the two countries might really have drifted into war."

On both sides tempers gradually cooled and the way was clear for arbitration. In Washington, Senator Lodge could not help crowing a bit. With his usual sarcasm, tinged with Anglophobia, he wrote Bamie again:

"The tone of injured love & the wonder that we do not love them as they love us which have appeared lately in English newspapers & speeches are very amusing. . . . I think England understands one or two things better than she did. . . . The whole thing is coming out right & we are going to carry our point."

Bamie surely smiled at this comment, so typically a "Pinkyism," even as she continued to scan this latest report from Washington for news of Theodore. The Senator was happy to say that the Police Commissioner had taken a much-needed vacation, and that Theodore and Edith had recently visited him in Washington.

"Theodore," Cabot wrote, "was in fine form—wonderfully better than when I met him on arrival. Venezuela has done him good & taken his mind off police & he was all himself, alert, energetic & full of interest in everything. He seems to have recovered his tone entirely."

PART II

Prelude to the White House

CHAPTER XI

"The Ambassadress" and "Sinbad"

WHILE Bamie was making every effort during her third winter in London to carry out Senator Lodge's instructions, which were "to make some of the people you see . . . understand the feeling here . . . for we don't want war," her brother, the police commissioner, had been privately but emphatically expressing quite the opposite sentiment.

"The clamor of the peace faction," Theodore wrote Cabot in the midst of the Venezuelan crisis, "has convinced me that this country needs a war. . . . I don't care whether our sea coast cities are bombarded or not; we could take Canada."

The extravagant belligerence of this comment was indication that, though Theodore was recovering his usual tone, he was still frustrated, overworked, and harassed by family worries. Theodore, poor darling, Edith would tell his sister, Corinne, was working himself to death. And she commented wryly, whenever they managed to get out to Sagamore Hill, he tried to kill himself with exercise—riding horseback, bicycling, chopping wood, and going skiing and sledding with the children. Invariably he returned to his Police Department with a bruised or sprained arm or leg and a nasty cold. The harder he worked at his job and his exercise, the more ills and ailments Theodore developed.

In spite of all this, Theodore was doing an excellent job as police commissioner and earning a national reputation as an incorruptible crime-buster. But he and Edith both missed their Washington friends and the easy society they had enjoyed there, and Bamie's life abroad, Theodore thought, sounded most enviable. "We see you in the papers, very swell," he wrote his sister, "going about with the highest in the land. It seems rather a contrast to the useful but grimy work [of] your affectionate brother."

Theodore actually loved the grime of it. Although occasionally he gave the impression he was only marking time until something better came along, he fully enjoyed the command the job gave him over a force of uniformed men, and he cleaned up the police force in remarkably short time. He had a fight all the way —with Tammany and with his own party machine, then dominated by Senator Thomas C. Platt, a wily character with an abiding interest in political power through patronage. Theodore's instinct, only barely held in check by repeated warnings from Cabot, was to break with the Republican machine and to attack Boss Platt publicly, which would have been disastrous for his political future.

The strain of holding his native pugnacity in leash was almost too much for the Commissioner. He admitted to a friend, "Though I have the constitution of a bull-moose, it is beginning to wear on me a little." The friend was Henry White, the new first secretary of the Embassy in London, who promptly passed her brother's remark on to Mrs. Cowles. This first use of the classic Teddyism, coupled with the very humor with which he described his "parochial problems" in his letters to her, only served to conceal from Bamie how miserable Theodore really was.

It was not the job alone that deviled the Police Commissioner during the winter of 1895–96. It was his own driving ambition, and the two most important people in his life who had fed it and materially supported it in the past were not immediately at hand to help. "I literally have no one here," he complained to Cabot, "to whom to unburden myself."

Cabot responded from Washington with well-meant words of advice and encouragement. "I do not say you are to be President tomorrow," the Senator wrote, "I do not say it will be—I am sure that it may and can be. I do say that the Senate, which is better, is well within reach."

Theodore undoubtedly had the same high ambitions for himself, but he felt it premature to talk about them. He wrote Bamie guardedly that he had been seeing a good deal of their friend, House Speaker Tom Reed, who was a preconvention candidate in 1896. "The struggle is very evident in his face," Theodore observed, "and I can see how hard it is. The Presidency is a great prize!"

As for himself, he wrote Bamie, how easy it was for "the delcious Caboty" to say the United States Senate was within his reach. He was trapped in a political backwash a long way from Washington. Didn't Cabot realize that, as a consequence of his thorough overhaul of the police force, he now had "not one N. Y. city newspaper or one N. Y. city politician" on his side? Even Bamie's friend, Whitelaw Reid, who ran the *Tribune*, had been given instructions by the Republican machine not to mention his name except to attack.

At home, Theodore continued to receive from Edith very little advice and less sympathy about his "parochial problems." When he mentioned them, she told him quite frankly she hoped Albany "would legislate him out of office," a possibility not at all remote. Involved in her own problem of rearing five small children on their modest income, Edith literally had no time for politics or New York society even had she cared for either. "Mrs. Roosevelt," Theodore wrote Henry White, "has had rather a harassing winter. She has hardly gone out at all. . . . For the past three months, it has seemed that we have never passed a week without at least one of the children being down with something, till at times I felt that we were running an amateur hospital. . . ." Whenever Edith managed to escape the hospital at No. 689, she sought refuge among the quiet book stacks of the nearby New York Society Library.

Things were so bad during the winter of 1896 that Fergie, who had always before looked on Bamie's home almost as his own, said he found it "not very encouraging" at No. 689. He ran into Theodore, dining out alone one evening at the home of the architect, Grant La Farge, and there they had a delightful time. Walking Theodore to his door later, Fergie was amused to hear him vow he was determined to go out more often socially—even if it meant attending Assemblies and musicales—and without Edith, if necessary. Theodore's reasoning, Fergie reported to Bamie, went like this: "Since Edith doesn't care much for public social functions, he would have to bring his children out before very long and so he begins a giddy career among the 400 to be ready for the strain when once it comes." Fergie asked, with his usual perspicacity, "How much have you had to do with this remarkable change in our all-round Commissioner?"

During that very trying winter, Bamie wrote Theodore repeatedly urging him to come to London, if only for a fortnight. She wanted him to meet Lecky and Bryce, the distinguished British historians whom he admired; and Augustine Birrell, a charming Liberal wit and scholar, and dozens of others. She urged him to lead a more active social life, and she wrote Cabot, "Judging from Theodore's letters, they go absolutely nowhere." She greatly regretted "not to be at home this year" because "we might have tried to have a congenial circle even if minute & I feel sure it is good for Teddy to see people sometimes who help divert his thoughts from the continuous strain of his position."

Under the circumstances, Theodore was finding his position almost unbearable. He could live up neither to Bamie's expectations nor Cabot's. And he would not let himself take Cabot's practical advice that he avoid, whenever possible, antagonizing the local Republican machine—though he did agree to skirt an open break—in order to carry more weight with the party regulars in the coming national elections. In this decision, Theodore had at least the warm support of Fergie, though he now saw that sympathetic friend only occasionally.

"Cabot's ideas," Fergie wrote Bamie, "could never work with Theodore & it is not likely that practical politics would in the least pay Theodore at present—As he says himself,—'Give way to the corrupt element in the least degree (as even his best friends & the strongest reformers like Choate & others have been advising him urgently to do!) and they squeeze you & throw you away like a sucked orange' (In his more emphatic words that imply somewhat the same meaning.)"

But Senator Lodge, who was a master at political maneuver, had other ideas for Theodore that were eminently workable and more to his young friend's uncompromising tastes. After the Republican convention of 1896 had nominated Major McKinley, the Senator encouraged Theodore to offer his services as a speaker to Mark Hanna, national boss of the G.O.P. In that critical campaign against William Jennings Bryan, Boss Hanna was delighted to put the popular young New York police commissioner on the stump for his man. Theodore drew surprisingly large audiences in Chicago and Boston, and, with Senator Lodge, he toured upstate New York, all with excellent results. The excitement of that campaign and Theodore's obvious success with the crowds dispelled the last vestige of his lack of tone and gave him a heady foretaste of his own future success on the platform. Having launched Theodore on the national scene politically by this maneuver, astute Senator Lodge now stood ready to help him collect his reward for services rendered from the victorious party leaders.

In London, meanwhile, the wife of the United States naval attaché was busily proving to her friend, the Senator, that she was, as he put it, "just as American and Republican as ever." She made light of her "officious position," which was the way her sister, Corinne, described her Embassy activities, and she thought it amusing when Fergie reported that he and Theodore had dubbed her "the Ambassadress." Still, she wrote the Senator, she "had done all that I could in explaining to people here" that Americans would stand firm on the Monroe Doctrine. This had been difficult because "many simply could not believe there was anything but admiration in the American feeling toward this country." Ambassador Bayard had done nothing to dispel this illusion, and the American colony abroad, with their blind adulation of everything British, only made matters worse.

Bamie's years abroad, in London and traveling on the Continent, had had a broadening effect in every respect but one. She could not stand American expatriates who thought they were endearing themselves to foreigners by denigrating their own country or their fellow countrymen. The more she lived abroad, it seemed, the more she loved her native land and wished it to take its proper rank among the other great powers.

"I am bound to say," she wrote Cabot with some indignation, in commenting on the inability of the British to understand that they were not worshiped by all Americans, "we do much to foster this feeling by the class of American who is most generally seen in this country & who after a short residence here cannot speak except slightingly of their home & people."

She had little patience with most of her compatriots in England. As an example of her difficulties, she described for Cabot one dinner party where at her end of the table she had "had a warlike time." Bret Harte took her in to dinner and "the conversation following on diplomatic manners & customs he firmly said that Willie Astor would be *the* best person for us to name as Ambassador here. To which I replied I should consider him quite the worst. Whereupon Bret Harte thought I meant that he was a parvenu, as he expressed it. I said that was not the reason. I suggested that a man who lived entirely away from his country hardly seemed a thorough representative, which disgusted my companion who had lived here for six years. He then said, 'Well, I consider that makes no difference & you would be in the minority here,' which of course was quite true as Daisy White, Henry James & John Sargent were all at our end. But is it not maddening to have Americans act in that way & all because the Prince of Wales had been stopping with Willie Astor for Sunday!"

It also seemed to Bamie a pity that most of her English friends took "no pains to know the statesmen of our country or even to know about them." She did her best to remedy this situation, she told the Senator, by quoting from his speeches—which he soon got in the habit of sending her quite regularly—not only on Venezuela but on America's growing difficulties with Spain over Cuba. "Thank you *very very* much for letters & reports," Bamie wrote the Senator, "as I am able to quote others them where I feel it is often really good."

Naturally, through her husband's duties, Bamie soon began to take a keen, though somewhat dilettante, interest not only in diplomacy but also in naval matters. "Our winter is passing rapidly & *most* satisfactorily," she wrote Cabot. "We are seeing rather intelligent, interesting people, a trifle of a potpourri but none the worse for that & as I always like people who are doing something, I find the side-shoots, so to speak, of naval work interesting. I like the big gun-makers, iron-plate and boiler-makers, with shipbuilders of various kinds."

On the eve of McKinley's election, Bamie's interest in the United States navy took a sudden spurt and a more serious turn. As a patriotic navy wife, she was gravely concerned about the nation's lack of preparedness, as war with Spain grew more certain. This concern was considerably reinforced when, with her usual dedication to her brother's advancement, she began to hope that, in this new crisis, Theodore might possibly be rewarded for his campaign activities with a Cabinet post. Secretary of the navy was the reward Bamie had in mind.

She now began to follow closely every bit of news about Cuba and the United States navy, and, more or less gently, to prod Cabot, who was already doing all he could to get Theodore shifted back to Washington and into an easier and better job. When the Venezuelan crisis had passed and as the situation in Cuba grew worse, she was sorry "after so much talk that the enlargement of the Navy & coast fortification could not have been started on a large scale"; she realized that "cutting out the Navy estimates was a disappointment to you & Theodore." Following immediately on this in her letter, Bamie wrote, "Theodore I think much about, for I hate him to continue wearing his soul out with constant small fights. . . ."

In the course of her long-distance campaign for her brother, Bamie managed to convey to Cabot how much she had enjoyed having him at No. 689 when he had needed a good rest after previous election campaigns and how she "longed to see him & see him satisfactorily"; she spoke of how pleasantly he was remembered by the English friends he had met through her; she recalled her brother's loyalty to him in earlier times, and she suggested that "if ever anything important turns up which I ought to know without delay," all the Senator had to do was use the Embassy cable address, start with "Anna" and the message "would come to me promptly."

The "delicious Caboty" was no doubt much amused and touched by Bamie's obvious campaign to further her brother's career. Soon after McKinley's election he assured her he would do everything possible for Theodore. Though he acknowledged Theodore "ought to go into the Cabinet," he was afraid "we may not be able to make it. I hope however we can at least get him the Asst. Sec. of the Navy which he says he would like. . . ." Cabot also reported that he was even then on his way to Canton, Ohio, to see the President-elect, and his "governing notion" in going was "to do what I can for Theodore."

Getting Theodore appointed assistant secretary of the navy at a time when the conservative wing of the Republican party, led by the President-elect and Boss Hanna, wanted to avoid war with Spain at almost any cost, took months and considerable doing on the Senator's part. Major McKinley, when pressed for Theodore's appointment, was not as frank with Senator Lodge as Mr. Blaine had been in telling Mrs. Lodge some years earlier that Theodore would probably disturb his slumbers and was much too volatile to make a safe assistant secretary of state— but McKinley's reason was the same. He would agree with the Senator that Theodore was more than entitled to a reward for his fine work in the campaign, and he promised, again and again, to keep him in mind. But even after McKinley took office as president, Theodore's appointment seemed not at all certain.

Theodore and Bamie both, with an ocean between, waited

impatiently as Inauguration Day in 1897 came and went, and still nothing was heard from the Executive Mansion in Washington. "I do not think there is much chance of my being made Assistant Secretary of the Navy," Theodore sadly wrote Bamie. And Bamie immediately posted another broad hint to the Senator in Washington—". . . Now the new order has commenced & we all look with interest to see how matters will go. . . ."

Early in "the new order," President McKinley delighted Senator Lodge by appointing John Davis Long, former governor of Massachusetts, to be his secretary of the navy, and now it seemed that Theodore's appointment would come in a matter of days. But even Secretary Long, who was the Senator's good friend, did not exactly leap at the idea of having Theodore as his understudy. The Secretary tried to put the Senator off by saying that, of course, he would love to have Theodore on board at the Navy Department, but the job of assistant secretary was really too small for such an able and brilliant man. Would Theodore be satisfied with anything less than a Cabinet post for himself and did the Senator really think Theodore could be happy in such a subordinate role?

The Secretary could not long withstand the Senator's insistence that the New York Police Commissioner, who was even then having a running public battle with his board, would make an excellent subordinate, and Cabot was soon reporting to Theodore, "The hitch, if there is one, is not with Long but at the White House. . . ." The Senator could not tell "whether there is any real resistance . . . and the only, absolutely the only, thing I can hear adverse is that there is a fear you will want to fight somebody at once."

President McKinley had good reason to be cautious. Theodore's public statements on Cuba and Spain during the campaign had been enough to give him pause. Had the President ever heard the Police Commissioner's private views, it is quite likely that Theodore's appointment would have been postponed indefinitely. For, along with the yellow press of the nation—which was busily building circulation on the atrocities committed by the

Spanish Governor-General against the Cuban revolutionaries and on the truly sad plight of hundreds of thousands of starving noncombatant *reconcentrados* herded by the Governor-General into festering refugee camps behind the lines—Theodore was the most rabid of jingoes. It was not so much that he was for recognizing the revolutionaries and then annexing the island, as many jingoes were. It was simply that Theodore, unable to string up the whole police board and Boss Platt by the thumbs, was, as Fergie put it bluntly in a letter to Bamie, spoiling for "bloody war." According to Fergie, "Theodore says he wishes we (England) had licked the Germans—You had licked Spain and then both had turned in together & cleaned up the Turk. And it does *look* so simple?" He added, "I hope he won't do anything rash before you get home."

Bamie was at the time busily making preparations to return, for the naval attaché had just received his orders for sea duty. This evoked an unusually flattering editorial in the *London Times*. The news that Commander Cowles had been given command of a ship, the *Times* said, "will be received by something like dismay here. For Mrs. Cowles has, in the three years she has lived in London, made herself almost indispensable." The *Times* noted that the little house on West Eaton Place, which Bamie was dismantling and preparing to close, had been "the pleasantest of rendezvous, a social international exchange" where "the most agreeable people of two continents were always sure of meeting each other."

In the midst of her plans for departure, early in April of 1897, Bamie received the long-awaited Embassy cable from Cabot informing her that, at last, Theodore had received his appointment as assistant secretary of the navy. This was soon followed by an ecstatic letter from Theodore telling her what she had undoubtedly surmised already, that ". . . It was Cabot's untiring energy and devotion which put me in."

Indeed President McKinley, still hoping that intervention in Cuba would not be necessary, had given in to the Senator only after he had mustered half of Washington and part of the President's native Ohio—including that rising young judge, William H. Taft—in Theodore's support. When the reluctant Secretary of the Navy finally summoned his new assistant to Washington, Theodore sent off a gleeful wire to Cabot that read:

"SINBAD HAS EVIDENTLY LANDED THE OLD MAN OF THE SEA."

CHAPTER XII

"He Cannot Help Being a Power"

AMONG the letters Bamie cherished long after she left London was one from a distinguished barrister in The City who closed his farewell note to Commander and Mrs. Cowles with "Confound the Navy!" as if it were his own. This was very generous of the London barrister, it reflected some of the "friendship and sympathy" that McKinley's new ambassador, John Hay, told Cabot Lodge he had found there on his arrival in the spring of 1897. Compared with the mighty British fleet built around forty-four majestic battleships, the navy of the United States was, in the 1890s, a disgrace—especially for a country whose industrial might had already set it among the great powers of the world. The United States navy then consisted of two second-class battleships, one of them being the *Maine;* twelve cruisers; nine gunboats; six monitors, with double gun turrets fore and aft; one armored ram; one torpedo boat—and that was all.

Commander Cowles's new assignment when he and Bamie came home in the spring of 1897 was the command of one of those nine small antiquated gunboats. Far from saying, "Confound the Navy!" when he boarded the *Fern* in New York harbor, the Commander took pride in showing her off to his wife and all his new Roosevelt relatives and friends, including Fergie, who lovingly christened that miserable little vessel, the *"Fern & Faithful."* The *"Fern & Faithful"* had scant armor and even less firepower, but she was at least seagoing, for which Commander Cowles was grateful. He knew only too well that the navy had more good officers than decent ships to go round. Leaving Bamie to settle in once more at No. 689, now that Edith and Theodore were happily back in Washington, Commander Cowles steamed away, all boilers burning, to the maneuvers off Hampton Roads, Virginia, where his new brother-in-law, the assistant secretary of the navy, would himself review the United States fleet from the deck of the *Dolphin*, another nondescript vessel that Secretary Long had put at his eager subordinate's disposal.

With little additional help from the cautious Secretary of the Navy, Theodore was, on the eve of the Spanish-American War, trying his best to get the navy ready to fight. His goal, he wrote Bamie, was "to increase our Navy by perhaps half a dozen battleships, besides cruisers and torpedo boats." With Congress almost as reluctant as President McKinley and the Secretary of the Navy, he found it very difficult "not to wish for a War with Spain, for such a war would result at once in getting us a proper Navy and a good system of coast defense." He succeeded in getting neither in the months before the *Maine* blew up in Havana harbor, but he did get enough money from Congress for a few new ships as well as better armament for the old. He put competent officers in strategic posts, as he had in dealing with his "parochial problems" in the New York City police force. He insisted, for example, that Admiral Dewey be made commander in chief of the Asiatic Squadron. And he kept what there was of the United States navy in the Atlantic in a state of combat readiness by ordering extra target practice and by holding frequent maneuvers.

On maneuver, the *Dolphin* often rendezvoused at sea with the *"Fern & Faithful."* The Assistant Secretary naturally invited the captain of the gunboat, who was a "Big Navy man" himself, to report to him regularly on the navy's needs as seen either from the rolling deck of the *Fern* or from No. 689 Madison Avenue whenever the *Fern* was at home in New York harbor.

Theodore assured Bamie, who thought this invitation might be taken too seriously, that Will's letters were "always welcome" and that he relied much "on his judgment about matters in the department," even as he repeatedly urged her—as Cabot Lodge did also—to come to Washington and take a house there so they could all be together again.

Bamie agreed with Cabot that Washington was "the place for Naval officers & their wives to dwell," but a number of activities and events delayed her departure from New York. She had spent her first summer home very pleasantly visiting old friends, at Newport, Wood's Hole, and Lenox, and now, in the early autumn of 1897, there were a host of other old friends coming over from England whom she wished to entertain. She felt she could, for the present, do this best in New York, and, since Theodore promised to get up from Washington for some of her luncheons and dinners, she decided to stay on.

As luck would have it, Edith was expecting her fifth child in mid-November in the crowded little house the Roosevelts had rented on Washington's N Street across from the British Embassy, and once again Bamie's sister-in-law, who cared so little for society anyway, was socially *hors de combat*. In this latest emergency, Bamie was delighted to provide, in New York during the autumn and winter of 1897–98, the circle of stimulating friends she knew Theodore so desperately needed. As if making up for the years Bamie had been away, brother and sister held long postmortems, at breakfast, over these interesting weekend gatherings at her house during the fall of 1897. With no third party present to put a damper on these early morning feasts of gossip about politics and personalities, table talk and the Roosevelt gift for mimicry went quite uninhibited.

Bamie would imitate to the life how her friend, the tall, long-lipped American diplomat who had sat on her right at luncheon, had discussed the situation in Turkey "with the ruminant air of a Smyrna camel." Or Theodore, ruffling his hair to stand on end and adopting a British accent, would take off Lord Bryce to perfection as he had discoursed on world history at one of Bamie's

dinners, exactly, Theodore said, like "a memory with hair on it."
Or again Bamie would dismiss another self-consciously erudite
friend with the general remark, "People so intelligent bore one
to death." These occasional sessions with Bamie were a delight
for, as Theodore wrote his sister from Washington, "I think I
enjoyed our breakfast à deux more than anything else."

But, soon the talk at No. 689, even as in Washington, lost its
frivolity and took on a serious tone, for all the Roosevelts were
caught up in the sorry affairs of that rich little island off the coast
of Florida that had been known for centuries as Spain's "key to
the New World," though Cuba had for many years already
begun to dance to the tune of her neighboring markets in the
United States. So, too, had some of her revolutionary leaders,
and these were now in the field against Spain's Colonial troops
and overrunning half the island, presenting United States jingoes,
including Theodore, with what looked like a golden opportunity.

All his Washington friends, including those in Henry Adams'
circle, Theodore proudly told Bamie, were for "Cuba Libre,"
but they were unable to convince the timid higher echelons in
the government. It was utter cowardice, Theodore said, for the
United States not to support the gallant Cuban revolutionaries
and recognize that island's independence—even before they had
won it. It had been sheer madness for the United States to neglect its army and navy—a condition he was doing his best to
correct—when anyone half blind could see that war with Spain
was imminent.

Together brother and sister discussed what each individually
could do when war broke out, as it was sure to do at any moment.
Bamie began to make plans with her friends, Mrs. Whitelaw
Reid and Mrs. Bayard Cutting, to train a corps of women nurses.
She thought they should be permitted to do actual field work
behind the lines, and Theodore greeted this as a capital idea.
Then, in those few remaining weeks before the Spanish-American
War actually did break out, Theodore told Bamie, much to her
horror though she could but sympathize, that nothing in the
world could stop him from going to the front the moment war

was declared. He would resign as assistant secretary of the navy. He would organize a volunteer cavalry outfit of his own. He would invite Fergie and all his other young polo-playing friends to join; he would send out a call to the Bad Lands for the cowboys and ranchers he knew and to the college campuses to enlist all the daredevil young men at Harvard, Princeton, and Yale.

On the eve of the conflict that John Hay, their friend in London, called "a splendid little war," Theodore's sorties to Bamie's in New York brought them very close together, and these weekend visits were frequent because Theodore often felt he simply had to get away for a few days from his home in Washington that now more than ever seemed to him like an amateur hospital.

To Edith, who was very ill herself for months after Quentin's birth, the behavior of her stepdaughter, Alice—now grown into a very lively tomboy going on fourteen and the leader of an equally noisy gang of boys her own age—made it also seem like a home for delinquent children. First, after Quentin's birth, Edith had a long siege of the grippe. Then she began to suffer from neuralgic pains so severe a trained nurse was required in constant attendance. Not long after Christmas, almost as if in sympathy, Ted, Jr., began having ghastly headaches.

Of all these unhappy developments Bamie heard only from Theodore, for Edith, in her weakened state, in her pride and stubbornness, in her fear that anyone other than Mother should exert an influence over her children, would not ask for help. Until she did, Bamie scarcely dared offer it. Again that frightening thought—if Edith turned against her, in time, so too might loyal Theodore.

Theodore's letters early in the year 1898 took on a grim, stoical tone that convinced Bamie something had to be done, even at the risk of alienating Edith completely. "Edith and Ted," Theodore wrote disconsolately, "continue exactly as they were. I had a consultation of doctors about Ted today, and the trained nurse that Edith has is fortunately very satisfactory. That is all that can be said about either." He would be up for another weekend late in January, he said, and Bamie decided to call in at that time an old friend, Dr. Alexander Lambert, ostensibly as just another guest for breakfast but in reality to act as a family counselor whose advice Edith as well as Theodore would respect.

Dr. Lambert told Theodore bluntly that he must, for his wife's sake, convince Edith that both Alice and Ted, Jr., would be better off with Bamie in New York for the rest of that winter. She could not get well herself while trying to cope with six children, ranging in age from a few months to fourteen, all cooped up together in that small house on N Street. Ted, Jr.'s symptoms, as Theodore described them, could be serious, and Dr. Lambert strongly advised sending the boy as soon as possible to New York where specialists could be called in to discover what was wrong.

Edith was not immediately convinced, especially when it came to sending Ted, Jr., off to Bamie, and she held out against letting Alice go until the second week in February. Alice, who was large and precocious for her age, had no doubt coasted once too often down the long hill on Connecticut Avenue with her feet on the handlebars of her bicycle. But the final straw was when Alice, hoping this would give her an evening out with her gang of teen-age boys, encouraged one of them to call for her in his sister's clothes. Alice's poor young friend was promptly unfrocked by a shocked Theodore, and so, on February 13, the day after her fourteenth birthday, Alice was put on the train for New York to join her "dearest and most terrifying Aunt," whom she adored.

The trouble with Alice was that she was in open adolescent revolt against her stepmother. Edith had tried, no doubt over-conscientiously, to treat Alice as her own. Alice, too, had tried; she even called Edith "Mother." But the child was growing up to bear a strong resemblance to her own mother, who had been an extremely pretty young thing, and this was a continual reminder to Edith, whose ill-health made her particularly edgy, that Theodore had first married Alice Lee. Feeling extremely annoyed at Alice's intransigent behavior one day, Edith had made the mistake of telling Ted, Jr., that Alice's mother had been such an empty-headed, frivolous young woman that, had she lived, Theodore would soon have grown bored with her. Ted had naturally lost no time in imparting this bit of family gossip to his half sister in the forlorn hope that this might stop her everlasting challenge of his natural male superiority. This had only served to make Alice's exploits as a gang leader even more daring and reprehensible in Edith's eyes. Whenever thereafter Edith spoke to her in that cold voice, with its high slight whine, "Oh, *yes*, my dear, Mother says you must," Alice went out of her way to do just the opposite. She resented most of all that neither Mother nor Father ever once mentioned her real mother's name in her presence. Auntie Bye, on the other hand, had been so fond of Alice Lee that she spoke of her often, telling Alice how pretty and attractive her mother had been. No wonder then that when Alice went to live with Auntie Bye that winter she became, almost overnight, quite a different and tractable young person.

No one could have been more astonished than Theodore at this sudden change in his daughter. He found her letters home "really interesting and amusing." He wrote Bamie, "Evidently you are doing her a world of good and giving her exactly what she needed. I quite agree with what you say about her; I am sure she really does love Edith and the children and me; it was only that running riot with the boys and girls here had for the moment driven everything else out of her head."

As for young Ted, who was still at home with Father and Mother, his headaches grew worse. Specialists from Johns Hopkins in Baltimore could find nothing organically wrong with the child and could suggest only that he was under some emotional strain that he would in time outgrow. Doubtless the high-strung little boy felt driven by his father's ambitions for himself and everyone near and dear to him; he also felt threatened whenever Theodore talked of going off to war, as he often did that winter, and of leaving his eldest son, who felt quite unequal to the task, to be the man of the family. And Ted worried most of all because his mother was so ill and seemed to be getting no better.

Early in March, the doctors told Edith that her illness was undoubtedly caused by an abscess, localized in the pelvic area, and that she must undergo an operation. Then at last Edith agreed that perhaps Ted, Jr., would be better off for a while with Bamie and Alice in New York. Again the change was miraculous. After a few weeks at No. 689, Ted seemed an entirely different boy. His headaches disappeared, and Dr. Lambert soon had no symptoms to diagnose.

There was, of course, nothing wrong with either Ted or Alice, as it turned out, that being away from their parents for a while could not cure, especially since the children were with Auntie Bye, who was loving, firm, and always predictably and consistently so. Loving, Theodore certainly was; no father ever enjoyed his children more. But Theodore could be quite unpredictable, sometimes bursting out in anger and exasperation in the midst of a happy romp, even though he doted on all his "bunnies." In this respect, Theodore was often a big, overgrown child among children himself, and this endearing trait had once prompted Edith to say to the Lodges, in Theodore's presence shortly after Quentin's birth, "Now I have *five* boys," including her husband in the count.

Edith, too, loved all the children, not excluding Alice, but she was much too reserved to be warmly demonstrative, and she had little patience with tempestuous adolescents. Her firmness toward Alice and Ted, both, amounted perhaps to a crippling repression of their natural rambunctiousness, for Mother's "No" was almost too predictable. Temporarily away from two such parents, however devoted, Ted and Alice soon began to blossom into happy, healthy youngsters.

At the end of March, while Edith was slowly convalescing from her operation, Theodore heard from Dr. Lambert that Ted, much to his father's surprise, was now getting along fine. He had had a kind of nervous breakdown, the doctor explained, and he told Theodore quite frankly that he himself was the cause of it all. Theodore should let Ted grow up at his own pace and not try to push him, and this apparently was exactly what Edith had been telling Theodore all along.

"Dear Alec," Theodore wrote Dr. Lambert contritely, "I shall give plain proof of great weakness of character by reading your letter to Mrs. Roosevelt, who is now well enough to feel the emotions of triumph. Hereafter I shall never press Ted either in body or mind. The fact is that the little fellow, who is peculiarly dear to me, has bidden fair to be all the things I would like to have been and wasn't, and it has been a great temptation to push him." To Bamie, Theodore wrote, "Evidently you have done as much for Ted as for Alice by taking him into your house."

It was just as well that both children were with their Auntie Bye when war with Spain was officially declared on April 24. For then, over the objections of family and friends and while his wife was still quite ill, Theodore went off to war just as he had told Bamie he would. He mobilized his regiment of volunteer cavalry, which was promptly dubbed the "Rough Riders," got the War Department to put his friend, Leonard Wood, in command as colonel, and, as lieutenant colonel and second in command of the Rough Riders, left for San Antonio, Texas, where his outfit would spend a few hectic months in training before embarking for Cuba.

Paradoxically enough, Theodore considered that this was "his one chance to do something for my country and my family." Senator Lodge, who had helped him to the administrative post of assistant secretary of the navy, had tried repeatedly to dissuade him, urging that it was Theodore's duty to stay home and run the Department of the Navy. But Theodore, as he said years later, would have gone "to answer that call," even if he had had to turn from the deathbed of his beloved wife.

Only Bamie seemed to understand why Theodore, who had always been ashamed that his father had not "joined the absolute fighting forces" in 1861, felt that he had to go to Cuba.

"My heart aches for him," Bamie wrote Cabot after Theodore's last visit to New York to say good-bye to her and to Alice and Ted. "He *cannot* see that the Department could be his duty, consequently his course to him is clear & go he will." She urged Cabot not to withdraw his personal support from Theodore in his seemingly quixotic decision because "I think it is a grief to an extent we cannot realize for him to feel that in this critical moment he goes, as it were, alone, against the wishes, & as he feels that means, without the good wishes, of those for whom & for whose opinion he cares." She was convinced "he will not stay & I feel that all we can do is to help him go in the best way."

Theodore went, with Bamie's blessing and with Lodge's, but this was the one decision of his career that he made absolutely alone. It was also the most important political decision of his life. He was warned on all sides that the country would not trust him again and that his political career was over forever. And here again, only Bamie had faith in his future, saying, "He cannot help being a power." Even as Theodore went off to war, she wrote Cabot that New York State, "unpatriotic as it always is," would realize that he had made his decision out of "unselfish thought of the country & not self-interest."

CHAPTER XIII

"Your Auntie Bye Has the Soul of a Hero"

MUCH to the surprise of everyone except Bamie, the Spanish-American War catapulted Theodore into the game of national politics. He went off to war under a cloud. In the eyes of conservative Republicans, he had confirmed their dearest suspicions; he was quixotic and unpredictable. He came back from Cuba, the swashbuckling hero of San Juan Hill, to a hooting, hollering New York now grown wildly patriotic—and to potential voters, of both political parties, who followed him everywhere singing the Rough Riders' favorite marching song, "There'll Be a Hot Time in the Old Town Tonight." In his own way, Theodore had become—as Bamie knew he couldn't help being—a "power," and even old Boss Platt could see that Colonel Roosevelt of the Rough Riders would be an asset to the Republican ticket at the polls.

John Hay's "splendid little war," which lasted only four months, had other repercussions on the Roosevelt family, though these were not of national importance. It brought a temporary truce, in the midst of war, between Bamie and Edith. In Theodore's absence, almost because of it, they were drawn together— first, by their common concern for him, and, second, by an event that had a decidedly softening effect upon Bamie.

By nature, Bamie had, particularly as she grew older, a "spicy" way about her. At least that was the adjective the family used to describe the scathing comments she was inclined to make about some individuals. She could not, for example, abide anyone who was "utterly incompetent" or "so very *pale* yellow," which meant pallid and uninteresting rather than timid. Theodore and her father, of course, were among the very few people in her life whom Bamie adored so completely that, contrary to her usual inclination, she never uttered a single "spicy" remark about them. On the other hand, Edith, who could be inordinately sharp herself, usually brought out all the "spiciness" in Bamie. Any small present or memento from Edith would very likely be dropped in the nearest and most convenient wastebasket or receptacle with the remark, "Another one down the *oubliette*." Even Alice, her favorite niece, did not escape a touch of Bamie's "spiciness." For example, if that high-spirited young lady forced a few contrite crocodile tears after some misdemeanor, Bamie would say, if only to show that she had not been taken in for a moment, "Alice came in with her amber-colored hair and shed an amber-colored tear." As for Bamie's attitude toward her devoted husband—with him, she could be most intolerant of all, even though he was her own dear "Mr. Bearo."

Much to her annoyance, Will Cowles did not share Bamie's intense interest in world affairs; her conversation and the conversation of her friends put him to sleep. He naturally preferred magazines and light fiction to the stacks of volumes of history and biography she kept piled high even by her bedside so that her reading would, as she put it forthrightly, "serve as mental manure." Commander Cowles, when not on naval duty, could and did play poker and bridge all day long and most of the night, and he resisted, passively but effectively, all his wife's determined efforts to woo him away from his pleasant pastimes into more serious pleasures and trains of thought. Still, she never ceased trying to get him to improve his mind and, in consequence, his conversation. "Mr. Bearo's" fondness for gold braid and a well-fitting uniform seemed particularly to annoy her at times, even though she took pride in the handsome appearance he made. She always helped the butler help the Commander don his full-dress regalia whenever they were to dine out formally, and yet, sometimes, she said he was "nothing but a cloth doll."

Will Cowles had the happy faculty of sensing only the affection that underlay Bamie's occasional scolding. He took things in easy, seagoing stride with his own gentle brand of humor, and this no one appreciated more than Bamie herself. For example, one evening after Bamie and the butler had bundled him up in his naval greatcoat and off in the carriage to attend a stag dinner, she was convulsed to find him, a few minutes later, back in the doorway where he complained in mock helplessness, "Someone forgot to put a scarf on me." Bamie delighted in "Mr. Bearo," without idolizing him; she was devoted to him and his naval career. For him, she once broke her longstanding rule, which was never to ask a favor of Theodore or Cabot for herself.

When the *Maine* blew up in Havana harbor, Commander Cowles was at Key West on the *"Fern & Faithful."* He was ordered to proceed at once to Havana and there act as floating headquarters for the United States naval officers assigned to investigate the cause of the explosion. Though a Spanish diver maintained that the bilge and keel of the *Maine* were so deeply buried in mud that no one could possibly tell what had happened, this United States board of inquiry reported, late in March of 1898, that the cause of the explosion had undoubtedly been an exterior mine. When this was headlined in the yellow press, war was inevitable, even though President McKinley, who "had no more backbone than a chocolate eclair," according to Theodore, still hoped to avert it. It was then that Theodore, to the cheers of the assembled Washington press corps and their guests at the annual Gridiron dinner, told Mark Hanna, the "Maker of Presidents," to his face, "We will have this war for the freedom of Cuba, Senator Hanna, in spite of the timidity of the commercial interests."

Public sentiment, whipped up by the yellow journalists, agreed completely with Theodore and, on April 20, Congress passed a resolution demanding Spain's withdrawal from the island. The next day the President declared a blockade of all Cuban ports, and Spain retaliated on April 24 with a declaration of war.

The *"Fern & Faithful"* had brought the board of inquiry safely home and its stalwart captain now asked to rejoin the Atlantic fleet, only to be told that his little vessel did not have sufficient armor or fire power even to be a despatch boat for the cruiser *New York*. He saw himself ignominiously riding the war out at anchor off Key West, even as preparations went on all around him for the United States naval attack on Santiago. Beside himself with frustration and despair, Commander Cowles at this point sent off to his wife what she described to Cabot as "that fatal woeful cablegram" saying, "Urge Theodore & Cabot obtain suitable command for me." Bamie knew that Theodore, who was then just about to leave for San Antonio, Texas, to join his Rough Riders, had already secured one extra gun for the *Fern* and had been trying to procure others. It went very much against the grain for her even to mention her husband's request to Theodore and Cabot. And yet she did.

One reason Bamie asked this favor for her husband was that she had just talked with one of Commander Cowles's brother officers who had been down at Key West. This officer, she wrote Cabot, "told me last night the *Fern* is utterly impossible. If they gave him more guns, he could fire them once & then be taken." Besides, "she is so slow and old" and "her guns of necessity would be so small that to be near enough to use them, she would apparently inevitably be caught." She wrote Cabot, "I hate to trouble, & if nothing can be done that is an end, but I felt I must speak."

Bamie spoke, and Commander Cowles was promptly transferred to command of the cruiser *Topeka* that joined the blockade off Puerto Rico. The other reason Bamie spoke was that she had only recently learned—just about the time that war was declared—something that Cabot perhaps did not yet know. She and Will were to have a child in October, and, of course, there was no doubt in Bamie's mind that it would be a son. That son's father deserved his chance, too, in the war.

Bamie's son, William Sheffield Cowles, Jr., surprised everyone by being born to her, at the end of the Spanish-American War, when she was only a few months short of forty-four. There were some members of the family who said that Bamie appeared to have managed this quite on her own. Others said she often ignored the part Will Cowles had obviously played in helping her achieve her great desire to have a son. But all agreed it was a near-miracle for Bamie to have her first and only child in her mid-forties, and nothing short of heroic the way she managed to keep up her war relief activity almost to the day Sheffield was born and even while harboring Edith's two eldest during the winter and spring of 1898.

In June, Edith came up from Washington and took Alice and Ted out to Sagamore Hill. These two were of an age to enjoy the war thoroughly, and Ted, Jr., began to glory in the news from Cuba as much as his father once had in Union victories during the Civil War. While Edith became increasingly grim-faced—over the news that United States troops would soon embark on the invasion of Cuba and that the army would there encounter malaria and yellow fever as well as stiff resistance from trained Spanish Colonial troops—Ted and Alice tramped up and down the broad veranda at Sagamore Hill shouting at the top of their lungs warlike stanzas from "The Saga of King Olaf," which Theodore used to read aloud to them, or martial verses, in their own variation, from an operetta Bamie had taken them to in New York:

> Unleash the dogs of war!
> The enemy will find us unrelenting.
> When our cannons roar,
> The little king of Spain
> Will be repenting!

For a few short weeks that summer, Bamie went out to Sagamore Hill, too, to be with all the children while Edith journeyed to Tampa, Florida, the embarkation point for the invasion, to bid good-bye to Theodore. On her return, Edith wrote Corinne, "These dreadful days must be lived and whatever comes Theodore and I have had more happiness in eleven years than most people in long lives." Then, in one of the few sympathetic asides mentioning her other sister-in-law, now five months pregnant—with her husband, too, out on the high seas, searching for the Spanish fleet—Edith wrote, "Bamie I do not dare to think of. She is so brave it frightens me." She wanted Bamie to stay on for the summer at Sagamore Hill where she could look after her, but that staunch soul insisted she had to return to the sweltering city and her duties as a member of the executive committee of Red Cross Auxiliary No. 3, whose most important wartime contribution, the training of women nurses for duty in the field—the very idea Bamie had discussed with Theodore before his departure—had a far-reaching effect.

When war seemed imminent, Bamie had written Cabot, "I would give anything on earth to be able to *do* something for the country, but I suppose we can but wait." Waiting was, however, not in Bamie's nature, and her friend, Mrs. Whitelaw Reid, was always in the vanguard of any effort to do good. Even before war began, they had raised funds for the relief of the starving, noncombatant *reconcentrados* of Cuba and, then for the first time, they had run afoul of that indomitable lady, Miss Clara Barton of the American Red Cross.

The American Association of the Red Cross had been in existence since 1881, but until the Spanish-American War, it was scarcely known as an organization. It was, instead, synonymous with the name of Clara Barton, its heroic, aging founder, and it was primarily her one-woman show.

The summer before the war with Spain, Miss Barton, fresh from her triumphant mission to the starving Armenians in Turkey, had offered her services to President McKinley, on one condition: If the Red Cross were named the sole agency of distribution, she told the President, she would herself undertake to feed and give relief to the *reconcentrados* of Cuba who had

123

so aroused the sympathies, and the warlike instincts, of the American people.

While Miss Barton was convincing the President that she should be sole distributor of all relief, New York society, as she felt, had gone off on a tangent of its own under the leadership of Dr. Louis Klopsch of the *Christian Herald*. Dr. Klopsch was bent on equipping and sending his own relief expedition to the "Pearl of the Antilles," and Bamie and Elisabeth Reid were, in the beginning, among his supporters. Nipping this scheme in the bud, Miss Barton convinced the President that he should give these "court ladies," as she called them, no countenance. Undismayed, Dr. Klopsch and the New York ladies next offered to send a ship with one hundred nurses to Cuba, but this time, acting on Miss Barton's recommendation, it was the State Department that turned their offer down.

At this point, Dr. Klopsch retired from battle; not so Elisabeth Reid and Bamie who, with all their usual diplomacy and tenacity, decided that rather than trying to fight Miss Barton, it would be better to join her. They then formed Auxiliary No. 3 of the American Red Cross and proceeded to work within Miss Barton's organization, giving it the pioneering spirit and the energy it had previously lacked.

As a result, when the President in due course designated Miss Barton as sole dispenser of all American relief for Cuban refugees, the New York "court ladies," whom she had so disdained, were among her most effective fund-raisers. Miss Barton's first Red Cross relief ship to Cuba, which arrived in Havana before the invasion by United States forces, carried $200,000 worth of medicine and food, and a large part of these supplies had been donated by the New York branch of the Red Cross and the "court ladies" who cared not one whit who took them if only they got there. Miss Barton's second relief ship, the *State of Texas*, was actually chartered by the New York branch. This vessel arrived at Guantánamo Bay, with 1,400 tons of food and medical supplies, immediately on the heels of the American invasion that deposited Theodore and his First Volunteer Cavalry Regiment on the coast of Cuba without a horse to its name because their invasion transport ship had been much too crowded to bring their mounts along.

Meanwhile, back home in New York, Auxiliary No. 3 had now turned Mrs. Reid's handsome town house into a training school for nurses who would, Bamie and Elisabeth Reid hoped, be used for active duty in the field. But here once again they met with powerful opposition, not only from Miss Barton, who did not approve of women on the battlefield, but also from the army's surgeon general, who was even more unalterably opposed to the idea.

In spite of this combined opposition, Auxiliary No. 3 persisted in training young ladies in wartime nursing in the hope that Miss Barton and the surgeon general could be circumvented. At least the nurses would be ready for duty as near the front as possible.

Bamie's determination to get nurses, as well as food and supplies, to the front in Cuba all through the summer of 1898 during the months of her pregnancy was undoubtedly sparked by her desire to help Theodore. He was, she wrote Cabot, "before my eyes continually, under that hot sky & the drenching rains struggling to make things right for the country & his men." Her farewell present to him had been a fully equipped medicine chest, which she knew, in view of Theodore's concern for his men, would be quite inadequate and soon exhausted. Despite her heroic efforts and those of the rest of Auxiliary No. 3 precious little of the Red Cross food and medicine aboard the *State of Texas* ever reached Theodore and his Rough Riders. After a few brief days of glory, following their brilliant charge, on foot, up San Juan Hill, the Rough Riders went into encampment outside Santiago where they soon felt doomed to die of malaria and yellow fever, if not from starvation.

As the war drew to its quick close, at the surrender of Santiago on July 17, Theodore grew more and more angry at the army's insane lack of logistical planning for the welfare of its fighting forces. He began to bombard the War Department and everyone else in Washington with letters exposing this condition; he begged to be sent on to Puerto Rico so his men could at least die fighting instead of like rats in a plague, without proper medical care, without nursing, even without enough food, which Theodore and his brother officers bought from the Cubans and paid for out of pocket. He also wrote home, with some asperity, to Bamie, who had done what she could under the circumstances, suggesting that if her fine Red Cross wanted to help them "in any practical way," then it could reimburse him "and Woody Kane and Willie Tiffany" for all they had spent and intended to spend for food and clothing just to keep the men of the First United States Volunteer Cavalry alive until the army chose to order them out of their steaming Cuban hellhole.

Later that summer, Bamie and Elisabeth Reid managed to get a few Auxiliary No. 3 nurses on board a hospital ship bound for Puerto Rico, but by the time this contingent arrived what little action there had been in this area, as elsewhere in the war, was over. The nurses' arrival, however, did cheer the men immensely, and it set a precedent that Bamie was later able to use with some force in her campaign for passage of the first Army Nurses' Bill in Washington.

But now, with her *accouchement* only weeks away, Bamie herself was *hors de combat*. She was much too heavy with child to put in an appearance at Montauk, Long Island, to greet Theodore and his returning Rough Riders. Nevertheless, Auxiliary No. 3 nurses were out at Camp Wyckoff in full force to take care of the sick and ailing men as they disembarked and were demobilized.

Bamie could at least take satisfaction in that, as she spent most of those long September days resting on the chaise longue in her sunny, orange-curtained morning room at No. 689. There Theodore, in his colonel's uniform, stopped in to see her even before his regiment had been fully demobilized. They discussed the offer Boss Platt had just made him, which was to throw the support of the regular Republican organization behind Theodore if he would run for governor of New York that fall. They also planned Theodore's strategy in dealing with the wily old Boss. Theodore could promise "to discuss" political appointments in advance with Boss Platt, as he had requested, without however tying himself down to accepting all his suggestions.

As Theodore, out at Sagamore Hill, prepared for his whirl-wind gubernatorial campaign, it fell to Edith's lot to play hostess to half a dozen Rough Riders, including Fergie, whom Theodore had made a lieutenant on the field for courage and gallantry. Fergie soon went back to his job with the Astor Estate, but quite a few of the other Rough Riders lingered on at Sagamore Hill, seemingly loath to tear themselves away from their beloved colonel and go home to their Western ranches or their studies at Harvard, Princeton, and Yale. The children enjoyed the visiting Rough Riders more than anyone else, partic-ularly Alice, who was quite grown up enough now to feel very much the daughter of the regiment. So, too, did little Ethel, who always seemed to Theodore so much like his older sister, the way she mothered and bossed her younger brothers around. One day toward the middle of October, Theodore told Ethel she should never forget that her Auntie Bye "has the soul of a hero," with which the child no doubt agreed, though she could scarcely have known why at the time.

Bamie, of course, had her sister, Corinne, with her, but Com-mander Cowles would be at sea when their child was born. Dur-ing those quiet, sunny days in the morning room, Bamie com-municated her perfectly reasonable fears only to him, in letters that fortunately never had to be delivered. These letters, which were read by no one in the family until many years later, would have done much to dispel the idea that Bamie reserved her "spiciest" remarks for Will Cowles.

The first undelivered letter was written on September 17, just a month before their son was born and while Commander Cowles was actually at home on a few days' leave.

"Bearo dear," Bamie wrote. "If things should not go rightly with me & if you are left to take care of Baby, please always, always love it for my sake and in the course of time you will for its own." Although she did not believe "in too firm last requests as they do not always prove wise," she urged him, since navy life was so unsettled, to let Corinne or Edith take their child to rear as "they care more for me than any others do & they are the best women I know as well as our own people." She assured him, "If this is the end, Bearo, of our married life, at least it has been a very happy one," and then on paper she permitted herself to go further in expressing her feelings than she ever did in spoken words:

"All these days since you have come, I can scarcely bear looking at you & feeling these may be our last times in the morning room where we have been so happy together. . . . I am crying so, Bearo, that I can scarcely see. You have just read me your letter to [Captain] Bradford and now you have gone to your room to take a dear Bearo rest. . . . Goodbye, Bearo. God bless you always & do not try to mourn me conventionally. Go with your friends, but remember your

"ARC"

Only eleven days before the birth of their son, she wrote Commander Cowles another undelivered letter, and this time he was back on sea duty. Again she told him that if "things should not go rightly," he should "let Edith & Corinne help you." She grieved "to feel there would be no home where we have lived together & where you would associate the surroundings with our mutual life, for, of course, this house would only be an expense & no pleasure." Then she began to think of the objects in that home that she wanted particularly to give to certain people. These were the things that always, for some reason, annoyed Edith, who would say to one of the children, "Why on earth does dear Bamie have so many *objects* around? One falls over these silly things, you know." But each one of those objects had for Bamie some particular, very strong sentiment attached to it and only death or the thought of it would ever make her agree to part with a single one of them. In some detail, she asked her husband to see that each of these mementos was delivered—

"Theodore, I have nothing appropriate for" and then, on second thought, he might like the "elk-foot inkstand on the morning-room table" that he had sent her years before when he had first gone out to the Bad Lands. Ted, Jr., was to have the silver tea set with the doves on top that had belonged to his great-grand-mother Roosevelt and so on, down the line, not forgetting "the Indian drum hanging on the gaslight" which "Mr. Bearo" was to give to Fergie. And now the letter is no longer written in ink but in a penciled scrawl added just two days before Sheffield was born in mid-October of 1898. "Darling, it is the 16th & I am very uncomfortable," she wrote. "If things go wrong, never mind. I have been so happy—ARC."

CHAPTER XIV

Theodore, Bamie, and the Boss

NOT long after Colonel Roosevelt had been elected governor of New York, he wrote Cecil Spring-Rice the exciting news. "Did you know," he asked this close friend of earlier days in London and Washington, "that my sister Anna Cowles has a baby?" The birth of William Sheffield Cowles, Jr., in the autumn of 1898, did indeed seem to all the Roosevelts one of the most impressive events of that year. Corinne was so carried away that she frequently brought unexpected luncheon guests home to Bamie's at No. 689 to show off her sister's wonderful new baby. Everyone was charmed by small Sheffield. As he grew into a toddler, completely adored by his mother and all his relations, his bouncing energy and most particularly his lively blue eyes made him unmistakably a Roosevelt.

Theodore, who always wanted Bamie's "blessed little Sheffield" to feel closer to him "than most boys did to their uncles," had many chances to cement his immediate rapport with his brand-new nephew. During his first winter as governor, he stopped in often to see Sheffield in the nursery at No. 689 where his own large and adored brood had spent part of their childhood. For, almost every weekend, the Governor came down from Albany to have breakfast conferences at Bamie's with Senator Platt, who controlled the Republican party in New York State.

Before his election, Theodore had promised the Senator he

would make no important appointment or executive move without first consulting him, and Theodore was determined, remembering Cabot's advice about never forcing an open break with the party, to live up to the letter of his precampaign promise.

Having recovered from a rather difficult childbirth with all her usual energy, Bamie managed easily to divide her time between the nursery and state politics. She was delighted to be weekend hostess in town for the Governor, even though some of her friends and relatives told her they never expected to come to her house and "meet people whom they knew only by their caricatures."

Nor did these gatherings at No. 689 altogether meet with the approval of Boss Platt. There was a fashionable, nonchalant air about these British-style breakfasts that unsettled him; he preferred getting Theodore off alone at the Senator's favorite pow-wow rendezvous, the "Amen Corner" at the Fifth Avenue Hotel. But the Governor usually got the jump on the Senator by simply writing him at the last moment that he was expected on such-and-such a date at Bamie's. Once there, Boss Platt would be told that the Governor's sister would sit in on their discussion because, as Theodore said with a disarming grin, "She takes such an interest in what I am doing." Being a politician of the old school, Senator Platt felt uncomfortable at having a lady present when such crass matters as patronage were discussed. He also suspected the Governor of planting Mrs. Cowles on him as a witness, and that disturbed him further. Another reason Senator Platt grew to dislike these breakfast sessions at No. 689 was that it became increasingly evident that "consulting," as Theodore construed it, meant that, after "consulting," the Governor would, if he felt he must on principle, go his own way.

This was not what Senator Platt had in mind when he had accepted his first invitation to breakfast at Bamie's; nor was it at all what he meant when he had originally exacted from Theodore—with a handshake—his promise to "consult." That was Platt's quid pro quo for putting Colonel Roosevelt, just returned from the war, at the head of the Republican ticket. Theodore's promise to "consult," the Boss grumbled to his henchmen, meant only that the Governor would harangue the Senator for hours and "then go and do just as he darn pleased."

There was something to be said for the Governor's high-handed attitude. After the 1898 election in New York State, it was apparent to all—and especially to the three around the breakfast table—that Platt's whole organization would have suffered utter rout at the polls without the hero of San Juan Hill at the head of its ticket. Without Theodore, the regular Republican slate would probably have lost by 50,000 votes, chiefly because the public could no longer stomach the previous Republican administration's extravagance and gross mismanagement of the Erie Canal. Even Theodore, with half a dozen uniformed Rough Riders aboard his flag-draped campaign train and his regimental bugler to blow the cavalry charge before each whistle-stop speech, had been elected only by the slim margin of 18,000 votes. Confronted, postelection, by these sober facts of political life, Senator Platt had often to swallow uncommonly bitter coffee as Bamie presided over the silver service at breakfast during the winter of 1899.

The "Easy Boss," as Platt was sometimes called, ran into immediate difficulties with the new Governor, and it was precisely over the Erie Canal that they first tangled. Theodore was determined to show the electorate that *his* Republican administration would be different. His appointees would be men of integrity, above reproach. Platt, hoping to set a precedent in his dealings with the Governor, offered the job of canal administrator to one of his machine politicians, an able man, but one who came from a canal county and was, therefore, vulnerable to local pressures. After the politician had accepted, Platt then told the Governor that here was just the man for him. Theodore knew very well he had to win the first round or the "Easy Boss" would move in, in exactly the same fashion, on all subsequent appointments.

There were many breakfasts over this one, and now the Senator encountered, for the first time, Theodore's tremendous staying power as a talker. First, the old man lost his temper, but Theodore kept on talking. Then, the old man just sat and listened with his head in his hands as Theodore lectured him about the ethical and moral principles involved. In the presence of a lady, Senator Platt could scarcely give vent to his disgust with such impractical, high-flown talk. When, after several of these sessions, Theodore produced a list of eligible names of his own, going over their merits one by one, Platt in sheer exhaustion finally nodded yes. The Senator never forgot this experience; he bided his time, but Theodore had definitely won Round 1 over the coffee cups at No. 689.

This early victory over the "Easy Boss"—a decided misnomer, Theodore learned in time—was a heady experience. It gave the Governor such immediate confidence in himself that the whole family soon began to feel very much at home in the Executive Mansion at Albany. Moreover, the Governor's salary, coupled with the increasing demand for magazine articles by Colonel Roosevelt, made it possible for Edith to run the family finances without endless skimping, for the first time in thirteen years of marriage. As for all "the bunnies," they had as much room to romp and play as they had enjoyed before only at Sagamore Hill. It seemed to Fergie, after an early visit to Albany, that they "looked ever so much stronger & better, being less rabbit-hutched in those big rooms & grounds." As he wrote Bamie, "It's a nice house."

Even Edith, who hated the rough-and-tumble of politics as much as she disliked being in the public eye as the Governor's lady, began to take an interest in the ugly, roomy Executive Mansion. Always a tidy housekeeper, she set about refurbishing the public rooms so that they would, as Theodore said, look less like the lounge of "a first-class Chicago hotel." Privately, Bamie did not think Edith capable of any such miracle. "Poor, dear Edith," she would say, "she never could make a home comfortable and attractive." But Bamie did not interfere in Edith's Albany domain. She was much too preoccupied with Sheffield, enthralled by the gubernatorial politics taking place almost every weekend at No. 689 and quite busy enough, for the time being, making "Oldgate," her husband's lovely old ancestral home at Farmington, Connecticut, into a cosily cluttered second home for her own small family.

Thus the first winter in Albany passed, most serenely and happily for the whole family. Edith had set a precedent of her own at the inaugural reception: While Theodore enthusiastically pumped six thousand extended hands, the Governor's lady merely smiled her quiet little smile and refrained from such vulgar, exhausting contact with the admiring multitude by holding quite firmly in her folded, white-gloved hands a large bouquet culled from the lilies of the valley Corinne had sent her in honor of the occasion and from Bamie's gift of wild orchids. Reporters noting this new custom in the gubernatorial receiving line decided that Mrs. Roosevelt was probably "not as frail as she looked." She was "winsome," they wrote; she was a fine little figure of a woman; her light chestnut hair was soft and lovely, but they also observed that her cool brown eyes were somewhat distant. This was scarcely surprising; a close classmate of Edith's at finishing school in New York had once remarked, "You could live in the same room with Edith for fifty years and never know what she was really thinking."

Edith's official manner at Albany was, as always, polite but reserved. As the Governor's lady, she encouraged no more intimacy than she ever had, with the result that Albany reporters learned to leave her strictly alone, which pleased her immensely. Besides, they found plenty of copy in the lively behavior of the small Roosevelts, their guinea pigs, their pony, and all their other pets, and almost more news than they could handle in the activities of the ebullient young governor himself.

In the spring of 1899, Theodore suddenly found himself in Round 2 of his running battle with the "Easy Boss." This was set off by the Governor's decision to support a bill taxing all franchises granted to corporations by the state. It was perhaps no coincidence that such a tax had worked out quite well in neighboring Connecticut and that Bamie had already begun to take a lively, observant interest in what went on in Hartford, Connecticut, that was so near her new summer home at Farmington. Senator Platt, whose very organization depended on sizable campaign contributions from grateful New York corporations, recoiled from this measure even more violently than he had, in Round 1, from the Governor's unusual display of independence in appointing his own canal administrator. He now told Theodore to his face that he was a dangerous, "altruistic" man. Bamie and Theodore, both of whom delighted in words and their use, were fascinated to learn that Senator Platt construed that adjective to mean the same thing as "socialistic." Concealing his amusement, Theodore very patiently, as if talking to a deaf man, tried to explain to the Senator that it was the height of practical politics for him to advocate the franchise tax.

"I believe that in the long run here in this state," he told Senator Platt, "we should be beaten, and badly beaten, if we took the attitude of saying that corporations should not, when they receive great benefits and make a great deal of money, pay their share of public burdens."

This caused nothing but snorts from Senator Platt, and now he began to dodge the breakfasts at Bamie's. Theodore tried another tactic. He wrote Bamie in mid-May, even as he pressed for passage of the francise tax, "You are having just the people I want at lunch. What do you say to asking Senator Platt? I have got to call on him that afternoon anyhow. I do not know whether he would come or not, but if he did, it might save me some bother, and then it is possible he would be pleased."

At this point nothing could possibly please Senator Platt. He agreed wholeheartedly with the corporation lobbyists at Albany who warned the Governor that, if he continued to press for the franchise tax, he would never again be nominated for any public office. No corporation would ever subscribe to a campaign fund, the Senator told Theodore, if he were on the ticket. This made the Governor mad. He told Platt he would not stand for blackmail, and, on his return to Albany, he sent a sharp message to the legislature urging immediate passage of the franchise tax.

The Speaker of the Assembly, who was one of Platt's staunchest henchmen, tore the Governor's message up. The Governor then went to the Executive Chamber of the Capitol and sent in to the Speaker a second version of his message, with the warning that he would appear before the Assembly in person and read it himself if necessary. This was Theodore's early strategy in the legislature—when he had been a young assemblyman—all over again, but with the authority of the governor's office behind him. His dramatic behavior, fully covered by the press, focused an unwelcome spotlight on a legislature only too vulnerable to the charge of serving the corporations better than the public. The tax bill went through both houses with a rush, and Theodore won Round 2 so handily he could not help crowing a bit. As soon as the bill was passed, he sent off a note to Bamie that may have caused her some apprehension.

"Darling Bye," he wrote, "I am pretty well satisfied with the triumph I have scored."

Theodore seemed perfectly oblivious that his "triumph" and the manner in which it had been achieved could have future repercussions. He understood the "Easy Boss" no more than Platt understood him, for he had, even in the midst of the battle over the franchise tax, told Cabot, "I am on excellent terms with Senator Platt," not having the least idea how one-sided that view of their relationship was. In June, still enjoying his victory over the machine, the Governor ended his first legislative year at Albany and, accompanied by Fergie, went happily off to Nevada, to attend the first of many rousing reunions with his loyal, war-whooping Rough Riders.

Theodore's trip out and back to Nevada in the private car of his and Bamie's friend, Paul Morton, vice-president of the Atchison, Topeka & Santa Fe, turned out to be a triumphal cross-country procession. Even Theodore was startled that so many people still wanted to see Colonel Roosevelt of the Rough Riders and shake his hand. "It would really be difficult to express my surprise at the way I was greeted," he wrote Cabot from Oyster Bay on his return. "At every station at which the train stopped in Indiana, Illinois, Wisconsin, Iowa, Missouri, Kansas, Colorado, and New Mexico, I was received by dense throngs exactly as if I had been a presidential candidate." The newspapers in the towns and cities through which he passed boomed him for the vice-presidency in 1900 and treated him as a candidate for president in 1904. Some of the small-town Republican papers were even for running the Colonel in 1900 in place of McKinley. "My reception," Theodore told Cabot, "caused some talk, so I thought it better to come out in an interview stating, that of course I was for President McKinley's nomination."

Still worried that McKinley himself might think the Governor of New York was planning to push him off the national ticket in 1900, Theodore followed this letter down to Washington. The President graciously put the Governor up for the night at the Executive Mansion and seemed quite unconcerned by Theodore's Western boomlet. Theodore also called on his good friend, Elihu Root, who had become one of his most influential advisers and had only recently been made secretary of war. He told Elihu he just could not see his way clear to running for vice-president, only to hear that great tease say solemnly, "Of course not, Theodore, you're not fit for it."

Somewhat deflated, Theodore discussed his future from every angle with Lodge, who was delighted with his friend's western reception. He assured Cabot he "was not taken in by the crowds in the West." "It would be five years," he said, before he could conceivably run for president, "and I have never known a hurrah to endure for five years." What should he do in the interim? "What I should really most like," he told Cabot, "would be to be reelected Governor."

But Cabot did not think Theodore could count on reelection in New York State, and defeat there would be a serious setback to his career. Cabot argued that Theodore's chances would be very much better on the national ticket with McKinley, who would surely be endorsed for a second term, and then after four years as vice-president, Theodore would be the presidential candidate in 1904. But what about the tradition that the vice-presidency was a political deadend? Nonsense, Cabot said, "The way to break a precedent, Theodore, is to make one."

Now began Theodore's year of great indecision. It lasted right up to the Republican convention in Philadelphia in June of 1900. On one side was arrayed his closest friend, Cabot Lodge, whom some called his political Svengali. Bamie tended to agree with Cabot, but she kept out of it as much as possible for fear of antagonizing Edith. On the other side stood Edith, firmly and unalterably opposed to the vice-presidency for her husband.

The Governor's lady now seemed to enjoy her position very much; she knew the governor of New York State was paid $2,000 a year more than the vice-president of the United States; with their large family, they could not afford to entertain in Washington as the vice-president and his wife should, and this would be most embarrassing. She quoted Theodore a favorite line of Finley Peter Dunne's "Mr. Dooley": "Though pollytics is a gran career f'r a man, 'tis a tough wan f'r his wife." It would, under the circumstances, be much tougher for all the family if Theodore were to become vice-president.

Having taken a house in Washington in the fall of 1899 to be with Commander Cowles, who had been transferred to the Navy Department as assistant chief of the Bureau of Navigation, Bamie was no longer available in New York as the Governor's weekend hostess. He missed those breakfast sessions at No. 689 and her astute political counsel.

Writing a friend in Oregon who took an optimistic view of Roosevelt for president in 1904, Theodore reviewed his chances and rather gloomily concluded they were not so good. He had no political organization of his own. Now he could no longer expect much in the way of corporate campaign contributions. And, worst of all, "I have no Hanna," he said.

CHAPTER XV

The Washington Breakfast and Other Social Events

WHEN Bamie went to Washington to take up residence there in the autumn of 1899, she was not altogether a stranger to that curiously backward world capital, so unlike the London she had known. She knew many of the diplomatic set, especially the British contingent headed by Sir Julian Pauncefote and his lady; and, through the Lodges, she was on good terms with some of the more powerful, and less corrupt, members of "The Millionaires' Club," as the United States Senate was then called.

Mrs. Cowles also had close friends in the Cabinet. Secretary of War Root thoroughly enjoyed Bamie in her "spicy" moods and had great respect for her political wisdom. John Hay, who had become secretary of state in 1898, was a family friend of long standing, and one who particularly admired her tact and social talents. Secretary Root at once enlisted Bamie's help in getting senatorial support for an Army Nurses' bill that would ensure, in future, that American soldiers wounded in battle would receive the prompt attention that had been so lacking in Cuba. And Secretary Hay called on Bamie to help him draft a new constitution for the American Red Cross that would make it a truly national organization.

The home that Commander and Mrs. Cowles bought was a modest, four-story brick house at 1733 N Street in the fashionable Northwest section of the city. It had a lovely garden and a pleasant oval dining room just big enough to seat sixteen at table but very little other charm except the comfortable clutter with which Bamie usually surrounded herself. The advantage of the location was that it was but a half hour's stroll—and Bamie enjoyed a walk as much as Theodore did—to almost every place in Washington that mattered.

The fashionable part of Washington at the turn of the century formed, in rough outline, a "T"—with Massachusetts Avenue as the horizontal stroke and Du Pont Circle as the point where Connecticut Avenue, or the down stroke, began and then sheared off at an angle straight for the Executive Mansion. The Lodges lived on Massachusetts Avenue just east of Du Pont Circle in a comfortable brick house to which they had added a large new wing for the Senator's library, and there Nannie Lodge, one of the quiet beauties of the capital with her soft violet eyes and her cameo-like profile, served afternoon tea to friends. Bamie's house on N Street was just three minutes' walk south from the Lodges on Massachusetts Avenue and only a few blocks due east from Connecticut Avenue, as if it were an "i" dot under the right horizontal arm of the "T."

Some of the diplomatic corps, notably the British, were still entrenched on Connecticut Avenue in the late 1890's, but Massachusetts Avenue, where the Lodges lived, would become known in later years as "Embassy Row." On Massachusetts Avenue, to the west of Du Pont Circle, there was, in addition to a scattering of new embassies and legations, the imposing residence of Washington's then most elegant party-giver, Mrs. Townsend. This daughter of an obscure but wealthy Erie, Pennsylvania, congressman and coal baron carried herself with the air of Alexandra, Princess of Wales, and was rewarded for her regal demeanor by being known simply as Mrs. Townsend, no further identification being necessary. Mrs. Townsend gave elaborate, delightfully conglomerate, sit-down dinners, for one hundred guests at a time. Her liveried servants, picked for their imposing height, often seemed to outnumber the guests. Terrapin, pressed duck; blue dinners, rose dinners, orchid dinners, altogether outdid everyone else in Washington. Bamie quite enjoyed these huge affairs, for all political Washington was to be seen at Mrs. Townsend's on one occasion or another. It was just like visiting Mme Tussaud's waxwork museum, only here the cast of celebrities was exceedingly animated under the stimulus of Mrs. Townsend's excellent cellar.

Not far from Du Pont Circle were the square brick residence of the three busy Misses Patten, who knew all the Washington gossip ("Telephone, telegraph or tell the Patten sisters," everyone said); the imposing mansion of the mineral-wealthy Thomas J. Walshes of Montana; and the huge Renaissance palace of the even more wealthy, conservative, and family-conscious Larz Andersons of Ohio.

Du Pont Circle itself was dominated by the white marble edifice built by Stanford White for Mrs. Medill Patterson of Chicago and by the grand ducal establishment of the Levi Z. Leiters, also of Chicago, whose department store fortune backed hospitality even more lavish than Mrs. Townsend's. Mrs. Leiter's forte was the costume ball, and these affairs set off to perfection her three really beautiful daughters, one of whom had become Lady Curzon, wife of the governor-general of India. Bamie enjoyed Mrs. Leiter most of all for her quaint malapropisms. "I went to the costume ball dressed as a nun and my husband in the garbage of a monk," Mrs. Leiter would say, or, "My dear, you should build a spinal staircase to your maids' quarters." The latest of Mrs. Leiter's remarks served to enliven any number of otherwise dull Washington dinner parties.

East of the Lodges on Massachusetts Avenue was a large, gloomy brick house with a porte-cochere perched high on a side carriage ramp as if overlooking the Elbe or the Spree, and here lived the German Ambassador. Beyond the German Embassy, on Scott Circle, was the handsome, white, stone house of former Vice-President Levi P. Morton, a wealthy New York banker, who had leased his Washington pied-à-terre to the Russian Ambassador, irascible Count Cassini.

Walking along the fashionable "T" formed by Massachusetts

and Connecticut Avenues, one might encounter almost everyone in Washington worth knowing, though some more or less eccentric folk lived elsewhere, among them, Mrs. John B. Henderson, wife of the Missouri senator, who had built her "Boundary Castle" out at the very end of Sixteenth Street on Meridian Hill. The John R. McLeans of Cincinnati did most of their entertaining in their imposing town residence off McPherson Square but they also enjoyed country living at "Friendship," and that was almost at the Maryland line. This was quite a trip in Bamie's brougham whenever she attended the meetings at "Friendship" to help reorganize the American Red Cross and put it on a more efficient basis, but it was important to convince the senators' wives gathered there by Mrs. McLean that the old ways of Miss Barton were perhaps not the right way to run that organization.

Sauntering from Du Pont Circle down Connecticut Avenue, past the British Embassy and the homes of many old Washington families, one was sure to see any number of friends and acquaintances—also on foot, on horseback, or in victorias or broughams. With a jog around Farragut Park, one then came to the most beautiful of all Washington parks—Lafayette Square. Facing the Square on the west was Decatur House, home of gallant, old General Beale, and in that same block, facing on Pennsylvania Avenue, the two Blair houses. Overlooking the Square from Sixteenth Street on the north were the twin houses, designed by Richardson, of Secretary of State John Hay and his good friend, the historian Henry Adams. Also facing the Square on the north was fashionable St. John's Episcopal Church. On the east was the residence of wealthy Senator Don Cameron of Pennsylvania and his beautiful young wife, "Lizzie," who was seldom in it. Also on the east, facing the Square, was the Washington residence of Senator Mark Hanna of Ohio. South of the Square, of course, was the Executive Mansion and President McKinley, whom Senator Hanna, Boss of the national G.O.P., had put in it.

Bamie's circle of friends when she first went to Washington did not include Senator Hanna, the "Maker of Presidents."

Nor was she ever invited, of course, to any of the Senator's famous political breakfasts, for these huge repasts of corned-beef hash and buckwheat cakes, though presided over by "Maggie," the Senator's jolly cook, were otherwise strictly stag. But Bamie often walked down to Lafayette Square on a Sunday morning to have breakfast with Henry Adams and his circle of friends, and these delightful people, men and women, young and old, were the only truly cosmopolitan society in all Washington. Everyone and anything worth knowing in the capital were sooner or later to be encountered at No. 800 Sixteenth Street.

These Sunday breakfasts on Sixteenth Street had been a delightful institution for a favored few in Washington ever since the 1880s when Theodore, the young civil service commissioner, had first attended them with his friend, Cecil Spring-Rice of the British Legation. "Sprice," who was "no madder than an Englishman should be," according to Henry Adams, naturally delighted the historian. And though Theodore's insistence on treating him and John Hay "as elderly sages" annoyed him, still Adams always welcomed Theodore, and Edith, too, whose reserve and occasional sharp sallies pleased him more than her husband's exhausting enthusiasms. On hearing that his sister had now joined that fascinating gathering, Theodore wrote her rather wistfully from Albany, where he was struggling with problems that he still regarded as "parochial"—"Give my love to John Hay and Henry Adams and tell them I wish I could stop in to see them."

By the time Bamie arrived in Washington, Henry Adams was a wispy little old gentleman with dark, brooding eyes and a bristling, gray Van Dyke who was, except for these Sunday breakfasts, a complete social recluse. When not traveling restlessly around the world, to which he seemed driven following the suicide of his wife, Marian, in 1885, he still wanted a few congenial souls around him. He never went out socially, but he welcomed his friends most hospitably almost every Sunday during the Washington season to his charming, English-style breakfasts. The table would regularly be laid for a dozen or more and a generous sideboard took care of any number of last-minute guests, the friends of intimate friends. To be added to Henry Adams' breakfast circle, the only group in Washington where intelligent conversation could be heard, was the one social distinction that city was then able to confer.

Nannie Lodge, who first took Bamie to these celebrated breakfasts, and Mrs. Don Cameron had both been close friends of Henry Adams' wife. For her sake and for their own lovely selves, Henry Adams adored them and all their growing children and was, in turn, christened by the youngsters and called by everyone in that intimate circle, "Uncle Henry."

The years made no difference at "Uncle Henry's" breakfast table. Bamie's young friend, Fergie, down from New York for the weekend, might be seated one time next to "Mrs. Decameron," as he called her, and the next time round beside her beautiful daughter, Rachel, who was more his contemporary. One Sunday, Bamie might spend the morning discussing the Hay-Pauncefote Treaty with the secretary of state and another, the geology of the Far West with Henry Adams's other good friend, Clarence King, or poetry with the Lodges' oldest son, brilliant young Bay Lodge.

Everyone, in short, who was endowed with youth, talent, wit, charm, beauty, or brains who came to Washington sooner or later gravitated to the breakfast table of moody, little Henry Adams, who never let his occasional dark forebodings on the future of the United States and the universe, interfere too much with the pleasure of his guests. Though no longer young herself, Bamie was generously endowed with her share of the qualities necessary for entrée and acceptance in the home of this great grandson of a wise old president. She, too, very much enjoyed, during her first months in Washington, observing the curious occupants of the Executive Mansion across the Square and the almost primitive social behavior of all official Washington.

The Executive Mansion, which was supposed to set the social tone, had been inhabited, since 1897, by the singularly uninspired McKinleys. One called at the Executive Mansion, of course, and attended, out of respect, the usual receptions during the official season, but almost everyone dreaded those appalling McKinley dinners. There was a flatness to these affairs scarcely relieved by the awful expectation that, at any moment before the dessert, the First Lady might become subject to one of her distressing epileptic seizures. Then the President, poor man, would himself gather up the stiff little form and carry it from the State Dining Room. In a few moments, he would return alone and, without once referring to the unhappy incident, politely, but firmly pick up the conversational lull at the point where it had been interrupted.

Bamie and her sister, Corinne, would never forget the uncomfortable quarter hour they spent when they paid their first call on poor Mrs. McKinley. The First Lady received them most graciously in the family's private sitting room, but there was no servant or nurse in attendance. They admired a tall vase containing one superb red rose, and the frail little woman, sitting erect like a child, piped with great effort, "My dearest love brought me that rose. He always brings me a rose every day. My dearest love is very good to me. Every evening he plays eight to ten games of cribbage with me, and I think he sometimes *lets* me win."

It was truly unfortunate, but Henry Adams was right when he said the tone of the Executive Mansion was "as dust and ashes, with a slight flavor of dish water." It was no wonder that the diplomatic corps, always Washington's liveliest set, regarded their assignments to that capital almost as a deadend to their careers. Certainly it was no stepping-stone to more glamorous and important posts in Paris, London, Berlin, or Vienna, and this had been true even before the McKinleys, chiefly because Washington played so unimportant a part in world affairs.

When young Cecil Spring-Rice announced to his friends in the British Foreign Office, after meeting Theodore and Bamie on shipboard back in the 1880s, that he would like to try Washington for six months, they considered him rather quixotic. "I hope you may get your exchange," a fellow Etonian loftily commented, "though why choose Washington which is out of all politics? It seems so off the line."

Washington was still very much off the line when Bamie first went there, but from the beginning, she tried to make things lively and entertaining for her diplomatic friends. As she had in London, she hired the best cook in town, and then for her gay, informal luncheons and small dinners, she invited only the people who interested her and each other, making a point to ignore stuffy protocol in her seating arrangements. Again, as in London, she was at home every Tuesday afternoon and soon the line of carriages depositing social and diplomatic Washington at the door of 1733 N Street on Bamie's regular Tuesdays was the longest in the city. Leaning out of the third-floor nursery window, Marsh, who was Mrs. Cowles's lady's maid imported from England, vowed she could identify, a block away, the brougham or victoria of important diplomatic callers by the coachman's cockade. "Here come the 'dips'," Marsh would say, and wherever the "dips" went, all the rest of Washington soon followed.

Almost overnight, even before the other remarkable Roosevelts descended on it, Washington discovered that it had an entrancing new hostess, one who entertained with the discrimination of a Henry Adams and a verve and energy all her own. Few may have drawn the comparison, but the town now boasted a social leader in the tradition of Mme Roland and Mme du Deffand and their famous French salons, for politics and society were one and the same to Bamie and both were equally fascinating.

Bamie reported all the fun she was having in long letters to the Fergusons, her adopted family in Great Britain, and these gave quite a different picture of the Washington they remembered from a visit there in the 1880s. It seemed to Sir Ronald, Fergie's older brother who was now a leader in Britain's Liberal party, that Washington had become quite an intriguing city.

"You talk of being quietly in politics," Sir Ronald wrote Bamie. "That is the only part of your letter one cannot quite understand. 'Quiet' has no connection with the content! You have seen everyone & some more. And there is no place half so adapted for seeing people pleasantly as Washington."

CHAPTER XVI

Theodore's Year of Indecision

WHILE Bamie was enjoying her first season in Washington, Theodore began his second year in office as governor of New York State with another huge New Year's Day reception. On this occasion, which celebrated not only the beginning of the young Governor's second year in Albany but the auspicious opening of the twentieth century, Senator Platt was noticeable by his absence. The Senator and his lady had sent their regrets, and so the year 1900 began on an uneasy note as far as Theodore's relations with the machine and the "Easy Boss" were concerned.

The Senator still came to breakfast with the Governor, during the winter of 1899–1900, at the home of Theodore's other sister, Corinne Roosevelt Robinson. But these breakfasts at No. 422 Madison Avenue were not going quite so smoothly as they had the year before at No. 689. Senator Platt seemed much less tractable and much more irritable, and from his point of view he had good reason.

To begin with, before the New Year's Day reception, the Governor had shown the Senator an advance copy of his message to the opening session of the legislature, and this contained a section that horrified Boss Platt. It is doubtful that even Bamie, with her tact and powers of persuasion, could have convinced the Senator it would be the height of political wisdom, in the long run, to regulate business for its own, and the public, good—which was what Theodore insisted his message was for. The very idea of regulation outraged the Senator's firm conviction that every man had a right "to run his own business in his own way, with due respect of course to the Ten Commandments and the Penal Code."

The Governor's message called for regulation of the trusts in rather general terms and then, more specifically, urged that all corporate earnings be given the widest possible publicity. These relatively modest proposals were far from being the sweeping reforms advocated by the radical Populists or by the Democrats and William Jennings Bryan. They had, moreover, been drawn up with the help of that distinguished corporation lawyer, Elihu Root, before he went to Washington as secretary of war; of President Hadley of Yale, who was Bamie's good friend; and half a dozen fairly conservative academic economists. And yet, over breakfast at No. 422, Senator Platt called all these gentlemen "visionary reformers," and he told Theodore his message was worse than "altruistic." It was, he now said, downright "socialistic, if not communistic."

Theodore delivered his message virtually unchanged, and the "Easy Boss" subsided into a heavy, brooding silence that the Governor mistakenly took for grudging assent. It was not Senator Platt's way to come right out and say the machine would no longer support Theodore if he chose to run for a second term as governor. Instead the "Easy Boss" now began to listen with an attentive and seemingly sympathetic ear whenever, over the coffee cups, Theodore argued out loud with himself about the merits of running for vice-president on the ticket with McKinley. What a wonderful opportunity, Boss Platt thought, to get rid of this man, who was no better than a Populist, for good! Oh yes, the Senator would agree, some people did think the vice-presidency a political deadend. On the other hand, the Senator would say, even though we *want* to renominate you for governor, can we be sure of reelecting you? Campaign contributions from the corporations had fallen off badly, said Senator Platt, and he, for one, was not surprised. We can't be sure, the Senator would say, shaking his head sadly.

In the 1870s, the Roosevelts posed with friends before going up the Nile. In the foreground (left to right) are Bamie, Conie, Tedie, and Ellie. Their mother and father are seated second and third from left; Bamie's beau, Mr. Jay, at far right.

Father was a gentle man.

Mother, a Georgia belle.

As a child, Theodore Roosevelt resembled Little Lord Fauntleroy, but he struggled manfully to turn himself into a robust youngster.

alice H. Roosevelt
Corinne Roosevelt Robinson
Anna Roosevelt

Pretty Alice Lee (left) was Theodore's first love. His sisters, Corinne and Bamie, were very fond of his bride.

The handsome bridegroom cut a dashing figure when he went to Albany as an Assemblyman.

Bamie took sole charge of Alice, whose mother died in childbirth four years after marrying Theodore.

Theodore Roosevelt Association

Theodore Roosevelt Association

When he met Edith Carow on the stairs at Bamie's, Theodore fell in love again.

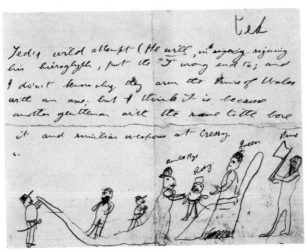

Ted, Jr.'s, drawing of Bamie being presented to the Queen.

Spring-Rice drew Bamie making her bow to Victoria.

In her elegant Court gown, complete with train, Bamie far outshone the hordes of other lovely ladies, both American and British, who clamored to make their bow in the Gay Nineties.

Bamie's great charm always eluded the studio photographer but not the unknown amateur who took this fine snapshot one sunny afternoon on Long Island while she was out visiting Admiral Mahan.

Bamie's friend, Fergie, served in Roosevelt's Rough Riders.

Bamie's husband was Admiral William S. Cowles, distinguished American naval officer. This oil portrait by Ellen Emmett Rand hangs at Bamie's beloved Oldgate.

At the peak of her power, socially and politically, Bamie also sat for her artist friend, Miss Rand. She posed in her middle years, wearing her white tea gown.

Bamie and her son, W. Sheffield Cowles, Jr., shown here in his carriage with the fringe on top, spent the hottest summer months at Camp Elsinore in the Adirondacks, which were then quite fashionable.

Franklin D. Roosevelt Library

Eleanor Roosevelt made a charming bride, of whom her "Auntie Bye" was very proud. Alone among all the Roosevelts, Bamie was for her niece's marriage to her handsome cousin, F.D.R. Eleanor married Franklin in 1905 in New York on St. Patrick's Day. At Bamie's request, the President was there to give the bride away.

Alice Roosevelt was very hard to please. All the family, including "dear Auntie Bye," wanted her to settle down, but Alice hated giving up all her "frivolous ways." Bamie endorsed her eventual choice of Nick Longworth.

Theodore Roosevelt Association

Theodore, family man, shown here with Archibald and Quentin, two of his four handsome sons, was a model father for all the nation.

Theodore, the president, was a heroic leader who tried to convince his people they should play their role in world affairs.

With a flourish of his topper, TR bade farewell in 1907 to the
"Great White Fleet" as it steamed off on its voyage around the world.

Senator Platt was so sympathetic that for a while he had the Governor completely fooled. "Senator Platt is fond of me," Theodore wrote Bamie who did not believe this for a minute. He thought the move to kick him upstairs into the vice-presidency, which happened to coincide with Cabot's wishes for him, came not from the "Easy Boss," but entirely from the "big politicians" and the "big Wall Street men" who "would like to see me put in the vice-presidency because they think I will be harmless there." He believed the "Easy Boss" had nothing to do with promoting this idea even after he had further angered Platt by refusing to appoint his man, Lou Payn, for another term as state insurance commissioner. And Payn was a key man in Platt's machine, a grateful friend to heavy Republican campaign contributors; his loss would be disastrous to Boss Platt. Theodore wrote Cabot that Platt "feels pretty bitterly" about the Payn matter, but the "Easy Boss" was still telling the Governor only what he wanted to hear—that "it would not be a wise move for me personally" to run for vice-president "as I should simply be shelved. . . ."

It came, therefore, as a surprise to Theodore, if to no one else, when he learned that Platt had been telling his henchmen the Governor would have to accept the vice-presidency because "events were shaping themselves so this was inevitable." "He gave me no hint of this," Theodore complained to Cabot, "taking exactly the opposite view and I do not understand what was up, or for the matter of that what is up now. . . ."

At this stage of confusion on the Governor's part, Senator Platt suddenly found he had a most formidable adversary, one on whom he had not reckoned, in the person of the Governor's lady. Edith had been unalterably opposed to the idea of her husband running for vice-president from the beginning of his Western boomlet the year before. Now she began coming down to New York with Theodore whenever he spent the weekend with the Douglas Robinsons. She never put in an appearance at political breakfasts, but her presence was felt. Occasionally Corinne would sit in because she, too, took "such an interest" in everything her brother was doing. But if, after Boss Platt left, Corinne and Theodore lingered too long over coffee to discuss strategy—usually on the subject of whether it would not be better after all for Theodore to run for vice-president—Theodore would suddenly look up and say to his sister, who had been Edith's devoted friend since childhood, "Pussie, I feel Edie's stern disapproval trickling down from the third floor."

Edith's opposition to the vice-presidency for Theodore, though she confined her remarks to members of the family and close friends, was obstinate and vocal. Even Cabot Lodge could not shake her conviction that Theodore should come out and openly declare himself *not* a candidate for that office. Lodge, with Bamie in agreement but maintaining a most unusual silence for fear of antagonizing Edith, advised waiting to see where Theodore's best chance of election lay. Again and again Theodore wrote Cabot, "Edith is against your view," and these letters, shared with Bamie in Washington, were a warning signal she dared not ignore. In her letters to Theodore during this period, Bamie was very, very careful to point out the advantages and disadvantages of either course he might follow, without expressing a firm opinion of her own.

Soon Theodore's letters began to read almost as if they had been dictated by Edith, the tidy housekeeper and overseer of family finances. "The money question," he wrote Cabot, "is a very serious one with me." He had to think of his children's education. Alice, of course, had an independent income from her Chestnut Hill grandparents, but the boys would be going to Groton and Harvard and Ethel to finishing school. And again that plaintive note of earlier years—"I am never certain when it may be necessary for me to try to sell Sagamore." Theodore explained, "As Governor, I am comparatively well paid, having not only a salary but a house which is practically kept up during the winter." If he were to become vice-president, even living in the simplest style possible in a rented house in Washington "would be a serious drain upon me, and would cause me, and especially would cause Edith, continual anxiety about money."

150

He would be in the position of a "poor man at a frolic." In this phrase, Bamie could almost hear Edith's voice. No one knew better than Bamie how much Edith's character had been molded into its formidable reserve by the straitened circumstances of her younger years. Theodore never thought of money whether he had it or not, which was perhaps one of their difficulties, and Edith, who was not exactly the soul of generosity, was the family business manager. After her father's early death, Edith, her sister Emily, and Mrs. Carow had had to spend a great deal of time abroad in cheap *pensions* in order to live respectably on their meager income, and Mrs. Carow had not been able to afford New York debuts for either Edith or her sister. They had, of course, attended the coming-out parties of their friends and contemporaries but in ball gowns artfully made over to last several seasons. Edith had, in consequence, very much the feeling of a "poor man at a frolic" in New York society, and this took the form of regarding all fashionable folk, including Bamie and some of her friends, with a sort of reverse snobbism.

In mid-February, with Edith at his elbow, Theodore took a step that Cabot and Bamie both deplored. He issued a statement to the press saying he did not want to be vice-president, and that he was a candidate for reelection for governor. The "Easy Boss" remained ominously silent. Theodore told Lodge he had made the statement to the press after "going over it with Edith and one or two men here." Then with a wry humor—and an exclamation point that further betrayed Edith's firm hand in the release of that statement—Theodore added, "Edith bids me say that she hopes you will forgive me!"

Heartened by this victory over the indecision she hated, Edith now felt so relaxed about the future and Theodore's chances of being reelected governor that she decided to take a winter vacation from her Albany duties. Feeling perhaps that she had checkmated not only the "Easy Boss," but the good intentions of Cabot and Bamie as well, the Governor's lady sailed off with her sister Emily to Cuba where, as guests of General Leonard Wood, who had commanded Theodore's Rough Riders, they made a tour of the Spanish-American War battlefields. Often thereafter, to Theodore's chagrin, Edith would say, with some amusement, that San Juan Hill was not quite the steep ascent she had been led to believe.

It was no longer possible, by the spring of 1900, for the Governor to harbor the illusion that Senator Platt was fond of him. The "Easy Boss" now avoided Theodore whenever possible, and whenever they did meet, he would mumble that Theodore's chances would be very much better if he ran for the vice- presidency, to which the Governor would reply that he would rather be a professor of history in some college. There was, however, another post on which Theodore set his sights not long after Edith's return from Cuba, and it fitted in perfectly with Theodore's abiding belief in the "Manifest Destiny" of the United States. Soon, after the army had completed its subjugation of America's unwilling "little brown brothers" in the Philippines, there would be need for a firm governor-general in those glamorous new island possessions. What could be more appropriate, with General Wood of the Rough Riders in Cuba, than for Colonel Roosevelt to be made governor-general of the Philippines? Theodore wrote Cabot and Bamie that the governor-generalship would be very much to his taste.

Bamie happened to be very much concerned herself with conditions in those newly acquired islands, through her continuing interest in Auxiliary No. 3 of the Red Cross. Over the opposition of the army's surgeon general and Miss Anita McGee, his assistant in charge of nurses who was not a nurse herself, she had managed, through Secretary Root, to have a contingent of seventy-five trained nurses, again financed by her friend, Mrs. Reid, sent out to Manila. These volunteer nurses, many of them of good family and the strictest propriety, were immediately subjected to a campaign of evil gossip back home. Sparked by Miss McGee and her supporters in the Daughters of the American Revolution, letters from sadly neurotic wives began to appear in the yellow press complaining that these nurse volunteers were corrupting the morals of wifeless army officers in the Philippines.

Undaunted by these canards, Bamie and her friends secured and circulated widely in Washington and to the press letters and reports from the islands attesting the brave behavior of their maligned volunteer nurses. In the end, the malicious campaign backfired on its perpetrators, for Secretary Root, using the shining example of the brave and noble nurses of Auxiliary No. 3, was able to put through Congress, with his Army Reorganization Bill, a simple rider that established the army's first regular corps of trained nurses.

Though very few people in Washington knew the part Bamie had played in this deserved defeat of Miss McGee and the surgeon general, it was a major victory. And when Secretary of State Hay appointed Miss Mabel Boardman, who was Bamie's personal choice, to be head of the reorganized American Red Cross in place of Miss Barton, who had finally decided to retire, and Miss Boardman's appointment was confirmed by the Senate, Bamie's quiet satisfaction in a job well done was complete. She could now give more concentrated attention to the political predicament of her brother.

Among her faithful correspondents in the Philippines was Admiral Sperry, a close friend of Will Cowles. Admiral Sperry had promised Bamie before setting off on his patrol of Philippine waters to write her all the news, and indeed his letters, some of which were twenty-four pages long, gave in great detail and with much perspicuity all the problems of government over a variegated and often belligerent island people then being encountered by an army not trained in administrative matters. These letters, with Admiral Sperry's permission, were made available to Secretary Root for his guidance, and some of them, of course, were quoted to Theodore. Bamie and Theodore both were much impressed with the Admiral's report on the laxness of army record-keeping, particularly in the collection of customs at the port of Manila. "We shall have a national scandal," the Admiral wrote, if the War Department did not act quickly to remedy this situation. Theodore now began to feel a definite call to be of use in the Philippines.

But Secretary Root, while tightening up on army laxity in the Philippines himself, did not take the hint. And so Cabot, faithful friend, called once more at the White House in Theodore's behalf. And there, once again, he met with bland disinterest. The President thought Theodore might be just the man for the governor-generalship when the time came, but it was much too soon, with Aguinaldo and so many of the other "little brown brothers" still on the rampage, to think of taking things out of the army's hands and putting in a civilian administrator.

Came June, 1900, and the impending Republican National Convention, where Theodore's year of indecision would have to end one way or another. Reports from the West indicated an overwhelming sentiment for Colonel Roosevelt as vice-president, and with this Boss Platt heartily agreed. But Theodore had promised Edith he would try to run for governor again even though he saw his chances there rapidly diminishing. He would go to Philadelphia, not as a vice-presidential candidate but as a simple delegate-at-large from New York, and Edith was going with him, to her first national convention. He wrote Boss Hanna bravely that he wanted "a box for Mrs. Roosevelt and her party," because "she takes the entirely rational view which I share that during these two years of my governorship we ought both of us to have all the fun there is," as if to say there would be no more.

Bamie would not be in Mrs. Roosevelt's party. When the hot weather came in Washington, she went to Oldgate, and there she heard from Fergie, who had seen Theodore at a Rough Riders' dinner in New York, that he still seemed in the best of spirits—"He talked from the soup until 2 A.M. when he wasn't singing battle hymns."

"Are you going to Philadelphia," Fergie asked, "to hold down that hot wave from the West? It'll be dreadfully exciting, for one's fears are the worst for Theodore's chances of *not* being nominated."

No, Bamie replied, she had no intention of going anywhere near Philadelphia during the convention. She was planning to leave almost immediately, with Sheffield and Commander Cowles, for Cousin Rosy Roosevelt's "Camp Elsinore" up in the Adirondacks near the Canadian border. With Edith so adamant against Theodore's running for vice-president, and Cabot and Bamie, herself, so very sure that this was now the wisest move for him to make, Bamie knew it would be much safer, for the sake of amicable family relations, for her to bow out of the political picture entirely and take herself off just as far away as possible.

CHAPTER XVII

"The Thing Could Not Be Helped"

SITTING next to Mrs. Roosevelt at dinner in Albany just before the convention, a well-meaning politician told the Governor's lady she would see her husband unanimously nominated vice-president in Philadelphia. "You disagreeable thing," Edith said, tapping him lightly with her fan, "I don't *want* to see him nominated for the vice-presidency."

As Theodore and Edith took the train to Philadelphia, he told his friend and adviser, Joseph B. Bishop, editor of the *New York Commercial Advertiser*, he was almost sure he could prevent his nomination. He told two other advisers who went with him, Nicholas Murray Butler of Columbia University and General Francis V. Greene, who was a vice-presidential candidate himself, that he would stop his nomination "by visiting the delegates in advance."

The Western delegations, chanting "We Want Teddy! We Want Teddy!" besieged the Roosevelts in room 521 at the Hotel Walton soon after their arrival and even before the convention opened. Reporters heard Edith whisper sternly to her husband as they went off to a secret luncheon rendezvous on Spruce Street with friends and advisers, "Now, Theodore, don't say anything."

At that luncheon it was decided Theodore should issue a press statement that very afternoon in order to head off the "hot wave from the West" Fergie had so accurately predicted. Edith,

Nicholas Murray Butler, and General Greene, who still had hopes for himself, urged Theodore to say unequivocally that he was not a candidate for vice-president. Senator Lodge just as strongly urged Theodore to say no such thing, but he had to leave right after luncheon to attend a caucus of the Massachusetts delegation. After Lodge left, Nicholas Murray Butler wrote out on the spot a draft of a brief statement and handed it to Edith, who read it and nodded agreement. Butler then gave it to Theodore, saying, "If you sign that paper and give it out this afternoon you will not be nominated." According to Nicholas Murray Butler, Theodore "screwed up his face as he had a way of doing when in perplexity." He said he was in favor of Butler's statement but thought he could improve it. When Butler read Theodore's version, which most modestly said he felt his "best usefulness to the public and to the party is in New York State," Butler told him bluntly his version was sure to get him nominated for vice-president. They argued heatedly over the point for half an hour, but in the end Theodore's version was given to the press at four in the afternoon of the day before the convention. For the first time, Butler said, he now began to suspect that Theodore was willing to be nominated.

The following night when the convention opened, the "Easy Boss" himself gave the coup de grâce to Edith's last stand for the governorship. He called Theodore to his hotel room and told him he had lined up most of the political bosses in the Eastern states, as well as Senator Joseph B. Foraker of Ohio, and since the Western delegates were already for Theodore, they could easily override the objections of National Boss Hanna of Ohio even though he still regarded Theodore as "that crazy cowboy." If Theodore did not take the vice-presidency now, the Senator told him, then the "Easy Boss" would prevent his renomination for governor. Theodore bowed and left the room. Then triumphant old Senator Platt called in the reporters and told them, "Roosevelt might as well stand under Niagara Falls and try to spit water back as to stop his nomination by this convention." Indeed the roar from the Western delegations, when a grim-faced Theodore took his seat on the floor with the New York delegates and looked up at his white-faced wife in the box above, sounded like Niagara.

It was truly all over but the shouting. Boss Hanna, when reporters asked him whether he thought Theodore wanted the nomination, growled, "He knows how to stop it." But no statement came from Theodore saying he would not accept the vice-presidency. He listened to Lodge who said, Take it. The vice-presidency, Lodge argued, would lead him straight to the presidency in 1904, or at least to the governor-generalship of the Philippines. He was only forty-one; he could afford to mark time for a while in the vice-presidency. He listened as well to Western delegates who said Bryan would surely defeat McKinley if Theodore did not run on the ticket. Theodore also heard that the President had wired Hanna he would not stand in Theodore's way if the convention wanted him as vice-president and that Hanna had told the President, "All right then, but it's your duty to *live*."

On the final day of the convention, Theodore had an hour's private conference with Boss Hanna. Grudgingly the "Big Boss" had at last given in to the "Easy Boss," who had played his hand so amazingly well. He, too, told reporters after his talk with Theodore, "Boys, you can't stop this any more than you can stop Niagara."

And so Colonel Roosevelt seconded Senator Hanna's renomination of President McKinley and was himself nominated for vice-president by acclamation, while the band played, "There'll Be a Hot Time in the Old Town Tonight."

"The thing could not be helped," Theodore wrote Bamie from Oyster Bay, and now he was going out West on the first of his strenuous cross-country campaign tours, while McKinley rocked comfortably on his cool, vine-covered porch out in Canton, Ohio, all that hot summer long in 1900. On many of these trips, Fergie managed to go along with Theodore, and from time to time he would report to Bamie, who was now up in the Adirondacks, how things were going.

"Theodore arrived home from the West," Fergie wrote her in mid-July, "in good shape & full of renewed youth & enthusiasm. A fickle condition of mind that seemed to be quite fairly irritating to Edith." Theodore wanted to believe that Edith was becoming "somewhat reconciled" but Fergie said, "She still feels that he has done a foolish thing in the vice-presidential business." Then, very much on Theodore's side, he added hopefully, "Theodore himself is quite convinced that he's in for a good & useful time of it. That there are big questions in the world that interest this country and that the campaign is to be fought out on many of them. Don't you guess he's right? The folk out West showed how much they wanted him—and they want him because they feel he can think with them from their standpoint and lead them from his own forcible one in the way a young people ought to wish to go."

To that Bamie said amen. While Theodore was away on his travels, she had Edith and the children up for their first visit to Oldgate that fall, just before the November elections, and she did her best to reconcile her sister-in-law to the idea of being the vice-president's lady. In her own way, Edith was touched by the enthusiastic reception Theodore received all during his nationwide, one-man campaign, and she began keeping scrapbooks of the clippings and photographs he brought home to Oyster Bay in huge batches from his exhausting trips. In due course, into these scrapbooks, along with an occasional clipping from "Mr. Dooley"—"'Tis Teddy alone that's runnin', and he ain't r'runnin', he's gallopin'"—went the final election count in November, 1900: More than seven million votes for McKinley and Roosevelt to less than six and a half million for Bryan and Adlai E. Stevenson, the largest plurality the Republicans had received in twenty-eight years.

Early in the morning on March 4, 1901, a cloudy day to begin with, two florists arrived at the door of 1733 N Street in Washington with a wagonload of flowers. This huge floral tribute costing $3,500, said the florists, came from an unidentified New York admirer. It may have been the "Easy Boss" or one of his well-heeled Republican regulars, for Senator Platt had told all his friends he would not miss for anything being in Washington that day "to see Theodore take the veil."

This excessive tribute, Bamie said, "was a great shock to the Vice-President facing life on a small salary," but the whole family assembled in her house for the day's stirring events thoroughly enjoyed the ridiculous spectacle as the two florists set up their funereal structure in her small drawing room, leaving no place at all for them and Bamie's other guests to sit down.

Bamie's house that morning was already full to overflowing. There were the guests of honor, Theodore and Edith, with all their six children; Corinne and Douglas Robinson with their three; and of course "Mr. Bearo" and Sheffield. There were Senator and Mrs. Lodge, Secretary and Mrs. Hay and Secretary and Mrs. Root, and an extra guest Theodore had included at the last moment, a visiting English journalist named Frederic Harrison. After breakfast at Bamie's, with champagne for a toast to Theodore and hot chocolate for the children, everyone rode in closed carriages to the Capitol in festive mood in spite of the heavy drizzle that now began to fall.

Theodore's swearing-in in the fusty old Senate Chamber, where he would preside for a few brief days only, seemed over in a minute. Then everyone crowded out on the central portico of the Capitol for the main event of the day. As President McKinley rose, once again, to take the oath of office, he stood with a sober-faced Theodore beside him, and when Mr. Chief Justice Fuller and the President raised their right hands over the Bible a sudden burst of hail and sleet lashed in between the Doric columns of the miniature Greek temple erected for the occasion. Almost everyone got sopping wet as they rushed for their carriages to gain good vantage points along the parade route.

The children went with Corinne and Bamie to rooms they had engaged above Mme Payne's Manicure Shop at Fifteenth Street and Pennsylvania Avenue, and from there they had an excellent, though bird's-eye, view of the presidential reviewing stand in front of the Executive Mansion where Theodore and Edith would be.

The sun came out just as McKinley's carriage rounded the corner at Fifteenth Street into Pennsylvania Avenue, and the President ordered a halt to take the top down, revealing to the delight of all the Roosevelt children their father, resplendent in top hat, sitting beside him. The younger Roosevelts and Robinsons, their coat fronts plastered with huge McKinley and Roosevelt buttons, leaned perilously far out of the windows over Mme Payne's Manicure Shop to shout hurrah and wave their American flags at father, but seventeen-year-old Alice sat curiously aloof studying President McKinley. She noted his corpulent paunch and, almost with satisfaction, his habitual deathly pallor, contrasting him with her father's military bearing and his healthy, ruddy complexion. She was wondering then, she later admitted, "what sort of a 'risk,'" President McKinley was.

Edith stayed over until the next day to see Theodore preside at his first session of the Senate that had only five days in all to run. He had teased Cabot and Edith, telling them, tongue in cheek, he was "going to be a very punctual, decorous presiding officer," but both had their reservations. With some relief, Edith wrote her sister, Emily, "He was very quiet and dignified," and then took the children back to Oyster Bay. Theodore remained at Bamie's for another week after the Senate adjourned, then he, too, returned to Sagamore Hill where he really had not much to do, except perhaps go hunting in Colorado, until December when Congress would be in session again. He and Edith had arranged to rent the Washington house of their Ohio friends, the Bellamy Storers, which was only a few blocks from Bamie, but as events turned out Edith never thereafter had to feel "poor man at a frolic" in a rented house in Washington.

CHAPTER XVIII

Side Trip to the Fair

FOR some reason, Bamie lingered on at 1733 N Street unusually late in the season after the new vice-president had left her to rejoin his family at Oyster Bay. She was one of the last in Washington to close her house that summer of 1901. All official Washington regularly decamped, as soon as dogwood bloomed in the Virginia hills across the Potomac, before the impending tropical heat for which that capital was so notorious. Throughout Foggy Bottom, along the banks of that slow-moving river, congressmen hurriedly stuffed winged collars into Gladstone bags, and the cheap hotels and boardinghouses all over town soon saw the dusty tails of their frock coats as they kited off for home and family. Certainly few could bring wife and children to live in Washington on a congressman's salary. Members of "The Millionaires' Club," including the "Big Four"— Senators Aldrich, Allison, Spooner, and Orville Hitchcock Platt, who was no relation—were already en route with their families to such places as Bar Harbor and Newport, there to be joined later by single members of the diplomatic corps bent on heiress hunting. Other Washington "dips" gleefully embarked for their own more salubrious capitals or for Paris, and, presently, even the McKinleys would be back in Canton, Ohio, for the summer, playing cribbage on the shady verandah of their modest little frame house.

Now, with her remaining house guests, Fergie and her god-child, Helen Roosevelt, who was Cousin Rosy's lovely young debutante daughter, it occurred to Bamie that it might be fun to take in the Pan-American Exposition in Buffalo, as a sort of side trip on her way to Oldgate at Farmington. When the McKinleys went to the Exposition in September for the celebration of "President's Day," it was sure to be much too crowded, and dull besides. Lloyd Griscom, that attractive young bachelor diplomat who had been Ambassador Bayard's secretary in the London days, happened to be in town, and his father had put his own special railroad car at his son's disposal.

And so, traveling by special car, a luxury she thoroughly enjoyed, especially when with such attractive young people, Bamie went up to the Buffalo Fair late in May, and from there, still in the Griscoms' special car, back down to Cousin Rosy's place at Hyde Park, adjoining the lovely home on the Hudson of Cousin Sara Delano Roosevelt and her handsome nineteen-year-old son, Franklin, just home from Harvard for the summer.

That delightful trip to the Fair in 1901 would never be forgotten, particularly by Bamie's young diplomatic friend, Lloyd Griscom. The best of it all was when Bamie and her godchild, and Fergie and Lloyd decided on the spur of the moment, after a few days at Hyde Park, to drive cross-country over the rolling hills from Cousin Rosy's to Farmington. They set out in a four-seated trap behind two fast cobs—Helen and Lloyd up front and Bamie and Fergie in the back seat. They drove through country lanes lined with fragrant lilacs still in bloom and, in fine spanking style to the envy of all, past elm-shaded New England commons, until on the evening of the second day they reached Oldgate. There they were greeted by genial "Mr. Bearo," who had escaped the Washington heat, and by small Sheffield, who was delighted with all the souvenirs Bamie had brought him from the Exposition. To top it all for Lloyd Griscom, Commander Cowles presented him with a telegram from Secretary of State Hay, which had arrived at Oldgate just before they drove up, appointing him, at the age of twenty-eight, American minister to Persia, the diplomatic post of his dreams. Young Griscom delightedly inscribed his name in Oldgate's guest book, adding after it, "His Oriental Excellency from Teheran."

There was indeed something special and almost magic about being at Oldgate for Bamie's friends, as well as for Bamie herself, and this became increasingly so with the years. No doubt her father's house on Twentieth Street had been her first love, or even briefly Sagamore Hill, of which she had been mistress for a while, but Bamie had fallen in love at first sight with Will Cowles's old family home the summer before that fast cross-country jaunt in the four-seater, and she had already started making Oldgate over into a relaxed American version, very much her own, of a fine old English country house.

Oldgate was, to begin with, of pre-Revolutionary vintage. It was a big, center-hall, white clapboard house with plenty of room for guests—and the most delightful room of all where everyone congregated, especially at teatime, was the snug, bright library, with its huge fireplace and its French windows leading out to the sloping lawn and the garden beyond.

On a table in the library at Oldgate—and not in Bamie's rather ugly brick house in Washington—she kept one of her most cherished mementos of London days, the handsome guest book in which young Griscom had inscribed his name with an Oriental flourish. Given her by her dear friend, Lady Alice Dugdale, this leather guest book was an exact reproduction of the one Marie Antoinette had owned, and it had been bound and tooled by the very same firm of fine Parisian craftsmen. Already it was beginning to grow into a joyful record of all the good times at Oldgate, for guests could, if they felt so inclined, write in it anything that came into their heads.

Bamie had written on the frontispiece herself, very simply, when she had first arrived—

"June 4th 1900—Anna Roosevelt Cowles
William Sheffield Cowles Jr."

Her very first guest, immediately thereafter, had been her beloved Uncle Gracie, whom everyone called "a saint with whiskers," and he had brought with him from New York two of Bamie's own nieces, Corinne, Jr. and poor, dead Elliott's daughter, Eleanor. Sixteen-year-old Eleanor had only that summer returned from her first year abroad at Bamie's old school— to which her "dear Auntie Bye" had prevailed on Grandmother Hall to send her—and she had many warm messages from Mlle Souvestre, who had moved her school from Fontainebleau to England.

Eleanor Roosevelt was, in fact, the first person to write something other than her name in the Oldgate guest book. No doubt she had, characteristically, been making herself useful to Auntie Bye as she went about putting Oldgate topsy-turvily in order for, on June 9, 1900, Eleanor had carefully penned in the guest book, soon to be filled with frivolous doggerel and other bits of nonsense, the Biblical quotation, "The laborer is worthy of his hire."

That summer of 1901, after the last of the young guests who had been to the Fair had left, passed very quietly for the Cowles family at Oldgate. The Roosevelts at Sagamore Hill were also having their own enjoyable quiet time, Theodore wrote, with lots of rowing and swimming and reading aloud in the evening. But, in July, Theodore was off again with Fergie, to another Rough Riders' reunion, this time at Colorado Springs. And again faithful Fergie reported to Bamie in full.

"It was 'great fun' as Teddy said and nobody cared for the time being whether school kept or not (or William McKinley either)." As they had traveled cross-country, again courtesy of Paul Morton of the Atchison, Topeka & Santa Fe, the reception that greeted the young Vice-President everywhere "was quite astonishing & touching, too, at times." "Altogether we came back thinking a devilish lot—& prepared to say as little as possible, hoping only that things will go their proper course & not be spoiled by anybody."

Cabot, at his summer place in Nahant, and Bamie at Oldgate, were also doing quite "a devilish lot" of thinking about Theodore's chances in 1904. It was not at all too soon to begin working very carefully within the party and without, and Douglas

Robinson was already quietly functioning as his brother-in-law's campaign fund-raiser, with instructions from Theodore not to approach "any man in any way that will by any possibility cause complications hereafter."

". . . There can be no doubt," Cabot wrote Theodore from Nahant, "that at this moment nothing could be better than your prospects. The real danger is the unknown quantity of the next three years."

On hearing that Theodore would be in nearby New Haven to receive an honorary LL.D. at the Yale Bicentennial in October, Bamie thought this an excellent early opportunity for him to meet and gain the support of the party powers-that-be in Connecticut, and she proposed having a reception for him at Oldgate before the event. Theodore wrote he thought this a capital idea, adding, "You will ask both the Senators and the Governor, will you not?"

Bamie's invitations to her reception in October for the Vice-President were out, and all the important acceptances had come in, when the kind and thoughtful editor of the *Hartford Courant* got word to her late in the afternoon of September 6, 1901, that President McKinley, while attending Buffalo's Pan-American Exposition, had been badly wounded, perhaps fatally, by some crazy anarchist.

PART III

The Washington Years

CHAPTER XIX

"She Will Get Used to This New Strain"

WITH the rest of the nation, Bamie froze into inactivity and hung on the news from Buffalo. For seven straight days, with not much variation, the President's doctors were quoted as saying he was "weak, but progressing satisfactorily," or he now seemed "on the highroad to recovery." Reassured by the doctors during a brief visit to his bedside in Buffalo the day after the attack on the President, Theodore wrote Bamie, "The President is coming along splendidly." He told her he would be at Oldgate, as planned, for the October reception, and, in the interim, he would join Edith and the children who were spending a few weeks in the Adirondacks.

Early on the morning of the eighth day, the *Hartford Courant* informed Mrs. Cowles that the President had died at 2 A.M. from gangrene caused by the bullet that Dr. Matthew B. Maine, the surgeon called in to operate on the President, had been unable to locate in the peritoneal cavity. This was followed by additional bulletins to Oldgate from the *Courant* telling her Theodore had managed to get to Buffalo to be sworn in twelve hours after the President's death, only by a hair-raising trip down the slopes of Mount Marcy, which he had been climbing, and a rocketing, all-night cross-country trip with the aid of three relays of carriage horses and a specially requisitioned train.

It was the thoughtful editor of the *Hartford Courant* who

also told Mrs. Cowles that her brother—who had become, just short of forty-three, the youngest president of the United States —had informed reporters in Buffalo that he was going to Washington on the special McKinley funeral train and that he would be staying at the home of his sister, who lived on N Street, in order not to embarrass poor Mrs. McKinley with his presence and to give her plenty of time to arrange her affairs.

Hearing this, Bamie left Oldgate Sunday night planning to go straight through New York to Washington. In New York, as the train pulled in, a telegram was delivered to her from Edith. The new First Lady had somehow managed to get down from the Adirondacks herself and back to Sagamore Hill with all the children, except Alice—for Alice, disdaining to appear too eager, had insisted on staying up in the mountains with friends. Edith's telegram asked Bamie to stop overnight in the city and go down with her and Ted, Jr., on Monday morning.

Early Monday morning Bamie was waiting at the ferry slip on the Manhattan side of the Hudson when Edith and Ted, Jr., finally drove up in a closed carriage with all the curtains drawn. Edith was wearing a long crepe veil she had stopped to purchase for herself, and Ted, Jr., wore a new mourning band on his arm. If they managed to catch the 10:32 express on the Jersey side, they could reach Washington several hours before Theodore and the funeral train pulled in at Union Station.

Once on the Jersey side, Edith got a foretaste, with a vengeance, of what it meant to be First Lady of the Land. She flinched but held herself erect when she saw the crowd that had somehow collected in the Pennsylvania depot in Jersey City to see her off. Several stalwart railroad policemen stalked interference for them through the silent mob as they made their way to the train and climbed safely aboard the Pullman car, "Olympia," for their own somber ride to Washington.

Union Station was heavily draped in black when they arrived, and there were many more silent mourners waiting here than there had been at the Jersey City depot. But all attention focused on the track where the funeral train and the new President were expected, now in a matter of a very few hours. No one recognized the two veiled ladies or the young man with the spectacles and the mourning armband who looked so like his father.

In time, Edith would grow used to staring crowds and to her position as First Lady. But those first days in the fall of 1901 were anything but an auspicious beginning; they were a nightmare from which she retreated, temporarily, even further into her cold, polite reserve. At Bamie's, while she was there, she was at home to no one, and she rarely took a meal downstairs with the family. She might have received Nannie and Cabot Lodge, but they were again on a trip abroad. Edith at first simply could not realize that almost everyone agreed wholeheartedly with Theodore's comrade-in-arms of Spanish-American War days, Winthrop Chanler, who told Cabot on his return, "He's too good a man to win on a foul—but there he is & thank God for it." Nor could Edith realize that people like Winty, and many others besides, could possibly have a kind thought for her.

"Poor Mrs. Theodore!" Winty said, "I am afraid she is heartsick with fear for him. Still she had a taste of it when he was in Cuba & after the first few weeks she will get used to this new strain."

"The Little White House" on N Street

ONE evening in September, 1901, after the funeral services at the Capitol for William McKinley but before he was
finally interred at Canton, Ohio, on the nineteenth, a portly
young newspaperman from Kansas presented himself by appointment for an interview with the President of the United States
at the door of No. 1733 on Washington's N Street.

The newspaper editor had come to this English-basement style,
brick residence on a tree-lined street just off Connecticut Avenue
in response to a wire from the new President, who was stopping
with his sister until the White House, as the Roosevelts always
called it, was ready to receive him. Some time before the tragedy
in Buffalo, the editor had been promised an interview on this
date, and the telegram had said it would take place as scheduled,
at this address, during a "quiet family dinner."

The editor would not find the new First Lady at this family
dinner on N Street. She had returned with her son to Oyster Bay
immediately after the ordeal at the Capitol. Standing next to
Grover Cleveland, Edith had said in a voice choked with tears,
"Oh, Mr. Cleveland, my husband is so young!" and the former
President, with his great kind smile, had tried to cheer her with,
"Don't worry, he's all right." But Edith had already noticed
with increasing perturbation how Theodore did his best to escape
Secret Service surveillance; she would return to Washington

from Sagamore Hill with the children as soon as she could possibly manage it.

As the young editor from Kansas crossed the small lawn and rang the bell at the grilled basement entrance to No. 1733 N Street, he wondered if this modest residence could really be "The Little White House," where, as the newspapers said, the new president was meeting with his Cabinet and conducting all official business. The editor was not familiar with Washington and its contradictory social ways nor with Henry Adams' boast that "We make a sort of headway against money." Out in the Midwest, where the editor came from, people of substance did their darndest to live in houses that showed it.

A rather undersized English butler opened the door, and the gaslight from a Tiffany chandelier in the hall shed a brief glow on two Secret Service men lurking in the shadow of a tree. For some reason, they looked a bit sheepish. This then was the right house but, since the young editor did not yet know the Roosevelts very well or realize that punctilious execution of all engagements was one of their more endearing Dutch traits, he continued to wonder, as Hopkinson let him in and took his hat, how the new president had managed on these first busy days in office to find time for the editor of a small Midwestern newspaper.

The editor was greeted in the drawing room, with its tiled fireplace and carved oak mantel, by a vivacious lady—somewhat on the plump side and a trifle deaf, though this was so carefully concealed from others the young editor was not aware of it—who made him feel instantly at home. While her husband, resplendent in the gold aiguillettes he wore as special aide to the new President during the obsequies for the late President, made the young editor comfortable with a tall drink, Mrs. Cowles told him that Mr. Roosevelt had gone out at dusk for a walk with Dr. Nicholas Murray Butler but that they would both be back very soon for dinner.

Waiting thus pleasantly for President Roosevelt and Dr. Butler—then striding briskly together along Sixteenth Street, two miles out and two miles back, without benefit of Secret

Service guards—William Allen White of the *Emporia Gazette* was delighted to learn that the President's sister knew him well by reputation as the author of "What's Wrong with Kansas?", an editorial of his that had been widely quoted in Republican circles a few years back. She congratulated him on that editorial's solidly Republican sentiments and agreed with him entirely on what was the matter with his benighted, pro-Bryan, Populist-infested state. Mr. White was also delighted to hear that Mrs. Cowles had read another of his editorials, the one in which, taking his cue from Kipling, Editor White had called on the Anglo-Saxon race, including all Americans, "to go forth" and fulfill their "manifest destiny." Jolly, up-and-coming Mr. White could not help finding the President's sister, then in her mid-forties without having lost any of her vitality or power to charm, a fascinating woman.

William Allen White never forgot that "quiet family dinner" on N Street. He was doubly fortunate, for he was gathering material for a magazine article on New York's Senator Platt, and Mrs. Cowles seemed to know as much about the "Easy Boss" as the President did. Both had a fund of anecdotes and the gift of mimicry, and Mr. White, as he wrote in his autobiography, was enthralled. "Mrs. Cowles and her brother, the young President," Mr. White recalled, "kept the conversation rippling." He thought their talk "the best I had ever heard," and he learned a good deal about New York politics. As Commander Cowles carved the excellent roast, and Hopkinson kept the glasses filled around the candlelit oval table, Mr. White could not help agreeing with Dr. Butler that the smartest thing the "Easy Boss" had ever done was to rescue himself from sure defeat in 1898 by running Colonel Roosevelt for governor.

After dinner, the conversation continued around Bamie's drawing-room fire, and now Mr. White was amazed to hear the new President discuss his future political course with extraordinary frankness. Standing with the tails of his frock coat hoisted before the fire and talking almost as if to himself out loud, the young President began to wonder whether he had done a wise thing in telling the Cabinet assembled in Buffalo, at Secretary Root's suggestion, that he intended to follow McKinley's policies. That statement had been made public, again at Root's urging, in an attempt to halt the stock-market dive on the news of McKinley's death, and now wouldn't that embarrass him sorely in future? He had every respect, even admiration, mind you, for McKinley's personal qualities, but when it came to McKinley's politics, that, by God, was another matter. This then was his dilemma: How could he possibly bring himself to follow in McKinley's footsteps and give the lie to all he had stood for throughout his own political career?

Dr. Butler hastened to tell the President that he would in time surmount this difficulty. Dr. Butler said that he, for one, had not the slightest doubt that Theodore's success as president would be "not only abundant but exceptional." At this point, Mr. White, who had been listening, as he said, "bug-eyed with wonder, sitting on the edge of my chair," was astonished to observe that Commander Cowles had slumped in his, and arms folded across his ample front, "had gone solemnly to sleep in the midst of the evening's pyrotechnics." Without disturbing his aide's well-earned slumbers, the President continued his dramatic monologue.

It was his private opinion, the President said, that Boss Hanna, now that his man, McKinley, was dead, wanted the nomination for himself in 1904. Had Senator Hanna not indicated as much in Buffalo when he promised his support to Theodore for the next three-and-a-half years without, very pointedly, making any promises for 1904? The President admitted, readily enough, that old Boss Hanna could be as dangerous as a grizzly, but he swore, chomping his teeth with relish, he had stalked bigger game out in the Bad Lands. He would beat Senator Hanna for the nomination in 1904.

Mr. White, quite unaware how much the year 1904 had already figured in family discussions long before McKinley's death, was properly impressed by the foresight and purpose of a president who, during his first days in office, was already plotting his political moves three years ahead.

Returning to his hotel after that memorable September evening, the young Midwestern editor had a new hero. He made copious notes for his magazine article on all that the President and Mrs. Cowles had told him about Boss Platt. He did not remember, perhaps with all the "pyrotechnics" he had not heard, Dr. Nicholas Murray Butler's miraculously prophetic words during the course of that evening. As recalled by Dr. Butler himself, these were:

"I do not fear for you in the presidency, Theodore. Your most difficult task will come when you finally leave the White House. You will almost to a certainty be there for seven and one-half years and then will come the job of your trying to be a Sage at fifty! It will be a lot harder for you, Theodore, to be an ex-President than President."

Theodore's very first days in office were the only easy ones he had. In his early sessions with the Cabinet he had inherited from McKinley, the President was careful to walk softly for he had as yet, politically speaking, no big stick. He spent much of his time at Bamie's working on the message he would send to the opening session of Congress in December, and he sought the help of a neighbor of the Cowleses who lived on nearby Scott Circle in drafting one of the most important sections of that 20,000-word document.

Chief Forester of the United States Department of Agriculture Gifford Pinchot called to pay his respects soon after the new President's arrival on N Street. He had visited the Roosevelts in Albany and had earned Theodore's admiration on two counts. First, Gifford Pinchot had been the first man to climb the western face of Mount Marcy in the Adirondacks, a feat Theodore himself would certainly have accomplished had it not been for that sudden call to Buffalo. Second, though Theodore had pinned Gifford, who was seven years his junior, to the mat in a friendly wrestling match during his visit to the governor's mansion in

Albany, when they put on the gloves, the Chief Forester, a lean and agile man, had knocked the Governor flat.

In Bamie's drawing room, the Chief Forester and the President, who had done much for conservation in New York State, discussed how they could best strike a blow to conserve the natural resources of the nation before, as Gifford Pinchot put it, the predatory interests made off with most of them. On one of his visits to N Street, the Chief Forester brought with him his friend, Frederick H. Newell, who also inspired Theodore the Naturalist, with his talk of wholesale land reclamation. The President told the forester and his friend to draw up their proposals, and it was, in essence, Pinchot's and Newell's ideas on conservation, thrashed out and discussed in Bamie's drawing room, that were incorporated into the President's first message to Congress. This lengthy document revealed in its many facets Theodore's basic antipathy toward all large, irresponsible entrepreneurs, but, in view of the new President's previously announced support of McKinley's policies, the contented business community paid it little mind. This first message called for publicity on corporate capitalization and earnings, the same proposal on a national scale he had fought for in New York. It also urged that only the United States should have the right to fortify any canal built across the Isthmus in Central America, and, of course, it started the conservation program that was to be Theodore Roosevelt's greatest achievement in office.

When Theodore moved into the White House, several days before Edith returned to Washington with the children, he simply walked there from N Street on a bright sunny morning, arriving at his office punctually, according to the *Washington Star*, at nine thirty on September 23. He was followed at a discreet distance—down Connecticut Avenue, with a jog around Farragut Square and Lafayette Park, to the White House—by two Secret Service men and by Jackson, the Cowles's colored coachman, driving their brougham, with Theodore's hand luggage, and Bamie, inside.

That night, his first in the White House, the President gave a small family dinner attended by his sisters and their husbands. The only other guest, the *Star* reported, was "another gentleman," who was most likely Fergie, down from New York, for this simple but moving occasion, with the Douglas Robinsons. At dinner, the President remembered that this day had been his father's birthday, and he called his sisters' attention to another curious coincidence. The dining-table centerpiece, arranged by Bamie, was a mass of yellow saffronica roses, the very flower their father had always chosen as his boutonniere! The President inserted a yellow rosebud from the centerpiece in his lapel and then presented each of the other three gentlemen with a saffronica.

Edith and the younger children joined Theodore at the White House on the twenty-fifth of September. She confided in a letter to her sister, "To me the shadow still hangs over the White House & I am still in constant fear about Theodore...." After a few days in residence, Edith was ready to admit her fear was probably "not quite justified"; perhaps the Secret Service guard, at her request, had been augmented, or replaced, by younger, faster-moving men. She took comfort in the fact that now they were "at least partly settled, though there is still much to be done."

The First Lady had already decided she would be her own housekeeper at the White House. She was spared the necessity of official entertaining during those early months, for there would be no White House functions out of respect for the previous occupants. Until January 1, 1902, Washington saw the First Lady only on Sundays when, with her children, she sat in the presidential pew at fashionable St. John's Episcopal Church across Lafayette Park from the White House. The President, following in the Dutch tradition of the Roosevelt family, went to Grace Reformed Church at Fifteenth and O Streets, usually alone, and this gave him an opportunity for the brisk walks he thoroughly enjoyed.

When the Lodges came home from Europe in mid-October of 1901, Theodore's Sunday walks through the Northwest section of the city began to set a pattern—with various and sundry zigs and zags en route home to the White House from church—that he was to follow almost religiously throughout his years in office. In fact, he often made the same waystops whenever he went on one of his frequent expeditions to Rock Creek Park—with the children, or with his friends, Baron Hermann Speck von Sternburg, the German chargé, and Jules Jusserand, the French ambassador. The people he dropped in on during the course of these rapid walks could be seen informally, or more "satisfactorily," to use Bamie's word for it, than if he were to have them at the White House under the eyes of the Washington press corps.

As Sir Ronald Ferguson had once written Bamie, there was "no place half so adapted for seeing people pleasantly as Washington," and the President took full advantage of the fortuitously homey nature of his capital city.

After services at Grace Reformed Church on a typical Sunday, Theodore might do a short zig two blocks west on O Street straight into the home of the Lodges on Massachusetts Avenue where his favorite rocking chair would be waiting beside Nannie's tea table in the library. This was the most satisfactory way to discuss with Cabot what Boss Hanna's next move might be or how far the Executive could afford to push the conservative senatorial "Big Four." From there, Theodore might take a zag straight down Sixteenth Street to the north side of Lafayette Park and into one of the twin houses of Henry Adams and John Hay, there to benefit by the sage advice of these two elegant, and astringent, older men of the world. Occasionally, Theodore could evoke a hearty laugh from sardonic Henry Adams at someone's expense, especially if it were their old friend, Cabot Lodge, to whom both were devoted. Cabot, Theodore said, didn't seem to mind at all when the newspapers called him the Boss of Theodore's "kitchen cabinet," but he was "simply livid" at the latest story: how Senator Cabot Lodge—whose horsemanship was superb—had been taking riding lessons in order to keep up with Theodore and the rest of the "kitchen cabinet" when they set out on horseback for Rock Creek Park. The cackles emanating from Henry Adams at such typical Roosevelt sallies could be heard almost halfway across Lafayette Park under the bronze statue of Andrew Jackson—the president who started "kitchen cabinets" in the first place—frozen forever in his heroic equestrian pose.

On yet another of his Sunday jaunts, Theodore might choose to go two blocks south from his church at the corner of Fifteenth and O to Scott Circle where the Gifford Pinchots lived, and there confer with the Chief Forester and any other zealous conservationists Gifford may have assembled. And, from the Pinchots on Scott Circle, it was but a one-block zag, due west, to Bamie's house.

"The Little White House" on N Street where Bamie and "Mr. Bearo" lived served its purpose, in many ways, for a much longer period than those first few days when the President had actually been in residence. It became a sort of annex for the overflow of White House guests who descended in droves, especially from New York, beginning in the Roosevelts' first extraordinary social season of 1902. But much more important than that, Bamie's house was always a ready haven for Theodore whenever he needed to talk out his complex problems. And so it remained, even when Bamie and Edith did not see eye to eye on the course each thought it best for Theodore to follow or on the people he should trust.

Edith's influence on Theodore was much like that of Abigail Adams on John Adams, second president of the United States. It was chiefly negative, in the best possible sense. She managed, with some measure of success, to curb her husband's natural impetuosity and to correct his lapses in judgment about people, though Theodore, with his abundant energy and goodwill, was much more often guilty of these faults than Henry Adams' shrewd old great-grandfather.

Edith was a good judge of people. Bamie once said the First Lady might seem to be "just sitting there mending Quentin's breeches," while in reality she was busily forming her own very firm opinions. These opinions, which Theodore was sure to hear later, were sometimes so bitter that the President could be thrown off the track completely. Edith might say, for example, of someone Theodore had instantly adopted as a friend, "I don't *dislike* him. I just don't want to live in the same world with him."

"*E*-die!" Theodore would protest, and then lapse into an uneasy, though temporary, silence. Edith's occasional intolerance of one of Theodore's instant companions could be extremely disconcerting if he had, on the spur of the moment, invited that particular person to luncheon or dinner at the White House. As likely as not in the early days, Edith would then absent herself from table with one of her neuralgic headaches, and Theodore would feel doubly guilty. Years later Edith would write a favorite daughter-in-law that she had eventually learned "one should not live to oneself." She admitted, "It was a temptation to me," but Theodore "would not allow it."

Bamie, on the other hand, always lived by the principle she often quoted, which was, "You must show your affection, or it will dry up," and to this Theodore and many others responded wholeheartedly. She was no more an initiator of his grander policies and plans than Edith, but she knew the world, accepted it, and was, above all, the world's best and most sympathetic listener. She rarely advised Theodore or anyone else to take a specific course of action because that went contrary to another of her guiding principles: To be helpful, advice should be offered only in general terms, not specifically. One should never propose a solution to another's problem; your solution might fit neither the will of the person seeking advice nor the real circumstances, since those who sought advice usually distorted reality in their own favor. Bamie, as well as Edith, had rare good judgment when it came to people, only hers was informed by a wide social experience and an abiding interest in the power play of politics.

These were the traits, in wife and sister, that made Theodore frequently seek refuge at 1733 N Street. The result was, as Bamie's niece, Eleanor Roosevelt, once said, that "Uncle Theodore made no major decision in foreign or domestic policy without first discussing it with Auntie Bye." Eleanor was in a position to know, for she spent two postdebutante seasons, when she had her own problems—chiefly the antagonism of Franklin D. Roosevelt's mother to their engagement—with her "dear Auntie Bye" on N Street.

Auntie Bye's other favorite niece, Alice, proved uncommonly skittish during the early days when Theodore and Edith first moved into the White House. She behaved as if she would rather be anywhere in the world than with her father and stepmother. Now, shortly before the holidays in 1901, she was still "just visiting"—this time with her maternal grandparents in Chestnut Hill.

Theodore, Edith, and Bamie all wanted Alice in Washington, but how to get her back in time for the family's first Christmas in the White House? In a wryly humorous acknowledgment of Bamie's influence, Theodore made a sure appeal to Alice's own budding interest in power struggles of every sort—personal or political, open or undercover—by writing his difficult daughter late in November, "Auntie Bye is as dear as ever and oversees the entire nation."

CHAPTER XXI

"Must *One Go Everywhere?*"

AT the height of the Washington social season of 1902, Senator Joseph B. Foraker of Ohio and his buxom wife, Julia, who had been among the town's liveliest partygoers in the time of the McKinleys, were visibly wilting at the pace set by the new family in the White House and all their friends and relations. Toward the end of January, as the Forakers wearily set out from home for the fifth consecutive evening that week, Julia Foraker could muster only a feeble smile when she heard her husband shout hoarsely to their coachman:

"Hurry, we're late for dinner at Senator Kean's. Come back for us there at ten and take us to the White House for the musicale. Come back at twelve and take us to the British Embassy. Come back at two and take us to the lunatic asylum."

The season had begun with a bang when the White House was thrown open on New Year's Day for the Roosevelts' first reception, the biggest crush Washington had ever seen at 1600 Pennsylvania Avenue. The description alone of that day and the week that followed, which Corinne Roosevelt Robinson wrote— to one of the New York cousins prevented from coming down only by dire illness—while she herself was trying to recuperate, at Bamie's on N Street, would cause the strongest mind to reel.

The afternoon before the reception, the Douglas Robinsons and their three children were met at Union Station by Ted who was down from Groton for the holidays. Father and Mother, he said, wanted them to come to the White House at once as "they were alone, and we could have a nice talk before all the functions began the next day." After "a lovely family time in the private sitting room upstairs" in the White House and "after establishing the children in their various quarters," Corinne and Douglas were driven to "The Little White House." Bamie and Will were still in New York at the Biltmore attending some social function, but the Robinsons were made comfortable on N Street by Hopkinson, Marsh, and Sheffield.

Bamie and Will, Corinne wrote her cousin, "did not get home until 9:30" the next morning "just in time for the former to hurry into her clothes, as at 10:30 we all started for the White House again. As we drove up the Back entrance we were greeted by nephews & nieces running informally through the garden paths & jumping on the steps of the carriage, which gave a lovely feeling of informality to the usually solemn New Year's Reception.

"Inside, the hall was already filled with the glittering uniforms of the Diplomats, & all of us who received soon congregated in the Blue Room & then the Band played a march & the President & Mrs. Roosevelt & all the Cabinet came into the room. Theodore was perfect in his manner, I thought, cordial and unaffected, but absolutely dignified, & Edith looked more than charming in a pure white gown, a lovely colour in her cheeks, & in her hands, an exquisite bouquet of orchids & lilies of the valley; her smile & bow were gracious and lovely, & I was very proud of my brother & his wife, as all the Ambassadors of foreign countries & their suites & then the Chief Justices, Senate & House of Congress, Army & Navy of the United States filed before them. I stood directly behind Theodore & thus heard all the introductions & was much interested to see so near all these 'people of importance.'"

Also in the Blue Room receiving the "people of importance" with the President and the First Lady were Cabot Lodge and Nannie, beautiful in steel satin and black lace with a cameo fastening the simple black velvet band at her lovely throat; Bamie in a striking white broadcloth gown with medallions of black velvet; and Alice, who had at last come home and now seemed to be enjoying the role of "the President's debutante daughter" almost as much as she had that of wandering off-spring, though still disdainful of the White House and its occupants. She had been promised an official debut at the White House, and this was to come later during that first hectic week. For the New Year's Day reception, eighteen-year-old Alice, her wavy, light-brown hair very much *en pompadour*, looked an extremely handsome and sophisticated young woman of at least twenty-eight in her molded white taffeta gown with its train and its high collar fastened at the throat by a huge diamond crescent.

Now, following the people of importance came long lines of "the hoi-polloi," the society columns reported, and the President's military and naval aides, Colonel Bingham and Commander Cowles, thought when it got to be half-past one in the afternoon that the President could, if he wished, order the gates of the White House closed. Theodore would not hear of it, Corinne proudly wrote, even though everyone in the Blue Room had long since been expected at the buffet breakfast Secretary of State and Mrs. Hay and their daughter, Helen, were giving for the entire diplomatic corps.

"Theodore said Edith must not receive any more," Corinne reported, "but that he would not disappoint people who had stood so long in the cold, so he stood until *everyone* had been admitted & shook hands in all with nearly 9,000 people!"

Having missed the Hays' buffet breakfast across Lafayette Park, Corinne continued, "We went back to lunch at Bamie's, & then almost immediately to the Roots where we had both been asked to receive, & from which we could not return until nearly dinner time.

"Bamie wished to take me to the British Embassy in the evening but my exhaustion was so great that I fell asleep & in spite of all that the Social Will & Bamie could do; I firmly refused to go, much to their astonishment as they of course went on the

Washington principle that one *must* go everywhere. I do not see how they stand the endless receptions."

The following day, a Thursday, it was so quiet in the morning at "The Little White House" that Auntie Corinne had a chance to play for a while "with darling Baby Cowles"—until Bamie's early luncheon party, and after that Corinne "was obliged to go to three teas," at the last of which, given by Senator Kean and his sisters, she "had to stay for nearly one hour," because she was "matronizing" not only her own daughter, Corinne, Jr., but her niece, Alice, who seemed loath to go home.

Back at Bamie's after the Kean tea, Corinne continued in her newsy letter to her cousin, "I had only ten minutes to lie down before putting on my best bib and tucker" to go to the first dinner for the Cabinet given by the Roosevelts at the White House.

"It was really a beautiful sight," Corinne wrote, getting her second wind, "we were fifty in number & the East Room was beautifully decorated from the Conservatory. We assembled there to await the Presidential party & then walked through all the other rooms to the State Dining Room, where the great table, shaped like an hour glass, was one blazing mass of exquisite pink begonias. Edith looked lovely in a pale blue, picture-looking gown, & many notabilities were present. Congressman Payne, the leader of the House, took me in to dinner & Senator Scott, Mark Hanna's close ally, sat on my other side & I had a very agreeable time with them & afterwards with Secretaries Root & Hitchcock & then a very gay 'back hair talk' with Edith & Theodore after all had gone."

On Friday, there was a luncheon at the White House for all the family gathered in Washington, and at four, Corinne had her "orders to meet Bamie for the awful teas again."

Corinne wrote, "I returned again exhausted." But she managed to lie down "for a few minutes before going to the George Peabody Wetmore dinner before Alice's Dance."

Alice's formal debut at the White House turned out to be the most dashing event of the social season on the entire Eastern seaboard. From the moment it was scheduled, it drew the attention of the spicy gossip sheet, *Town Topics*, that everyone in Washington as well as New York read. "Miss Roosevelt's dance on Friday," *Town Topics* had said, "is to be a small affair, only five hundred cards being sent out." At least a fourth of Alice's invitations had gone to her young friends in New York society, *Town Topics* reported mischievously, and the White House list for her party had consequently ignored quite a few of the many daughters of official Washington, including those of some irate congressmen and senators—which augured ill for Theodore. *Town Topics* also reported maliciously that in the midst of a formal White House tea given by the First Lady for her sister, Miss Emily Carow, during the week before Alice's debut, that that young lady had sauntered into the Blue Room munching a sandwich held in one hand while carrying a spare in the other.

Oblivious as always of nagging gossip and whatever consequences it might have, for such was her sunny nature, Corinne wrote her cousin that she had thoroughly enjoyed herself, just before Alice's dance, at the Wetmore dinner. Bamie might say that her charming younger sister's success in Washington could be partly credited to Corinne's intense "do-tell-me-all-about-yourself" concentration, between the soup and the fish, first on the dinner partner to her right and then on the gentleman to her left. And Alice might call this "Auntie Corinne's elbow-in-the-soup manner." But both were proud that, from the beginning, Corinne Roosevelt Robinson was extremely popular in Washington.

At the Wetmore dinner, Corinne wrote her cousin, she "sat between Mr. Wetmore & Percy Wyndham, the English Secretary & afterwards had a real talk with Cabot & then we all went on to the Dance."

At the dance, it was Auntie Corinne's opinion—though apparently not that of Alice, as her subsequent behavior revealed—that "Alice had the time of her life, men seven deep around her all the time." Though Alice, looking quite lovely and almost demure in white chiffon and pearls, was good enough to give that impression, she was really very annoyed, for two reasons. First, Edith had said it would not be necessary to take up the carpet in the East Room for dancing. She had directed that a layer of waxed crash be laid over the carpet and gave it as her opinion that this would be perfectly adequate for ball room dancing. Alice, who loved to dance and did it very well, could not agree. Second, Mother had decreed "no cotillion" and consequently no favors, and, since these were all the rage at the coming-out parties of Alice's social peers, she feared this taboo might cause her to appear as provincial as the rest of social Washington in the eyes of her New York contingent. This included the daughters of some of the wealthiest captains of industry—whose party favors ran to gold-mesh evening bags and silver cigarette cases—and a goodly proportion of the eligible young college men Alice had encountered as a subdebutante in New York and Boston, and at Ivy League proms. And so, even with "men seven deep around her all the time," inside, Alice sulked. She had her own independent income. She could have afforded appropriate favors for her guests. To Alice, it seemed that Edith had only been unusually stuffy when she insisted that Mother and Father were giving the debut party at the White House for their daughter and that that party was to be the best *they* could afford. Alice had cried a bit on Auntie Bye's shoulder at the injustice of it all. As Auntie Bye said, "Alice came in with her amber-colored hair and shed an amber-colored tear." She could sympathize with Alice's unfortunate predicament, but, following one of her own wise principles on this occasion, she had been careful not to intercede with Edith.

During the dance, the First Lady had arranged for a simple supper to be served in the State Dining Room and even here, as the ubiquitous correspondent of *Town Topics* seemed happy to report, discontent was evident in yet another quarter. At supper, he heard several of "the old beaux of Washington" complaining; "they were exceedingly disgruntled because they did not dance with the debutante," surrounded as she was by all the young beaux she had imported from out-of-town.

Viewing Alice's dance from Auntie Corinne's point of view, which doubtless reflected the sentiment of the majority of older guests, the First Lady, wearing a gown of white lace over white silk with a corsage of pink orchids, was "a gracious hostess" and "Theodore perfect again." Then, lapsing into poetic vein, Mrs. Robinson rhapsodized for the benefit of her absent cousin:

"Such a band! Such Strauss waltzes, & such go to it all! We did not leave until two o'clock & I think every one had a good time. The beautiful conservatories were perfect for sentiment & it was so pretty to see the girls' gay dresses & many a uniform & college athlete hidden among the palms."

The following day at Bamie's, Corinne was so exhausted she stayed in bed right through another of her sister's gay luncheon parties, or so it seemed "from the sound of the voices downstairs." If she could but last the week out, she concluded in her letter to her cousin, there would be only three more Washington affairs that she had to attend, and this was only the beginning of the most active social season Washington had ever known. Tomorrow, Corinne wrote, there was Senator Kean's dinner in honor of the President's sisters. She could hardly avoid going with Bamie to that one. Bamie herself was giving a dinner party at "The Little White House" in Corinne's honor on Monday. And on Tuesday, there was the Diplomatic Reception, if Corinne could make it again to the White House.

Somehow Corinne got through that incredible first week. She attended the Diplomatic Reception and then, with relief, boarded a train for New York, leaving the rest of the Roosevelts to carry on at the same gruelling pace. Somehow Edith, who made up in will for what she lacked in energy compared to the Roosevelts, also managed to carry on. She had one or two fainting spells, but she continued, most gallantly, to act through it all both as White House hostess and housekeeper, straight through until mid-February when Lent, mercifully, put an end to official functions that winter.

The evening reception for the Diplomatic Corps, the Washington *Star* reported, had been the most colorful ever held at the White House. As the President, the First Lady, and their receiving party "came down the West stairway, two buglers standing at the East Room heralded their approach. Colonel Bingham and Commander Cowles walked in advance of the President and Mrs. Roosevelt." The *Star* also noted that it was not the First Lady but Miss Roosevelt and Mrs. Cowles—"in white satin with many jewels and a spray of green leaves in her hair"—who "relieved the crush by leading the way to the East Room from the Blue Room."

Hearing of all this, Henry Adams, that shrewd old recluse across Lafayette Park, cackled it would serve Bamie right if Edith sooner or later barred her from the White House and, as for Theodore, *he* was courting trouble by "playing the king" a bit too much.

CHAPTER XXII

Ambassadors Extraordinary

"WE must always remember that the President of the United States *has* no sisters," Bamie had cautioned Corinne when Theodore and Edith first moved into the White House. This was easier said than done, as Bamie herself soon discovered.

Did one refuse an invitation to dine with Senator and Mrs. Mark Hanna, whom one scarcely knew, even though one suspected it had been extended only because one was the President's sister? Not Bamie, who welcomed the opportunity to become better acquainted with Theodore's formidable political adversary. Early in February of 1902 when Bamie received this invitation, she was one of the few people who knew Theodore was about to drop his first bombshell on the business community—his suit to dissolve that huge railroad holding combine, the Northern Securities Company. Prominent among those who headed the combine was Mr. J. P. Morgan, whom Bamie knew socially better than Theodore did, but she had no more patience with the irresponsible exercise of unbounded power than her brother. Theodore had told Bamie that, although Boss Hanna had warned him to "go slow" about business after reading his first message to Congress, he had decided he would "rather be full President for three years than half a President for seven." She had applauded Theodore's secret decision not to follow in McKinley's footsteps.

Bamie knew that when the Northern Securities suit was announced in mid-February she might never again have such an excellent opportunity to study Boss Hanna at close, informal range, so of course she accepted the invitation to dine with Senator and Mrs. Hanna, whose guests on February 9 also happened to include one or two of the Senate's conservative "Big Four" and their wwies. Bamie took with her to that dinner a secret any Wall Street bear would have given his soul to know in advance. As usual, that secret could not have been safer; all her family and friends knew, as Hector, youngest of the Fergies once said, "Bamie has never given anyone away." No one could have been more surprised than Boss Hanna and the "Big Four" when, little more than a week after the Hanna dinner, the President's first big antitrust suit sent the stock market down more sharply than the death of McKinley.

There were other social duties that made it impossible for Bamie to take the advice she had given Corinne. How could the President's sister refuse invitations to all the official functions arranged for the visit, at the height of the 1902 season, of the Kaiser's younger brother, Prince Henry, when that attractive royal personage came to America to pick up the yacht built in Philadelphia for the Imperial German family? How could one refuse when the First Lady so obviously needed Bamie's sure assistance with protocol and other matters connected with the State banquet at the White House held in Prince Henry's honor? And who else but Bamie was available to chaperone Alice at all the other gala affairs given for the Prince in New York as well as Washington?

Mrs. Cowles had always believed, with the rest of conservative society, that a lady's name should appear but twice in her life in the newspapers—once when she was married and again in the obituary column. But now in America's gay Edwardian period, things had changed. As Washington's preeminent social leader and as the President's sister, Bamie could not help being very much in evidence. She almost eclipsed the First Lady, and this caused her some distress and discomfort, especially when she saw that Edith had started keeping a scrapbook of clippings and on its cover had written "Social World." Bamie was eclipsed in that scrapbook, as time went on, only by "Princess Alice."

Unfortunately for Alice, the gossip sheets and the newspapers called her "Princess Alice" from the moment when, on the invitation of gallant Prince Henry, she had stepped up and cracked a bottle of champagne over the receding prow of the Kaiser's yacht as it slid down the Philadelphia ways. Surprising as it seemed to everybody but sharp old Henry Adams, the American public's reaction to this cognomen by which the press of the nation always thereafter referred to the President's eldest child— as well as to Alice's own rather imperious manner—caused trouble for "Princess Alice," for her father, and for the whole Roosevelt family. When the English papers and the French journals picked up and bandied that silly title about, and this got back to America, it made matters even more embarrassing for the President of the United States.

The world in which "Princess Alice" made her debut in 1902 bore amazing similarities, in tone, to the way things were in the world, particularly in the United States, fifty or sixty years later. Many of the problems, domestic and foreign, confronted by the thirty-fifth President of the United States, who was when he took office almost as young as Theodore, were but proliferations and further developments of the very same ones the twenty-sixth President of the United States had had to deal with as they were first emerging. As Bamie might say, *"Plus ça change, plus c'est la même chose."*

For one thing, despite noticeable change in style of dress (which became more modish though perhaps less flattering for the ladies and much less dashing for the gentlemen) and in behavior (a bit more relaxed, but not so much more so in public), the Democratic occupants of the White House better than half a century later comported themselves in much the same manner and were subjected to the same glare of publicity that dogged the doings of all the Roosevelts, at home and abroad. The only difference in this respect between the Roosevelts and the Kennedys was that there were even more of the former actually living in the White House, and there were consequently even more stories about pets and ponies, that, in 1902, were reported to be riding in the White House elevators. Another difference was that Jackie Kennedy seemed to combine in her own person, through the almost mythological role in which she was cast by the press of the 1960s, some of the dignity and reserve of Theodore Roosevelt's First Lady and the sophisticated dash of his daughter. Which was why, no doubt, Alice Roosevelt Longworth —who had thoroughly enjoyed *her* role as "Princess Alice" and who continued as one of Washington's traditional social leaders well into the 1960s and was still the world's staunchest Republican—not only approved of the Kennedys in the White House, as she had of no other occupants since 1909, but was also utterly fascinated by them.

There was yet another similarity between the first decade of the twentieth century and the 1960s that might cause one to observe that the more things change, the more they are the same. In 1902, the United States was already an international force. The odd thing was that, though all the chancelleries of Europe and most educated Europeans recognized this new fact of international life in Theodore's day, very few Americans chose to.

It seems impossible that they could have ignored the evidence before their eyes—the astounding growth of their manufacturing, which had already outstripped England's and Germany's, and of their towns and great cities; the thousands of miles of railroads criss-crossing the continent; the huge combinations of capital and labor, growing ever larger; the new territories acquired in the Caribbean and in the Pacific; the plans for an Isthmian Canal; the rapidly expanding trade with Europe and the Orient. But ignore this evidence most Americans did, choosing to regard themselves, erroneously, as a predominantly agrarian people, luckily isolated by the oceans for all time from the rest of the world and never to be drawn into the complex power politics played by industrial England and decadent Europe. In 1902, as later, they would recognize neither the signs of their industrial might nor its attendant problems. And this attitude—the most important problem of all—bedeviled all subsequent occupants of the White House right through the first half of the twentieth century and beyond.

It was no doubt because Theodore was the first president courageous enough to try to tackle all these problems head on, when they first became evident, that he and his daughter received such a bad press before he had a chance to go to the people in 1904 for their vote of approval. The antagonistic press knew well enough that the title "Princess," reiterated often enough, would disturb the democratic ideals of an agrarian-minded nation impatient always with the idea of a governing aristocracy of any kind, whether of birth or of brains.

There was but one important editor and publisher in the whole United States, not counting the editor of the *Emporia Gazette,* who gave all the Roosevelts, almost all the time, a consistently good press, politically and socially, and that was the *New York Tribune*'s Whitelaw Reid, whose wife was Bamie's closest friend, beginning even before the days of Auxiliary No. 3 and the trained nurses spurned by Miss Clara Barton. Early in Theodore's career, he had told Bamie he would have nothing to do with Whitelaw Reid because the *Tribune* had been most unfriendly to him as police commissioner and even as governor. To their mutual benefit, Bamie had brought Theodore round in time, and now, in January of 1902, the President gave Whitelaw Reid an appointment eminently suited to his exquisite taste and the largesse to which he had become accustomed as the husband of the daughter of Darius Ogden Mills, one of America's wealthiest old captains of industry. The President appointed Whitelaw Reid of the *Tribune* Special Ambassador Extraordinary and Minister Plenipotentiary to the Court of St. James's for the august coronation ceremonies in June at Westminster Abbey of that gay old blade, Edward VII of Great Britain and Ireland, who had at last succeeded Victoria.

On January 14, courtly Mr. Reid acknowledged that welcome presidential appointment with a few well-chosen words: "It will be my hope and earnest effort that the duties you thus impose may be so discharged that you will be satisfied with your personal representative, and the country benefited by the service."

On February 29, en route in his private Pullman to his California ranch at San Mateo for the winter, Mr. Reid sent off, from Chicago, a hurried telegram to the President of the United States marked "strictly personal." This read: "Cheerfully accept of course any conclusion you think wisest. Personal impression at first thought, even if you decide on that course best no publicity now, lest in connection with other things should be maliciously interpreted as back-down. Great faith sometimes in strength of silence, and letting things blow over. Naturally disappointed over decision, but anything you feel best satisfactory."

This ominous communication cloaked, not an important change in the coronation plans of the President or Edward VII; it was Mr. Reid's knowing way of acknowledging, reluctantly, Theodore's decision not to let his daughter, Alice, go as the guest of Mr. Reid's daughter, Jean, to the coronation. The news that "Princess Alice" was going to the coronation had somehow leaked to the press and this had evoked many rude comments about "American royalty." Theodore, always acutely sensitive to public opinion, had decided that Alice had best stay home. The "other things" hinted at darkly in Mr. Reid's wire referred to Wall Street's rage and the furor raised in the venal press at the President's suit to dissolve the Northern Securities Company, much of which had polarized around "Princess Alice" as well as her father. Cautious Mr. Reid was probably right in advising Theodore not to announce his decision to keep Alice at home for, in its current mood, the press would certainly have gleefully labeled such a public announcement a backdown by the President.

Though Bamie and Corinne each frequently wore in her coiffure of an evening three small, rather regal-looking white ostrich feathers—adapted from the headdress of the armored knight on the Roosevelt family crest—and, although Corinne often blithely referred to these as her "Presidential sister plumes," the press did not single them out for the caustic treatment it gave "Princess Alice" in abundance and ad nauseam. "Princess Alice" was better copy, of course; besides, Mrs. Cowles and Mrs. Robinson were so obviously conservative society matrons of well-entrenched power and prestige that they seemed above reproach.

Following Whitelaw Reid's advice, the White House put its faith "in the strength of silence" and made no official announcement about the change in Alice's plans. Perhaps in an attempt to draw some of that unwelcome attention away from "poor, dear Alice," the White House gradually let it be known that Mrs. Cowles was going to the coronation, but simply as the wife of Commander Cowles who had been appointed naval aide to Ambassador Extraordinary Whitelaw Reid. It also became known that Mrs. Douglas Robinson would be in London, too, at the time of the coronation. She was going over chiefly because she wished to enter her daughter in Mlle Souvestre's excellent finishing school at Wimbledon, near London, where Corinne, Jr., would join her cousin, Eleanor, now, as her Auntie Bye had been before her, very much teacher's pet and given by Mademoiselle the affectionate nickname, "Tottie."

Special Ambassador Reid spared no effort or expense to make his mission to the coronation of King Edward VII the envy of all the crowned heads of Europe who would be attending the ceremony. By spending so lavishly, out of his own pocket, for his mission, he took the chance that he, too, might arouse antagonism at home, for Americans were notoriously suspicious of their own diplomatic representatives abroad and certainly most niggardly with the salaries and official expenses allowed them. Then, as now, as one Iowa congressman phrased it in the 1900s, "It takes a young man to be President of these United States and a millionaire to be an ambassador." It was typical that for years, before the turn of the century, the State Department was housed in Washington's old orphan asylum.

Mr. Reid's advance planning for the American mission to the coronation entailed many letters to his personal representatives in London who were told to obtain a suitably elegant establishment in which to house it. They were likewise to get horses and carriages—"the best turned out of all the Special Embassies," even down to such details as "blue liveries with red stripes and silver buttons" for the two coachmen and two grooms, a pair each for the Landau and the victoria, as "Mrs. Reid and I will often need to be going in different directions at the same time." These letters reveal a meticulous mind at work as well as the role Bamie played, for the second time in her life, as an unofficial ambassador abroad.

From his California estate, on March 8, Mr. Reid congratulated one of his London agents, Isaac N. Ford, Esq., of 18 Old Queen Street, on having rented for him Lord Tweedmouth's house at 5,000 pounds for the three-week period during which his Special Embassy would be officially in residence for the coronation and its attendant festivities. In the same letter, he congratulated himself on being in California "as we are fortunately out of range of the New York reporters and of the endless questions of New York Society; the announcement will probably pass without undue notice." Concurrently he wrote J. P. Morgan, Jr., who was also acting as his agent in London, to spare no expense in fixing up Lord Tweedmouth's house as friends had told him it "looks pretty shabby."

Mr. Reid confided in Mr. Ford that Miss Roosevelt definitely would not be one of the party. "The sensational press," he wrote, "made a disgusting fuss about it; but this was of less importance than the President's own feeling that it was unwise to let his daughter attract so much attention. There seem also to have been some hints that in view of the Prince's visit here, and her christening the Emperor's yacht, she might be expected, if she went to London, to go also to Berlin, and this naturally seemed to the parental mind to be making too much of a state personage out of the young girl."

"My understanding," Mr. Reid also told his agent, "is that Mrs. Cowles is to go."

Why Mrs. Cowles was to go in Alice's place, or who exactly had decided this, Mr. Reid did not say. He did write the President it was Senator Lodge who suggested to him when he was in Washington that Alice's "visit to London might have entailed the embarrassment of an invitation for another visit not less noticeable."

The fear that "Princess Alice" might be invited to Berlin as well as London at this ticklish stage in world diplomacy could well have been first expressed by Cabot Lodge. As a member of the Senate Foreign Relations Committee, he knew the tension building up between Britain and Germany and the explosive involvement of all major powers in the Far East. Since Secretary Hay's health was failing, the Senator was soon to go to London himself on a much more important mission than Special Ambassador Reid's for the President of the United States. On that secret mission, the Senator would assure the British Foreign Office that the United States, on the word of the President unratified by the Senate, would support the Anglo-Japanese Alliance —and this Alliance, with secret American backing, gave Japan a free hand in China against the Russians. It would then have been most embarrassing, while the President was trying to give the British every assurance of his support, for his daughter to be royally wined and dined, first in England, and then to hop right across the Channel to be perhaps even more royally entertained by King Edward's nephew, Kaiser Wilhelm, who was so violently anti-British. And, to complicate matters further, through America's much unappreciated regular representatives abroad, Theodore, Lodge, and Bamie all knew—what the British Foreign Office also certainly knew—that Edward's "Nephew Willy" was then feeling very much pro "Cousin Nicky," and consequently for the Russians against Britain's allies, the Japanese, on the eve of the Russo-Japanese War.

Considering all these treacherous undercurrents tugging at what seemed a perfectly innocuous official visit to the coronation by Mr. Reid and his Special Mission, Theodore also had to take into account that the British might be offended when "Princess Alice" did not come to the coronation. Why not then simply let it be known that another member of the President's family, his sister, Mrs. Cowles, whom many people in London remembered with affection, was coming in her stead? The advantage here was that Mrs. Cowles knew Edward VII quite well and the Kaiser not at all. There would be no embarrassing invitation from across the Channel.

Bamie herself was not very anxious to go. She wrote Corinne, just before they sailed, "If it had been possible to avoid going this year, *nothing* would have taken me to London, but, on account of Will's appointment and at the time it was decided, on Alice's account, it would have seemed churlish to refuse, and as I *am* going, of course, I am only too happy at the thought of seeing my friends."

Since Corinne was sailing on an earlier ship, Bamie gave her sister some last-minute advice on how to behave and what to wear when she was presented at Court before the coronation. Bamie herself, having already been presented in the time of the old Queen, would not have to wear a court dress with a train when she was received by her old friend, Edward VII, and Queen Alexandra.

First as to behavior—"In your position," Bamie advised, "you must do things in a very quiet but very dignified manner. However little either you or I, for our own as well as for Theodore's sake, would ever use the relationship to him, still for his sake, whenever people do realize who we are, we must do him credit. . . ."

Then, as to dress—"Do not let *any* one lure you into any combination of things; unless marvelously handsome and costly they give a poor effect. Having watched so many gowns, I know them well, and the ones that were handsome—except, as I say, the very costly ones—were those that were distinguished by a certain simplicity that is not mixed-up looking. Try your veil beforehand to see how it is most becoming."

This was sound advice for any lady about to be presented at

court at any time. Then Bamie gave Corinne some specific tips on where to purchase her clothes:

"Ina Colgate will tell you who is best for gowns in London. In my day Jay made really very handsome ones, but things change quickly. Worth now has a London house. I, of course, do not need any court train, but for day clothes will reach the other side in simple rags, as I prefer getting them there and do not wish to take over any more than necessary, on account of duties when returning, as we pay for the glory of the relationship to that brother in being unable to, in any way, try to evade the Custom House."

Mrs. Cowles was also in a position to be helpful to Mr. Reid on the matter of dress. On the eve of the Mission's departure, Mr. Reid wrote from New York to his personal representative in Washington.

"Can you ascertain quietly for me at the State Department just when the present agreement with the British Foreign Office on the great clothes question went into effect. . . . I know [Ambassadors] E. J. Phelps and Thomas F. Bayard wore the present costume on ceremonious occasions, but want to know how much farther back it went—whether to Adams (Charles Francis). . . . And what was it Buchanan did on the same subject?

"P.S. Please be sure Mr. Bayard wore knee breeches. Mrs. Cowles will be sure to know."

It was a pity that Mr. Reid, who was tall, lean-limbed, and most distinguished looking, did not have a chance to wear knee breeches at Westminster Abbey in June of 1902. After the Special Mission had moved into the Tweedmouth house, after Mr. Reid had received an honorary degree at Cambridge, after the presentation of Mrs. Robinson at court, and Bamie as well, without train, and after the dinner at the United States Embassy, given by the regular ambassador, Joseph H. Choate, for Queen Alexandra and King Edward, the King had to have his appendix out, and the coronation was called off.

The United States Special Mission sailed for home, leaving

Bamie behind to spend some time with all her old friends. It was no surprise to Theodore, when, not long after his victory at the polls in 1904, he received an extremely warm message of congratulation from Edward VII, asking the President to ". . . Bring me to the remembrance of your sister, Mrs. Cowles. . . ."

CHAPTER XXIII

Extra Eyes and Ears

ONE fine September morning in 1902, after her return from England, Bamie was sitting out on the veranda of Cousin Rosy's rustic hideaway two thousand feet up in the Adirondacks enjoying a breeze off St. Regis Lake when she saw a thin, unfamiliar figure disembark rather gingerly from a rowboat. At this distance, through the spruce and sweet-smelling balsam bordering the winding path up from the lake to Camp Elsinore, she was unable to recognize her unexpected visitor. It could not be Whitelaw Reid, whose summer camp was only half a mile away on the Upper St. Regis, for this man was short. Besides, Bamie knew Mr. Reid would never choose to pay a call, good friends though they were, at such an inelegant hour of the day. It might be some restless early riser among the many guests staying at the Reids' Camp Wild Air, perhaps one whom she had met at dinner there the evening before.

These dinner parties in the wilderness given by her friend, Elisabeth Reid, Bamie thoroughly enjoyed. Though she knew "Lizzie's" remarkable talent for organization fom the Spanish-American War days when they had turned the Reids' town house in New York into a training school for nurses, Bamie never ceased to wonder how Lizzie managed each summer to transport so many of the rich comforts of her various establishments—the house on East Fifty-sixth Street, her country place, Ophir Hall, and her California ranch—to the Adirondacks. All this Lizzie Reid accomplished with the ease and efficiency of a brilliant quartermaster general, in full charge of garrison and supply, to the army of some splendid monarch always on the march. It was to Bamie an unending source of delight, and some amusement, to find the Reids "roughing it," whenever she went to stay with them up in the Adirondacks or with Cousin Rosy, surrounded as usual by their retinue of servants—chef, valet, butler, maids—and to note among the many luxuries and conveniences at Camp Wild Air, a misnomer if there ever was one, not only hot and cold running water but also, in the spacious bath off Mr. Reid's master bedroom and dressing room, an imported French bidet.

As her visitor came into full view around the last crook in the trail, Bamie immediately recognized, by his drooping walrus mustache and his baggy but immaculate white ducks, Mr. Edward H. Harriman, the railroad financier, who was indeed one of the guests at Camp Wild Air that week. Somewhat out of breath, Mr. Harriman, who was then fifty-four but looked a good ten years younger, gratefully accepted a chair on the porch and sat there for a long while silently fanning himself with his oversize straw boater. To cover his discomfort, shyness, or whatever it was, Bamie congratulated him on being up and about so early in such delightful weather and asked whether he might be on his way down to Saranac Lake to visit Dr. Trudeau's Sanatorium, of which she had been told he was a trustee. No, said Mr. Harriman, shyly pulling his long neck down into his stiff collar and averting his eyes behind thick-lensed spectacles, he had just wanted to stop by for a brief visit to improve their acquaintance of the evening before. Then, continuing to fan himself with his hat, he again lapsed into complete silence.

At this temporary impasse, four-year-old William Sheffield Cowles rescued Mr. Harriman by toddling out of the house in bathing suit and waterwings. On request, he shook hands solemnly with his mother's guest and received in turn a gentle, almost loving, pat on his curly head as he set out with his nurse for a morning paddle down at the pier. Mr. Harriman now relaxed and told Bamie he had a fine boy named William, too, who would be eleven in November, and all about his two lovely daughters who were his pride and joy.

During this proud paternal recital, Bamie's mind was busy with other thoughts. She realized, of course, that Mr. Edward H. Harriman was the third and lesser known of that bold financial trio—Morgan, Hill, and Harriman—who had formed the Northern Securities Company and that Theodore's antitrust suit against that huge railroad combine was still pending. Surely Mr. Harriman would not be so naïve as to think his little surprise visit could in any way affect *that*, for, as Theodore himself had said with some relief, the matter was now in the courts where it belonged. But what sort of man, Bamie wondered, was this Harriman, who had risen, as everyone said, from Wall Street runner to become the financial wizard first, of the Illinois Central, then the Union Pacific, the Southern Pacific, and, more lately in his long struggle to out-pace the Morgan-dominated railroads, the Northern Pacific?

Bamie recalled having heard that Mr. Morgan had been none too happy at having to include Mr. Harriman in the Northern Securities combine, and she also suddenly remembered something her Uncle Jim had told her back in the late 1880s. James West Roosevelt had, with several others, represented the Morgan interests on the board of directors of some small railroad out West, and along had come Mr. Harriman who wanted that road for himself and his Illinois Central. He had secretly bought up all the outstanding stock of that little railroad and had, almost overnight, wrested control right out from under the sizable nose of the great J. P. Morgan himself. Harriman, Uncle Jim had grumbled, was a shrewd and ruthless operator. Recalling this story, on the porch at Camp Elsinore, Bamie couldn't help being intrigued, in spite of her guest's shy, circuitous behavior and his strange, tortoise-like appearance. She listened carefully to what he finally got around to saying and then, after her visitor had left, she immediately sat down to write a letter to her brother.

"Dearest Theodore," Bamie wrote. "The Edward Harrimans happen to have been up here for the last few days & he came over just for a quiet call this morning & was so very, very friendly & interested about you, then talked of various matters. Just before he left, he said he hoped some time to have the chance of talking with you—that the idea was you could not do it all alone & they ought to stand by ready to help & that he was ready at any time only he never wished to seem to intrude."

Bamie continued, suiting the action to the words, "I think the latter part of the conversation was meant for me to repeat to you." Though she did not exactly suggest that Theodore could, if he wished, see Mr. Harriman sub rosa at her N Street house, she did add, rather pointedly at the end of her letter, "Remember our Washington house is ready for you at *any* & *every* time."

Within the week, Bamie heard from Theodore, "I am very much obliged to you for what you told me about Mr. Harriman. It was important and I appreciate your writing me. Give my warm regards to the Reids."

Thinking of 1904 for Theodore, Bamie could not help wishing for at least one big financial backer who would feel friendly towards the President and his policies and who would remain so long enough to contribute to his campaign for election in 1904, provided, of course, he received the nomination. Theodore's prompt response to Bamie's letter indicated his strong interest in this possibility, too, but its noncommittal brevity also conveyed his wariness of Mr. Harriman's offer, tentative and indirect as it was. Why should one of the very men against whom he had instituted suit want "to help" when all the rest of Wall Street was attacking him so violently for thus interfering with business? He had heard enough about the little railroad wizard to know that no one could ever guess what was on the mind of Edward H. Harriman. Perhaps he was following that tried and true political tactic—If you can't fight 'em, join 'em. In which case, Theodore could afford to wait and let Harriman come to him, and less obliquely at that. Besides he had his hands full just then trying to talk some sense into the heads of quite another breed of businessman, the tough, intransigent coal operators who said the miners could stay out on strike until doomsday before they would deal with the union. And in the course of his difficult negotiations with these hard-headed characters, Theodore was already getting effective, first-rate help—not just some vague offer of future aid—from yet another surprising quarter, from the most powerful member of the Northern Securities trio, J. P. Morgan himself. Morgan and his partners, notably Bob Bacon, who had been Theodore's classmate at Harvard, were actually working behind the scenes to make intransigent old George F. Baer, president of the Philadelphia & Reading Railroad, who spoke for all the coal operators, listen to the President's "unofficial" request that the strike be settled by a board of arbitrators.

During the anthracite coal strike that dragged on dangerously close to cold weather—and the off-year Congressional elections of 1902—Bamie again felt encouraged to act as extra eyes and ears for her brother, especially since he had found her Harriman communication important. Most of the information she passed on to Theodore came from Mr. Reid who was, of course, as editor and publisher of the *Tribune*, in a better position than she was to know what was really going on. Sometimes Mr. Reid wrote the President direct, but he had a tendency to preachify, and Bamie sensed this annoyed Theodore. Nevertheless, she told her brother, the Reids were very helpful because they "tell me any political things they know." Since Mr. Reid often called on his paper's correspondents, at home and abroad, for special private reports on any given situation— the alignment of the Republican machine in New York, for example, or how Congress might be expected to vote on a particular issue—such information was often invaluable to Theodore. Moreover, Mr. Reid led a very active club life in conservative circles, and what the Wall Street crowd was saying, as it thought off the record, in such establishments, when conveyed to the President by Mr. Reid or indirectly through Bamie, gave him a preview of any concerted move on the part of his entrenched opposition.

By mid-October, Theodore had made some progress in the coal strike. "Acting unofficially," the President of the United States had, in an unprecedented executive move, "invited" the coal operators to Washington to meet with him and, incidentally, with Mr. John Mitchell, the lone representative of the coal miners' union. The operators came, grudgingly enough, and were somewhat annoyed to find the President dramatically ensconced at the conference table in a wheel chair. This may have seemed to them a calculated play for sympathy, but Theodore had, in fact, been temporarily lamed, while in New England making a speech, when his carriage had collided with a runaway horse-drawn tram. He was in the wheel chair on doctor's orders, though otherwise in fine fettle.

Mr. Baer and friends listened to the young President with obvious impatience. They objected when he invited Mr. Mitchell into the conference room, and they greeted the miners' representative with stony stares. Then they addressed their angry remarks directly to the President, completely ignoring the physical presence of gentlemanly Mr. Mitchell. Under the circumstances, Theodore kept his temper remarkably well, insisting only that Mr. Mitchell was entitled to state his case for the miners, which he did quietly and well.

The precedent-setting conference had seemed utterly fruitless. But now there was a break in the solid phalanx of the operators who had attended that meeting. Morgan interests were working behind the scenes to bring the diehards among the operators around to the President's idea of submitting the issues to an independent board of arbitrators. At this stage of the negotiations, the President received from Mr. Reid via Bamie one of the many private communications, on every sort of issue domestic and foreign, that he received while president from this particularly well-situated combination letter-drop and listening post. Mr. Reid was now back at Ophir Hall and Bamie at Oldgate for the early autumn. No doubt their communication regarding Wall

Street sentiment on the strike made the President urge the friendly Morgan partners to redouble their efforts, for the good of the Republican party at the polls in November and to improve Theodore's chances for election in 1904, as well as for the good of millions of Americans who might otherwise freeze to death in the cities during the winter of 1902–1903.

"My dear Mrs. Cowles," Mr. Reid wrote Bamie, and she, of course, sent his letter on to her brother, ". . . The situation is not getting any better, and I am disturbed at the angry tone which begins to be taken by large numbers of the representative New Yorkers one meets at the Clubs or in business circles. . . ." Mr. Reid hoped the President would not be tempted to "interfere" again to settle the strike. This would no doubt ensure popular victory at the polls that November, but lose Theodore himself the support of the entire business community. "Would that a settlement or the elections were here!" Mr. Reid almost groaned. ". . . What I dread is the danger of carrying the Congressional elections now at a price that may cost us the National elections two years later. . . ."

Further identifying himself with the occupant of the White House, Mr. Reid was sorry to hear of the President's accident; he, too, had been "kicked by a horse on exactly the same spot in Syria" and had gone "on crutches for weeks, after a fortnight in a palanquin."

On October 16, the President answered Mr. Reid in a letter to "Darling Bye," who was now visiting at Ophir Hall on her way back to Washington.

"I was very much interested in Mr. Reid's letter," Theodore said. He was happy to report that the operators had finally agreed to arbitration "and parenthetically, may Heaven preserve me from ever again dealing with so wooden headed a set, when I wished to preserve their interests. . . . Our great trouble was that the little world in which the operators moved was absolutely out of touch with the big world that included practically the rest of the country. . . ." Nor could Theodore resist a slight dig at the circles in which Mr. Reid moved. "One prominent member of my Cabinet," he said with some satisfaction, "remarked that in his judgment Manhattan was our most troublesome insular possession . . . New York is not representative of the country. . . ." Moreover, said Theodore, "The trouble with the excellent gentlemen who said that they would far rather die of cold than yield on such a high principle as recognizing arbitration with these striking miners, was that *they* were not in danger of dying of cold. . . ."

For the most part, the American press, including Mr. Reid's *Tribune*, though happy to have the strike settled before winter and the elections, continued to regard Theodore's masterly handling of the coal crisis as an act of supererogation. It was left to the *London Times* to give him his due in an editorial that said: "In a most quiet and unobtrusive manner the President has done a very big and entirely new thing. We are witnessing not merely the ending of a coal strike, but the definite entry of a powerful Government upon a novel sphere of operation. . . . His personal prestige and reputation are enormously enhanced by the immediate public service he has rendered, and they will be immeasurably enhanced when the American people grasp, as they rapidly will, the far larger issues involved in his striking departure from precedent. . . ."

Rather belatedly Mr. Reid admitted in a letter to Theodore on Election Day, "I believe the results today will show an immense gain from your interference in the coal business—hazardous as I thought it at the time."

Bamie would have to placate Theodore for her friend, Mr. Reid, over the reappearance of that word "interference." It grated on the President at a time when he was literally reveling in his political triumph. Emboldened by his success, he had even written Boss Hanna, "I feel most strongly that the attitude of the operators is one which accentuates the need of the Government having some power of supervision and regulation over such corporations."

This was notice to Senator Hanna that the President was now his own man. The footprints of McKinley had been completely obliterated, and Colonel Roosevelt, mighty hunter, intended to spend the rest of his days in office openly stalking corporate big game whenever it seemed to him to be acting against the public interest. But, as an outgrowth of the coal settlement, Theodore had quixotically promised not to let the government poach on one fairly obvious large business preserve. *In camera* and off the record, when J. P. Morgan, who had so effectively helped the President bring off his first important executive triumph, asked him point blank whether he planned any future antitrust suit move against Mr. Morgan's huge new combine, the United States Steel Corporation, Theodore in spontaneous gratitude had replied, of course not. Since U.S. Steel, as everyone knew, was bigger than Northern Securities or any other holding company in the United States, it was thereafter sometimes embarrassing to Theodore when anyone referred to the relative freedom from unwelcome government attention enjoyed by the Morgan interests, while almost everyone else in the business community seemed to be under investigation by his new Bureau of Corporations or threatened with some other kind of Rooseveltian "supervision and regulation." The President's instant and unconsidered magnanimity toward his powerful and helpful colleague in the coal crisis was the sort of thing that made Edith remark, on more than one occasion, "Theodore has tied so many knots with his tongue that he can't undo with his teeth."

The friendly feeling the President had for the Morgan firm was naturally helped along by his personal friendship for his Harvard classmate, Bob Bacon. Bamie, too, was very fond of Jack Carter, another Morgan partner who had been devoted to her since the London days when he was on the United States Embassy staff. These agreeable and informal connections with the House of Morgan, which in Theodore's terminology usually lined up in his mind on the side of the "good trusts," boded ill for any of the other financial or industrial groups whom he suspected of being "bad trusts." Some years later, Otto H. Kahn of Kuhn, Loeb, the investment bankers who supported Edward H. Harriman, often in opposition to the Morgan interests, was to say that there had developed something he called "The Harriman Extermination League" and that the League had "played its trump card by poisoning President Roosevelt's mind against Mr. Harriman, with whom he used to be on friendly terms. . . ." This was, of course, a partisan observation, but it had more than a grain of truth. Besides, where Mr. Morgan came right out bluntly with anything he wanted or had to say, the circumlocutory and often silent Mr. Harriman was not Theodore's sort of man. He made the mistake of circling round and round the White House, and when he finally got his chance to talk to Theodore and help him in the 1904 national campaign, with very substantial contributions, he made the additional mistake of expecting, as Boss Platt had done, a definite quid pro quo that Theodore, who could be the most ruthless of Roosevelts, stoutly maintained he had never promised.

As things turned out for the wizard of railroad finance, he would probably have been better off if, in September, 1902, he had never stepped ashore from that rowboat to pay a call at Camp Elsinore on the banks of St. Regis Lake. Considering Mr. Harriman's shy persistence following that initial visit, it should be said that his complete failure to charm the Roosevelts was not for lack of trying.

CHAPTER XXIV

The Boat Train to Sagamore Hill

WHENEVER Bamie was away from Washington, at Oldgate in the spring and early fall or in the Adirondacks during the hot months, and when, concurrently, the President and his family were at the "Summer White House" at Oyster Bay, she wrote her brother regularly, as he wrote her, almost every week. Most of Bamie's letters during Theodore's first three and a half years in office, while he was serving out another man's term in the presidency, began with the intimate salutation, "Dearest Theodore" or "Best of Brothers," and there would follow some bit of news or political insight that might prove useful to him in planning his 1904 campaign. This was also the focus of all their private conversations at 1733 N Street when Bamie was in residence during the Washington season.

After Theodore had swept the country in 1904 with the largest popular vote a Republican candidate had ever received, the tone of Bamie's letters changed—from general advice tactfully offered to general approval conveyed with loving respect. Once he had become Chief Executive on his own, her letters usually began "My dearest Mr. President," "Beloved Mr. President," and sometimes, "My dearest Mr. P." It was as if that best of brothers had now earned and were entitled to a certain affectionate deference from his elder sister since he had now achieved all she had hoped he would. Very much on the grand scale, he had beaten the machine with which their gentle father had been too ill and too politically inexperienced to cope. And he had climbed his own political Mount Marcy to the summit with, relatively speaking, very few of the secret commitments that encumber others who reach such peaks. This was a source of pride to Bamie and Theodore both. Heaven help those who dared besmirch that record with insinuations that he had ever made a single deal on his way to the top. Woe betide anyone who tried to compromise him by angling for favors.

Just before she left for Washington in the fall of 1902, having spent a few days with the Reids in New York and at Ophir Hall, Bamie wrote "Dearest Theodore" letting him know that she had, in connection with the coal settlement, picked up "many odds & ends that in retrospect will be amusing." She would reach Washington the following week "& will hope surely to see you on Sunday." If he wished to have one of his private conferences at her house, "We would love to have you & any man you choose to bring for lunch or dinner." But, of course, she added, "If this is not feasible then somehow I will see you."

After Bamie's return to Washington, she discovered she had something to tell Theodore besides the latest disgruntled remarks of the President's Wall Street opposition. One evening, following her usual round of teas and receptions, she came home to find that her drawing room, which had once overflowed with the ridiculous floral tribute to Theodore when he became vice-president, had now been turned into a sort of railroad roundhouse for the most elaborate miniature train anyone had ever seen. With Hopkinson's help, small Sheffield had unpacked this lavish gift addressed to him and had set it up, with its intertwining tracks, and its wonderful little tunnels and bridges, so that there was hardly an inch on the drawing-room floor for anything but the train to move. Sheffield burst into tears when his mother, after reading the card that came with the gift, instantly told Hopkinson to pack his beautiful train away in a closet. It never reappeared, for Bamie politely but firmly posted the Union Pacific

Railroad, in miniature, back to its sender, Mr. Edward H. Harriman.

After this episode, Mr. Harriman's name did not come up very often in Washington or at the "Summer White House"— until the following autumn when that gentleman paid a second visit to his friends, the Reids, at Camp Wild Air. He missed Mrs. Cowles in the Adirondacks only by a few days. "We are all sorry at your leaving so soon," Mr. Reid wrote Bamie who had returned earlier than usual to Oldgate.

Mr. Harriman did not, therefore, figure in Bamie's annual roundup of news from the Adirondacks or in Theodore's letters to her at that time. Their interchange of correspondence during August of 1903 was significant in another respect, for it indicated that the President was beginning to find Mr. Reid useful not only as a source of information but as a disseminator in certain quarters of the presidential point of view.

Bamie had sent Theodore a letter Mr. Reid had received from Mr. Fahnestock, the eminent stock broker. In that letter, Mr. Fahnestock had written Mr. Reid that he and his friend, Mr. Stillman, president of the National City Bank, hoped the President was not planning to tinker with the currency. Times were hard that summer and credit was dear. There was near-panic in the market. They hoped the President, who usually had one ear cocked to the West, would not be tempted in the direction of greenbackery or, for that matter, to any further acts as upsetting to the market as his suit against the Northern Securities Company.

"Darling Bye," Theodore wrote Bamie at Camp Elsinore, "I re-enclose the letter. Please read this letter to Mr. Reid.

"I have had both from Mr. Fahnestock and Mr. Stillman very interesting letters written along the line of the one the former sent Mr. Reid. I agree entirely with the position therein taken. Our currency system as a whole is good. We are on a sound money basis. It would be disastrous the year before a Presidential election to try to remodel our currency laws. . . ." Then he gave Mr. Reid something to pass along where it would do the most good—his own evaluation of what the still-pending

Northern Securities suit had really accomplished. "The only effect," Theodore stoutly maintained, "... has been that the action in the Northern Securities suit undoubtedly stopped a movement for the wildest speculation in railroad and other combinations—a speculation which would have resulted probably by this time in a real panic—not such a stringency as we have seen this summer but a time of disaster like 1873 and 1893."

The task assigned Mr. Reid was to present Theodore as a true conservative interested only in preserving business from its own excesses. This evaluation of the President's intentions was correct, but Wall Street's antagonism to him did not make Mr. Reid's assignment an easy one. He apparently began his campaign of education at home. In a few days, Bamie wrote Theodore that Mr. Reid's father-in-law, Mr. Mills, "who more or less represents the wealthy class who are opposed to you (he is not)) feels you have strengthened your position greatly during the year by showing a greater grasp of business matters than they expected & by being conservative."

Also before leaving the Adirondacks, Bamie reported further rumors of softening in the Wall Steet opposition. She had lunched with her friends, the Bayard Cuttings, who were at their lakeside camp only six miles away by steam launch, and they, too, had spoken of this surprising new trend. "As usual," Bamie wrote, "he is a devoted adherent of yours & so is Olivia, but what was interesting was hearing them talk as to the change in New York among the wealthier men, that many of them began to realize that only through your administration were their interests safe."

In view of this reported shift in sentiment, it was no surprise to Bamie to learn, in the long letter she received from Mr. Reid soon after her return to Oldgate, that Mr. Harriman now wanted very definitely to be considered among the early conservative recruits who were jumping aboard Theodore's bandwagon a good year before the 1904 national election. There was nothing wrong with that, of course, but again, as in the episode of the train, there was something distasteful to Bamie about Mr. Harriman's devious methods. They were altogether different, for example, from the straightforward approach of Mr. Fahnestock and Mr. Stillman, and, as she could readily see from the contents of Mr. Reid's letter, Mr. Harriman's remarks were not freely and generously offered, as had been those of the Bayard Cuttings and old Mr. Mills. Why must the man be so circuitous and roundabout?

Between the railroad financier's first visit to Camp Wild Air and his second, the President had, in the course of events, been happy to sign into law, in February of 1903, the Elkins Act. This federal bill made it illegal, for the first time, for railroads to grant rebates to large shippers. Many railroads, though not Mr. Harriman's so far as he himself knew, were finding loopholes in that law and continuing to grant rebates. And now all the smaller shippers in the country were complaining louder than ever about this unfair practice. Astute Mr. Harriman could see the handwriting on the wall; the President would surely push for tighter laws to prevent this kind of unfair competition. Mr. Harriman had some good ideas himself about how a better law might be written, and he had, of course, every right to go straight to the President, as almost everyone else did, and give him the views of the smartest railroad man in the business. But the direct approach was apparently not in Mr. Harriman's impressive array of talents. Besides, he was linked by friendship and other ties to the regular Republican machine in New York and, in particular, to Governor Odell, whose loyalty often leaned away from the President towards old Boss Platt. Exposed through his long association with state politicians to their horse-trading methods, Mr. Harriman was evidently expecting to bargain with the President in the same manner, and this may have increased his natural circumlocution.

Mr. Reid's letter to Bamie on her return to Oldgate described in some detail the conversations he had been having with his important guest. Mr. Harriman's approach to the President by this means made no better impression than his first attempt.

"My dear Mrs. Cowles," Mr. Reid wrote. "The day he

arrived, Mr. Harriman casually mentioned to me that he had seen Mr. Pierpont Morgan the previous day shortly before starting up; that Mr. Morgan began talking in a critical way about the policy of the Administration and the probability that the President would be defeated by a conservative Democrat, as well as the certainty that he would not get the necessary support from the moneyed classes on account of their present dissatisfaction.

"Mr. Harriman went on to say that he had suggested to Mr. Morgan the overwhelming probability that the President would be renominated, and the certainty that it was to the interest of the moneyed classes to have the Republican nominee elected rather than take their chances with the Democracy. He then intimated that at present the labor unions seemed to be putting the President under more obligations to them than to the capitalists, and that it seemed to him to the interest of the capitalists to relieve that situation; and have at least as much claim upon him as the labor unions would have."

Whether or not Mr. Harriman had himself used such euphemistic phrases as "putting the President under more obligations" or having "as much claim upon him" to describe the tactics he said he had urged on Mr. Morgan, it was clear that he put his faith in the old quid pro quo technique. One other thing was certain, he wished to convey the impression that Harriman, not Morgan, was Theodore's friend. "All this," Mr. Reid assured Mrs. Cowles, "came out voluntarily and in the course of casual talk." Mr. Harriman had also mentioned "that he expected before long to see the President—qualifying this afterwards by saying at any rate he supposed he would have the opportunity. . . ."

Mr. Reid continued, "He has not referred to the matter since although he has spoken quite positively as to his belief that Mr. Morgan's political policy has been a mistake, and as to the desirability of securing the support of capitalists for the Republican nominee. He is also quite confident that there is nobody else in sight at present with any chance for the nomination, and he believes that the nominee can be elected. . . ."

Then, knowing Bamie's continuing interest in things political in the state of New York, particularly as they might affect Theodore's chances overall, Mr. Reid added, "I drew him out a little about Odell, to whom he is obviously as devoted as ever. He had no doubt about Odell's playing fair, but asked, rather significantly, whether the President had always been equally fair to Odell. I did not know exactly to what this referred, and hardly thought it expedient to inquire."

Mr. Reid concluded, "Of course, all this is confidential; but everything led me to suppose that he was not likely to object to the President's knowing what he said, and, in fact, was likely to welcome an opportunity for saying about the same thing himself to the President."

Mr. Reid's letter, which revealed the extent of Mr. Harriman's naïve and rather old-fashioned trust in cracker-barrel politics—while others almost equally powerful financially were beginning to acknowledge that Theodore was really trying to save them from impending social revolution—was probably delivered to Theodore by Bamie in person on one of her trips that fall across Long Island Sound in the presidential yatch, *Sylph*. This vessel had now begun to ply more or less regularly back and forth between New Haven and Oyster Bay whenever Bamie, or Sheffield and his nurse, were at Oldgate in Farmington and the Roosevelts in residence at the "Summer White House." There was a train each morning from New Haven on the Sound to Farmington not so many miles inland and a regularly scheduled return trip to New Haven every afternoon, and this convenient boat-train connection with the "Summer White House" was, over the years, a shuttle for all the young Roosevelts who went to stay, periodically, with Auntie Bye at Oldgate. It was also a convenience to small Sheffield, of whom Aunt Edith was extremely fond, whenever Bamie's son went to spend part of the summer with his cousin, Quentin. Occasionally, this direct route by train and boat was used by Auntie Bye herself whenever she felt she had something to discuss with Theodore that could not wait until they were all back together again in Washington for the season.

The decision this time on what to do about Mr. Harriman and his pussyfooting approach was undoubtedly Theodore's, for his native political acumen had been developed to an acute degree. In Lincoln Steffens' bowdlerized words, written for publication, in his halcyon days, Roosevelt "thought with his hips." And certainly here, once again, Theodore's political instinct was quick, sure, and ruthless: Harriman was on the hook; let him fish or cut bait.

The Roosevelts and the Cowleses returned to Washington in the late autumn of 1903 with plans for the gayest social season ever, one that seemed to draw all of New York to the White House except the Harrimans. That winter season in Washington, the society columns reported, was "significant for its size and brilliance." It was also observed that the Roosevelts were attracting to Washington "many of the great social and financial leaders of New York, who had never previously considered these official White House functions of sufficient importance for their attendance."

Down to White House functions came the Bayard Cuttings and the Whitelaw Reids, and the Vanderbilts, the Lorillards, and the Townsend Burdens. Many of the New York contingent stayed with Bamie or with her friend, Miss Mabel Boardman, head of the American Red Cross. Also, for the first time, artists and writers in number were asked to the White House and made welcome—the sculptor, Augustus Saint-Gaudens; John Burroughs and John Muir, naturalists; the painter, Frederic Remington; the muralist, John La Farge, and his son Christopher Grant, the architect; the writers, Booth Tarkington, Owen Wister, and Hamlin Garland; and favored journalists by the dozens, including Joseph B. Bishop, who was writing Theodore's biography, and the President's devoted admirer, Mr. William Allen White of the *Emporia Gazette*.

The whole tone and feeling of the social life that now revolved around the White House seemed to reach a fever pitch in the months before the Republican convention of 1904. In all these festivities, Edith was bearing up remarkably well. She had achieved a confidence and competence as First Lady that almost seemed to merit the friendly *Tribune*'s comment that she was "the most gracious and hospitable First Lady the White House had ever seen." Certainly Edith was presiding with dignity and tact, if not with warmth, over the largest social, literary, artistic, and political salon the White House had ever harbored. It dwarfed Theodore's own early dreams of the political-literary salon he had told Bamie he hoped for years before when he had been a young man ranching all alone out in the Bad Lands.

Handsome and statuesque, though not at all modish in dress, Edith seemed even to the Old Guard Republicans in Washington a perfect foil for her exuberant husband. Having overcome much of her shyness, her very reserve apparently endeared her to many of the regulars in "The Millionaires' Club" on Capitol Hill who were finding it increasingly difficult to get along with a president who wanted to lead rather than follow the wishes of the august Senate. It was, indeed, Mrs. Senator Foraker who observed that "At the Roosevelts' there was a great bubble and hum in the air, with Mrs. Roosevelt, loveliest and wisest of hostesses, keeping table talk off the rocks," and somehow, Julia Foraker added, in a dig at the incumbent who was also a candidate in 1904, the First Lady managed this, "in spite of our monologistic, aggressive, brilliant host."

CHAPTER XXV

"At Lunch with You We Find Life Gay"

THE fountainhead of all the frenetic activity at the White House was a president more active perhaps than any man in his mid-forties should be. Theodore always made up in enthusiasm and variety for what he lacked in natural skill, and he continued, long after a hearty appetite and sedentary hours at his desk had given him a paunch, to play a slashing bad game of tennis, to box, to wrestle, to scramble over hills and across streams, and to ride and jump his favorite heavyweight hunter, Bleistein.

A busy day in the Executive Offices and a cram-packed social calendar were never permitted to interfere with the fun he shared with his children and the more active members of his "tennis cabinet." If one of them happened to be ill, the President would say, for example, with the disappointment of a child, "Speck von Sternburg can't play with us today," even though Billy Phillips of the State Department, Chief Forester Pinchot, or James Garfield of the Bureau of Corporations and his two sons were always ready for tennis or a rampageous gallop through Rock Creek Park with the President and his children.

Nothing pleased Theodore more than to have Edith, who was an excellent horsewoman, go along with him on these rides. But, increasingly, the First Lady begged off because of pressing White House duties. After a year or two in residence, Edith was beginning to enjoy the White House much more than she had the Executive Mansion in Albany. Congress, during its early honeymoon with the new President, had appropriated funds for the first renovation and face-lifting the White House had received since it was burned by the British in 1812, and Edith, with the professional assistance of the New York architectural firm of McKim, Mead & White, took complete charge of all alterations. She did the whole place over to suit her own, and Theodore's, taste, and soon the State Dining Room bristled with the heads of buffalo, elk, and moose, even as the corridor to the first-floor dressing rooms was flanked by the white plaster busts of all the First Ladies.

Edith spent hours selecting the right chintz, the right wallpaper for each room. She supervised to the last detail everything done by Mr. Charles F. McKim, and he, poor man, went along as best he could with all the First Lady's wishes. Her wishes had the force of commands and were expressed in no uncertain terms.

"I do not like my writing desk at all," Edith told Mr. McKim, "I think it ought to be made to match the furniture which is rosewood, carved with big birds, I should say about fifty years old. Perhaps it would be a good thing to have a photograph taken of the bed. In any case I think the drawing of the writing table is ugly and inconvenient. About the Blue Room samples, before deciding I would like to know how the room is to be decorated, whether the silk is for covering the furniture or hanging on the walls, or whether you mean to use blue and gold brocade with it. . . . My daughter and I are rather converted to your dark blue, but the President still thinks it would make an ugly evening room, so to satisfy him I would like to know exactly how you propose it should look completed. . . ." and so on. Bamie had great sympathy for Mr. McKim, a friend from the days when, as a Lady Manager, she had worked with him on the Chicago world fair of 1893, but she dared not interfere.

Edith made other significant changes at the White House and

in its routine, and these considerably lessened her early dependence on her sister-in-law for advice on protocol and other social matters. Though the First Lady continued to be her own careful housekeeper, she took on a most efficient social secretary, Miss Isabelle Hagner, for she had come to realize that White House entertaining could further Theodore's candidacy in 1904, and prolong their pleasant days at 1600 Pennsylvania Avenue. Gaining confidence from her recognized success as a White House hostess, she also began to extend her activities even into the Executive Offices in order to be helpful to the President. All his personal mail went first to her, and Edith decided which letters should be brought to his attention. Moreover, since Theodore was much too busy to follow the newspapers closely, as he had once been in the habit of doing, Edith had the White House secretaries make abstracts of all important news comments, while she herself read three or four newspapers carefully each day. Again it was the First Lady who decided which items of news should be called to the President's attention, and now Edith, too, had become an extra pair of eyes and ears for Theodore.

Even as these new self-imposed tasks succeeded, Edith came to feel less threatened by Bamie's influence over Theodore and their children. Her occasional notes or chits to Bamie, from the White House and from Oyster Bay, now bespoke a more tolerant attitude, though they still carried a sardonic edge.

"I am delighted that you have disciplined Ted—Hurrah! Hurrah! Hurrah!" Edith wrote. "Perhaps you may have more effect than I have." Or, "You are most amiable to say that Quentin has been good—but I don't know whether you are truthful." Or, "Alice merely said, or rather wrote, that she had had a lecture from you, & I answered that it was probably needed. Let us hope it may do good, but Alice just loves to be looked at and talked about. She writes most amusingly from Bar Harbor." And again, after Theodore had been over to N Street without her, "Theodore says he ate a good lunch and does not feel languid so he is to have a milk punch tonight."

Following the advent of Belle Hagner, Bamie's presence at

the White House was not required so frequently as it had been though she and Captain Cowles were always included on the First Lady's guest list at all important official functions. Besides, just as midday dinner at Bamie's on Christmas Day became a tradition for family and close friends, holiday fun at the White House would have been no fun at all without Auntie Bye when they rolled back the rug in the State Dining Room, and everybody danced the Virginia Reel.

Though Bamie did not run in and out of the White House quite as often, she now seemed to see more of Edith herself than ever before. The First Lady's new attitude toward her sister-in-law, who was beginning to be plagued with twinges of rheumatism and arthritis, also took the form of encouraging her to take long, brisk walks. Since this seemed to help, Edith frequently dropped in on Bamie early in the morning to take her out walking or along to the inexpensive little dressmaker the First Lady had discovered on H Street or on the train with her to Baltimore for a secret shopping trip and a visit to an art gallery.

Despite rheumatism, arthritis, and increasing deafness, of which few were aware, Bamie participated with pleasure in these impromptu command expeditions without letting them interfere in the least with her own social life. Outside the White House, she remained supremely Washington's foremost hostess. No important dinner party or ball was complete without Captain and Mrs. Cowles. She was also in constant demand, from Cabinet and ranking senatorial wives to pour at their teas or, whenever they were ill or out of town, to preside for them, with their husband's delighted approval, at their dinners. Bamie's own entertaining was like nothing else in Washington, lively, informal, and graced by good conversation. Her luncheons, in particular, attracted many of the younger men who made the wheels of government and diplomacy run smoothly, and these were once memorialized by Jonkheer R. de Marees van Swinderen, Minister from The Netherlands, in a grateful note of acceptance in these rhyming words:

Dear Mrs. Cowles:

A line to say,

At one o'clock on Saturday,
   I lunch with you no matter what
   May be neglected or forgot
Within the office where I sway.

You add your "lunch is short alway;
That busy guests may run away."
   But such a one be sure I'm not—,
      Dear Mrs. Cowles.

Van Swinderens go, van Swinderens stay
As any other mortals may
   And find life runs within a rut
   Alike for Dutch and Yankee—but
At lunch with you we find life gay,
      Dear Mrs. Cowles.

In short, the bubble and hum that Mrs. Senator Foraker had observed at the White House often reached its gayest crescendo on N Street, and this was assured whenever, as frequently occurred, two or more Roosevelts gathered there on the spur of the moment. It was exhausting, as Corinne Robinson Roosevelt wrote her daughter on one of her visits to Washington, but it was wonderful how everyone naturally gravitated to Auntie Bye's. After "a chatty evening" at the White House, Corinne "stayed in bed till about eleven and all the rest were going to ride on horseback. Such a cavalcade! Uncle Ted, Aunt Edith, Father, Cousin John, Mr. Fergie, Ethel and Archie and Ted. We were all at lunch at Auntie Bye's and the riders came in just as they were, liberally sprinkled with mud. Sheffield, Quentin and Archie looked so cunning at their own little side table."

The younger Roosevelts, in particular, had a way of dropping in without notice at N Street whenever they found out from Pinckney, the White House steward, that one of their number had drifted over to Auntie Bye's or that something might be going on there. One day, for example, Bamie had set the tea hour aside for a potentially rewarding tête-à-tête with a diplomatic friend who was likely to be a heavy contributor to Theodore's 1904 campaign, only to have this plan, much to her amusement, completely disrupted.

"I had promised to be in by 5:30 for a quiet visit from Larz Anderson," Bamie told Corinne in describing this particular afternoon, "and I wish you could have seen the result! Ruth Morgan walked around with me. In two minutes we were joined by blessed Ethel who said she could not resist coming in for a jammy bread and butter tea. Alice in five seconds appeared, having heard from Pinckney that Ethel was here, then the Cameron Winslows drifted in and Sheffield was brought down." After that, "other men came in" and "on this composite group entered Larz, most elegant and wealthy and disgusted!"

Bamie's own reaction to such interruptions was chiefly one of delight, for Roosevelts of every age were welcome at any hour, for a day, a week, or a winter. After her debut in New York, Eleanor Roosevelt, who had no other place she could really call home, came to spend two winters in a row at 1733 N Street with her "dear Auntie Bye." As for Alice, who could not stand the Blue Room, the Green Room, or the Red Room for informal entertaining, she virtually lived at "The Little White House" during her five winter seasons in Washington before her marriage.

In 1903 and 1904, when Eleanor was living with Auntie Bye and going everywhere with her in Washington, she frequently encountered her more glamorous and sophisticated cousin, Alice, but their paths merely crossed on N Street, as they had on occasion before, making no lasting impression on either of them. They had nothing in common, before or later, and each had already branched out in her own social direction.

First cousins, with Eleanor the younger by less than a year, Bamie's two very gifted nieces were, from childhood, poles apart. Where Alice had been a beautiful, headstrong child, beloved first by Auntie Bye and then alternately spoiled—by doting grandparents and by Theodore—and held in leash by Edith, Eleanor had been entirely orphaned at a very early age and reared, almost as in a convent, in a gloomy old house on the Hudson by a fanatically religious grandmother. Had it not been for Auntie Bye, who had Eleanor with her as much as she could, and for Mlle Souvestre, Eleanor might never have come out of her shell at all.

When Eleanor was very young, Grandmother Hall, who wished to have as little to do with any of the Roosevelts as possible after Elliott's death, had allowed her to go on an occasional visit to Uncle Ted and Aunt Edith at Sagamore Hill. From the first, Eleanor had been no match for rambunctious Alice, who rode her pony hell-for-leather over high jumps and tried in a dozen other tomboyish ways to outdo Ted, Jr. Yet Eleanor had not been a coward. She, too, had trailed Uncle Ted, "Mr. Fergie," and all "the bunnies" in that perilous game of follow-the-leader up Cooper's Bluff and down, in a precipitous two-hundred-foot slide, to the water's edge. She, too, had jumped, with eyes tight shut and holding her breath, into the water over her head when Uncle Ted threatened to throw her off the dock if she wouldn't at least *try* to swim. It had mattered to Edith, who had to make the necessary repairs before Eleanor could be returned more or less intact to her grandmother, though not to Eleanor at all, when Uncle Ted in an ebullient game of blindman's buff had inadvertently ripped all the buttonholes in her petticoat and all the gathers out of her best frock. Whatever Uncle Ted did, Eleanor adored him extravagantly.

After one of Eleanor's too infrequent visits to Sagamore Hill, Aunt Edith had written Bamie, "Poor little soul, she is very plain. Her mouth and teeth have no future, but the ugly duckling may turn out to be a swan." Always acute in her judgments, Edith never made a better prediction. As she grew older, Eleanor's unfortunate teeth could almost be ignored as she developed the grace of a tall, gawky cygnet. Her eyes were truly lovely, and she had an endless capacity for interested listening that reminded the family of Auntie Corinne's "elbow-in-the-soup" manner. She also had some of Auntie Bye's warmth and vitality. Bamie's godchild, Helen Roosevelt, once remarked that "Eleanor reminds me so much of Auntie Bye sometimes that she makes me jump."

It was no doubt this combination of charms that attracted haughty, handsome Franklin when he first encountered Eleanor as a grown-up young lady at a holiday party given by the Douglas Robinsons at their place in Orange, New Jersey. They became secretly engaged in the autumn of 1903 at the beginning of Franklin's senior year at Harvard, the year following Eleanor's New York debut.

Though Eleanor had been launched in New York society under the kindly wing of her cousin and godmother, Mrs. Henry Parish, she had found the experience an excruciatingly painful one. It would have been even more so, perhaps, if "Mr. Fergie," that handsome older man-about-town and loyal family friend, had not beaued her everywhere and seen to it that she never lacked partners.

While staying on with Mrs. Parish and waiting for Franklin to break the unwelcome news of their secret betrothal to his doting mother, Eleanor had tried, after her debut, to evade as many social engagements as possible. She had been brought up by her grandmother to prefer the path of duty to society, and she had always hoped to find affection and her reward in being useful to others. Now, she embarked, with a few other serious-minded postdebutantes, on a round of good works that included instructing underprivileged young women in morris dancing down at the settlement house in New York's lower East Side. It was when Auntie Bye heard that her old friend, Sara Delano Roosevelt, had, in true matriarchal fashion, taken Franklin out of college for a brief winter cruise in the Caribbean in the hope that he might forget his infatuation for his fifth cousin, that Auntie Bye came to "poor, dear Eleanor's" rescue. She urged Eleanor to come to Washington and stay as long as she pleased.

During the winter seasons of 1903 and 1904, then, 1733 N Street harbored both Alice and Eleanor, Auntie Bye's two favorite nieces, both refugees from what they considered intolerable situations at home. But where Alice was as quicksilver, a dashing, modern Atalanta or Diana of the Chase, in turn pursued by an assortment of swains, Eleanor felt very much the shy sit-by-the-fire, in love with one man, and rejected. Only Bamie took the trouble to encourage in her the potentialities that would one day make her, through that man, a veritable Athena to the modern democratic world.

Though Eleanor was shy, she was no fool. Under the wing of Auntie Bye during those two winters in Washington, she attained a certain deeply simple wisdom that helped her through many later crises, and there she had her first taste of the kind of life she herself would one day lead in the White House. She listened and took in everything. She knew from studying Aunt Edith, as she said later, "what it meant to be the wife of a President"; it "was the end of any personal life" of your own. She knew also how important Auntie Bye was to Uncle Ted, for, as Eleanor recalled, "There was never a serious subject that came up while he was President that he didn't go to her at her home on N Street and discuss it with her, before making his decision. He talked things over with her, that was well known by all the family. He may have made his own decision, but talking with her seemed to clarify things for him."

The winter season of 1903–1904, Eleanor's first in Washington, was a particularly busy one. That winter Bamie's social calendar had already been filled right through into spring even before she left Oldgate in the autumn. Eleanor, who went with Auntie Bye to many official functions, may often have wished herself back in the comparative calm of the New York social whirl. As for the frivolous young set led by "Princess Alice," the hectic social pace in Washington on the eve of the national elections in 1904 was apparently not quite fast enough for them.

CHAPTER XXVI

A Curious Double Diplomatic Mission

THE year 1904 was a trying one for all the Roosevelts. Unusually edgy about his chances for nomination and election, Theodore was alternately cast down and overconfident. He could laugh, but not very much, at Edith's remark, "My lot is harder than yours. You only have to live with me, while I have to live with *you.*" Giddy "Princess Alice" was getting into all sorts of mischief that all too often made headlines in the gossip sheets and the yellow press. This caused Theodore to be even more irritable. In an election year, Alice's widely reported little eccentricities—taking with her to Newport a pet green lizard named "Emily Spinach" or driving in a racing Panhard nonstop, at an average of forty-five miles per hour, completely unchaperoned, from Newport to Boston, in six hours—could seriously affect his standing at the polls.

It was under this mounting family tension that the Roosevelts held their New Year's Day reception of 1904. *Town Topics* said it was the most brilliant of all, as the dazzling uniforms of the diplomatic corps vied with the "ravishing toilettes" of the ladies. In its account of this White House occasion, society's favorite gossip sheet made no reference to the sedate British delegation or to little Commander Kogoro Takahira, the Japanese ambassador, in his somber blue naval uniform—the one guest present who knew exactly, to the day and the hour, when

231

during the very next month the Japanese navy would shock the whole world by launching its surprise attack on the Russian fleet at Port Arthur. All the dazzle and ravishment at the White House on New Year's Day in 1904 seems to have been supplied by the Russians and their allies in Far Eastern affairs, the Germans. But the whole effect was such that Henry Adams, who came out of seclusion occasionally to attend Roosevelt functions, had to acknowledge that "this place is now the political center of the world."

Baron "Speck" of the German Embassy, with his lovely wife, the former Lily Langham of Louisville, Kentucky, went down the presidential receiving line in the most picturesque uniform of all. The little Baron was wearing the sky-blue tunic of a colonel of Saxon Hussars and shiny black Tartar boots to the knees. The Speck von Sternburgs were eclipsed only by irascible old Count Cassini and his pretty twenty-year-old daughter, Marguerite, Countess Cassini. The Russian Ambassador, who had a tendency to throw "pink fits," so Secretary Hay said, whenever he visited the State Department on his diplomatic errands, bristled with waxed mustachios and gold braid, and, on his arm, the little full-blown Countess looked more ravishing than all the other diplomatic ladies in a filmy white gown, Russian sables, and a huge black picture hat. This was annoying even to the Teutonic ladies of the corps who should, following the Kaiser's lead, have felt friendly towards the Russians, but the egret feathers atop the pompadours of Mme de Quadt, wife of the counselor of the German Embassy, and of Baroness Hengel-müller von Hengervar, wife of the Austrian ambassador, quivered alarmingly whenever they saw the little Russian. Night after night, dining out in Washington, they had to give precedence to that naughty, precocious young lady. She always went in to dinner before them on the arm of their host, to which, of course, she was entitled simply because her father's lengthy sojourn in Washington made him the dean of the diplomatic corps.

Naturally, the lively little Countess and "Princess Alice" very soon discovered they had in common, among other things that included the attentions of young Congressman Nick Longworth of Ohio, an overpowering desire to *épaté les bourgeois*, and they became, for a while, fast friends in their joint effort to shock staid Washington society.

Chiefly because it was a source of embarrassment to the family in the White House, the girlhood friendship of the Countess and the "Princess" was of short duration, but it was fun while it lasted. The undisciplined ways of the pert-faced little Countess, who was indeed wise beyond her years, were not at all to Edith's taste, yet she could scarcely forbid the daughter of the dean of the diplomatic corps the White House. Theodore tried hard to be friendly and *gallant* whenever he encountered the Cassinis, startling the Countess with his hearty handshake and his booming, "You're a dead ringer for Anna Karenina." He believed, nonetheless, that the Countess encouraged Alice in her frivolous ways, quite forgetting that his daughter was more apt to be leader than led in all the social pranks they concocted. He trusted the Count even less, for the Russian Ambassador was both knowledgeable and wily, and, from Theodore's point of view, he was proving extremely difficult to deal with. From Count Cassini's point of view, the American State Department was "only a branch of the British Foreign Office." He had good reason for this belief as Theodore's foreign policy, shared all along in advance with his somewhat Anglophile sister, began to crystallize and take shape.

While one of Bamie's nieces refused, as her father said, quite fiercely, to have any "pronounced serious tastes" and continued to "lead the life of social excitement," the other profited by her two winters at Bamie's on N Street by attempting to understand some of the serious subjects usually under discussion between Uncle Ted and Auntie Bye. They would become so engrossed in these tête-à-tête confabs that Theodore often lost complete track of time. Suddenly he would pull out his watch, groan,

"Good heavens, E-die will be wondering where I am," and bolt for the door, his coattails flying.

After Uncle Ted's precipitous departure, Auntie Bye was always happy to answer young Eleanor's questions, and these were many and probing, for she, too, had been early exposed to Mlle Souvestre's world view. Unlike Alice, who was to come by her keen interest in politics and people much later, Eleanor was from the beginning quietly and shyly enthralled by all the exciting palavers and the discussions about diplomacy on N Street.

One of the serious subjects that came up in Washington while Eleanor was making her home there was that sudden revolution in Panama in November of 1903 that enabled Theodore to boast indiscreetly some years later, "I took the Canal." Of course Theodore's pounce on the Canal Zone was entirely his own, and merely a forerunner of other executive gambles he was to take later, especially in foreign affairs. No one in the family, and certainly not Eleanor, ever thought Auntie Bye had had a hand in the Panamanian Revolution—except perhaps to know all about it, as Theodore seems to have, well ahead of time—any more than they credited her, keenly interested as she always was in naval affairs, with sparking Theodore's brilliant idea of sending the American fleet around the world in 1907. That idea could well have been a spontaneous and perhaps simultaneous inspiration ignited by one of Bamie's quite frequent summer visits to their old friend, Admiral Alfred Thayer Mahan, that strong advocate of sea power, who was then in retirement on Long Island. The President always regarded this circumnavigation of the globe by the United States fleet, with its brand-new battleships painted a sparkling white, as his most important single act in office, a necessary show of American force to all other great powers, including the Japanese, after Russo-Japanese hostilities had ceased. Bamie may certainly be credited with endorsing this idea and with following very closely every detail of advance preparation for the long voyage since Will Cowles was then assistant chief of the Bureau of Naval Operations.

There is no doubt that Bamie was privy to all of Theodore's skillful power plays in foreign affairs while they were being hatched, just as she was an early confidante in his trust-busting activities, his campaign tactics, and his conservation program. But no one will ever know—since Bamie held the view that women should remain in the background and this conviction was enforced by her fear of antagonizing Edith—to what extent, as Eleanor once put it, she "clarified" Theodore's ideas. She herself covered her traces entirely. Her letters to Theodore were eventually burned by Edith, along with all such very personal family letters, and Bamie herself, as an old lady, burned many of Theodore's letters to her. There is no longer a single photograph extant showing brother and sister together in their political prime.

On the other hand, despite her innately bossy nature, she may have gone no further in her advice to Theodore than to others in whom she was, conceivably, not quite so extravagantly interested. Nieces, nephews, and the children of her friends, who tended increasingly to bring all their problems to her, insisted that her advice was always "general." As Eleanor recalled, Auntie Bye would say, "Now this is what I think. I can only give you my best judgment. It is of course for you to decide."

However Bamie dealt with her "Best of Brothers," and as he later became, her "Dearest Mr. P.," whether by subtle suggestion, by simply listening, or more forthrightly, as was her nature, she was undoubtedly most helpful to him in foreign affairs, keeping the channels open to the British, through her friends in their Washington Embassy and in London. These channels between the two great English-speaking nations had, since the War of 1812, shown a surprising tendency to become clogged, and Bamie in her time certainly helped unclog them. There had always been, according to some experts in these matters, more United States diplomatic controversies with Great Britain—over Newfoundland fishing rights, over the location of the Canadian border, and over British interests in Latin America

—than with any other nation. But such difficulties had always been resolved, more or less amicably, and of course they always had to be in the face of some greater, common danger.

The President's sister, through her continuing correspondence with friends in England, and as this new intelligence was applied against her thorough understanding of British politics, customs, and temperament, could not only interpret for Theodore the often obscure attitudes of the British Foreign Office, but sometimes even anticipate them. This was invaluable to Theodore who, more than any other president up to that time, acted as his own secretary of state, particularly during 1904–1905 when Secretary Hay was a dying man. In the diplomatic maneuvers leading up to the Peace of Portsmouth, which was Theodore's greatest international coup, he acted quite on his own, without consulting the State Department or relying on his regular ambassadors abroad, but he had the benefit of Bamie's sound judgment and general advice. Frequently, only Bamie—and Edith—knew what he was up to, and it was with Bamie's help that Theodore set up one of the strangest extracurricular missions in Anglo-American diplomatic history. This mission, entrusted to the Roosevelts' close friend, Sir Cecil Spring-Rice, was highly unorthodox, but it was most effective in helping Theodore achieve status as an international peacemaker at the end of the Russo-Japanese War. And the Peace of Portsmouth, which Theodore brought about, as he and the British put it, "quite off his own bat," was a diplomatic milestone that marked, as all the world would see, America's entry into the international arena as a world power.

During the Russo-Japanese War, which began on the night of February 8, 1904, with Admiral Togo's surprise torpedo-boat attack on the rickety Russian squadron anchored at Port Arthur, the British behaved as though they feared to trust the word of the President of the United States. The suspicious Foreign Office, headed by Lord Lansdowne, the Conservative party's foreign secretary, took a dim view not only of Alice's chum, Russian

Countess Cassini, but more especially of Theodore's close friendship with Baron Speck von Sternburg, who had now been elevated to full ambassador at the German Embassy in Washington.
Suppose, through his fondness for Baron "Speck," the President
were being taken in by the blandishments of the militaristic,
flamboyant Kaiser? Suppose he were being lured to the side of
Wilhelm, and therefore of the Czar, in the Far Eastern conflict
between Russia and Britain's allies, the Japanese? The British
were counting on Japan as a buffer against Russian expansion in
the Orient that they feared might extend even into India.

The British had assurances, of course, from Cabot Lodge on
one of his visits to England, that the President promised to be
a silent partner to the secret agreement Britain had made with
Japan giving her a free hand in China. But this, skeptics in
the Foreign Office pointed out, was purely a personal assurance.
It carried with it no guarantee, other than Senator Lodge's own
educated guess, that the Senate, which must ratify all United
States treaties and foreign agreements, would go along with the
President. A gentleman's agreement was binding, so the British
Conservatives then in power said, when the Foreign Office made
it, because, under the British Cabinet system, it spoke for His
Majesty's Government. This was obviously not so under the
American system and Constitution. Unless the President could
win over the Senate, and the people of the United States as well,
what was his personal promise worth?

In their dubiety, the Foreign Office under Lord Lansdowne
made the mistake of sending to Washington in the fall of 1904,
as the new British ambassador, Sir Mortimer Durand, a rather
stiff, unbending sort with whom Theodore just could not sit
down and talk freely as he did with Baron "Speck" and French
Ambassador Jules Jusserand, both of whom were charter members of his "tennis" or "kitchen cabinet." Theodore found Sir
Mortimer, whose seniority in the Foreign Office made him eligible for the Washington vacancy created by the death of Sir
Michael Herbert, more inscrutable than any Oriental. Bamie,

too, considered "poor, dear Sir Mortimer" not quite up to the usual British best in nimble diplomacy. The President kept trying to convince the Foreign Office, through regular diplomatic channels and through friends of Bamie's, that he would much rather have with him in Washington, their old friend, Sir Cecil Spring-Rice, who was then stationed at the British Embassy in St. Petersburg. This was unthinkable to British protocol. Lord Lansdowne was sorry but Sir Cecil, no matter how persona grata he might be to the President, was distinctly junior to Sir Mortimer. Besides, Durand's recall would mean his public disgrace; no British diplomat, however uninspired, deserved such treatment when he had but a few years to go before retirement.

But Theodore saw the immediate need for open and direct communication between Britain and the United States. They had to decide together what the picture in the Far East should be when the Russo-Japanese War ended. He knew, and Bamie knew, that "the honest broker" in any peace negotiation often gained some territorial or trade advantage out of the bargaining around a conference table. If Germany, for example, or even England, were that "honest broker" at the end of the war, Theodore wanted to be sure that American interests, now extending into the Pacific and across, would be protected.

Just before the New Year in 1905, with Russia getting the worst of the war, Theodore wrote urgently to First Secretary Henry White at the American Embassy in London: "I intend to appoint you Ambassador to Italy after March 4. Now I wonder if you could arrange to have the Foreign Office send Spring-Rice over here to see me for a week? There is no one in the British Embassy here to whom I can talk freely, and I would like to have the people at the Foreign Office understand just my position in the Far East, and I would like to know what theirs is.... I do not know whether it is my fault or Sir Mortimer's but our minds do not meet; and in any event, I should be unwilling to speak with such freedom as I desire to anyone in whom I had not such absolute trust as I have in Spring-Rice, both as regards his intelligence, his discretion and his loyalty."

On the same day, the President wrote two other letters, one to Spring-Rice himself: "It is always possible that Japan and Russia may come to terms of agreement.... I wish to Heaven you could come over, if only for a week or two...." The other letter, on the same day, to House Speaker Joseph G. Cannon, indicated the President was canny enough not to trust any great power when nations sat down together at the bargaining table: "No one can tell how long the war will last, or whether when peace comes a great effort may not be made to save the honor of both combatants at the expense of the remaining outsiders, or by the aid of some outsiders at the expense of the remaining outsiders." To insure that American interests in the Pacific and in the Far East would not suffer at the hands of any "honest broker," including the British, the President urged the Speaker to support his program for building up the American navy.

Exactly what commitments Theodore exchanged with the Foreign Office through "Springy" during that special emissary's mysterious visit to Washington, official diplomatic history does not disclose. One American historian hazards the guess that Theodore managed to convince the Foreign Office, through Springy, that American interests in the Far East were identical with those of the British. Then the President agreed that, though he would act on his own in relation to any developing Far Eastern situation without consulting the British Foreign Office in advance, he would keep them fully informed of any move he made, not through their Embassy in Washington, but in code via Springy in the British Embassy in St. Petersburg! Whatever the specifics of the secret agreements were, Theodore thus got Springy for British ambassador, in spite of Foreign Office protocol, and since Springy was strategically situated at St. Petersburg, he, as well as the regular American ambassador there, would keep the President well posted on the rapidly deteriorating situation in Russia proper.

Interestingly enough, the way was paved for Springy's unusual visit by his good friend and Bamie's, Sir Ronald Ferguson, whom she invited to stay with her at 1733 N Street in January of 1905 just before the Foreign Office finally agreed to let Springy himself come over. The details of Sir Ronald's advance visit were arranged through his younger brother, Fergie, who wrote Bamie from New York in mid-December: "As to Ronald —unless you really find him handier on the 1st of the year— I imagine he would be as well suited himself if he came after the excitement [of the usual New Year's celebration at the White House] is over—for I fancy he's going kind of slow & easy and cares more to see the few he knows at a quiet gate.

"He'll probably go to the Durands' for a couple of days—and any time the White House says will of course suit him.... I'll warn him not to get too entangled at the Embassy—tho' I fancy they'd let him do just as he likes.

"If this suits you, he cd. take in Corinne's dinner on the 3rd (arriving 31st) & come next day to you till the Reids or others arrive ... and after that go to the Embassy or the Grafton Hotel."

When Sir Ronald arrived in Washington, he himself had something of the Foreign Office's suspicious attitude. He wrote Springy that "a proposal from our F.O. commits the more vulnerable empire to every consequence, whilst that of the most autocratic President commits his country to nothing." But, after several sessions with that autocratic President, arranged by Bamie, Sir Ronald began to change his mind. He put the question quite bluntly to Theodore, "What, Sir, can you do to implement your understanding with us on China?" As the intimate friend and right-hand man of Sir Edward Grey, who was in line for foreign secretary when the Liberals, as soon happened, took over from the Conservatives, Sir Ronald had every reason to ask the question. Theodore replied, equally bluntly and honestly, "I can't tell you that. All I know is that I would do my best to carry my people with me." He undoubtedly reminded Sir Ronald that he had managed to carry the Senate and "my people," *post factum*, with him on Panama. And he also reminded Sir Ronald that *he* had managed to act more boldly than either Balfour or Lansdowne of the Conservatives when it came to matters of foreign policy. Sir Ronald, solid Liberal party man, was impressed. He wrote Springy, "Our people have not yet grasped the full significance of this President's status." Sir Ronald was also happy to report that he had paved the way for Springy's special mission with Sir Mortimer, who now realized how badly understaffed he was at the British Embassy in Washington. "All here agree," said Sir Ronald, "that you should come on leave as a sort of unofficial go-between." Sir Ronald, eldest of the Fergies, took home with him a signed photograph of the President, and this, as he later told Bamie, always hung in a place of honor in his library because "the Colonel" was "the public man to whom I gave most confidence."

From shipboard en route home, after seeing his brother, Bob, in New York, Sir Ronald wrote Bamie thanking her "once & again & with all my heart" for her hospitality and for the opportunity to know her brother better. He hoped Springy's mission for Lord Lansdowne, which immediately followed his own visit, would be successful. As for himself, he would do two things as soon as he got to London: He and his wife, Lady Helen, were going to the Greys immediately on arrival. "The best thing I can do now is to put things to Grey & consult as to our action" when the Liberals come into power. Then he would go personally to the Foreign Office, to which he had already "sent a stinger," and warn them that the real trouble in Washington was that poor Sir Mortimer just did not have enough competent help at the Embassy.

Fergie, too, wrote Bamie after his brother's visit. "I'm satisfied," he said. "How about you? You were certainly good to him down your way to judge by the smile that wouldn't come off when he returned to New York.... He's well worried about things (under the smile) & it will do him a lot of good & he may do others (good) on both sides, I hope, and that is precisely the frame of mind I wanted him to go home in.

"Also he found things out for himself & with no aid of mine (but of others!) which was also desirable—for the information is now his own & he knows it—for he naturally told me none of it (nor found me anxious to know!)

"He really was very nice, wasn't he? And you were probably altogether too good to him—(But you have the right!)

"I enjoyed my little end of it very keenly."

Following Sir Ronald's highly successful preparatory mission, Theodore was, toward the middle of January in 1905, delighted to receive a cable in code from First Secretary Henry White in London: "Spring-Rice sailing next Wednesday steamer Baltic. Would like to stay with Henry Adams. . . ." Theodore sent this cable to ailing Secretary Hay, with a triumphant little note: "This is very interesting. Won't you ask Henry if he can put up this distinguished member of the kitchen ambassadorial circle— if there are members of the Kitchen Cabinet, why cannot there be kitchen ambassadors?"

Springy spent his week in Washington at the home of his old friend, Henry Adams, who enjoyed being party to Theodore's irregular diplomatic methods even as he grumbled about them. He was devoted to Springy from his earlier days in Washington, but still Springy was "mad, of course, but not more mad than an Englishman should be." As for Theodore, he could, "thus playing the king and avowedly acting without Secretary of State or Cabinet . . . fetch us up somewhere with our heads against a stone wall," said fierce old "Uncle Henry."

During Springy's visit, there were conferences with Theodore at Henry Adams's house and also at 1733 N Street, with Cabot Lodge in attendance. Just before Springy left Washington, he paid an open, official call on the President with "poor, dear Sir Mortimer" in tow. And Sir Mortimer may or may not have known it at this time, but, for the remaining months of Russo-Japanese hostilities and all through the peace negotiations, the British Embassy in Washington was being snatched right out from under his nose and transferred—by Theodore, Bamie, Sir Ronald, and Springy—to St. Petersburg.

En route home aboard the *Britannic,* after his busy week in Washington, Springy wrote Bamie: "I am now at sea. I mean literally. . . . I can't tell you how strange it seems to be really gone—I suppose I ought never to have returned to America as now I have more friends on that side than at home and who knows when I shall see them again. But I do hope I shall see you and that in some small way I may be able to repay part of the kindness shown by you and Teddy."

Before returning to St. Petersburg, in his curious and unprecedented double role as diplomatic representative of His Majesty's Government as well as personal emissary of the President of the United States, Springy naturally went first to London. He saw, of course, Sir Ronald and Lady Helen and altogether agreed with the Fergusons that there was no one more astute politically, as Sir Ronald always said, than Bamie when it came to "political judgment," and, as Lady Helen said, that Bamie "was the best of the bunch and the most satisfactory to meet." He reported to Lord Lansdowne the mysterious specifics on which his special mission had come to agreement with the President, and then he was rewarded by an audience with the King himself. King Edward asked Springy what he thought the President of the United States would like as a gift to cement these close new ties between England and America, and Springy had the temerity to suggest the Hampden miniature from the King's own Windsor Castle collection. Since John Hampden was that famous British gentleman who once stood up against Charles I himself and refused to pay the king's ship-money tax unless parliament voted it, and performed this brave deed almost 150 years before any American ever thought of dumping tea in Boston harbor, Edward VII was immensely tickled with Springy's suggestion. He promptly sent the Hampden miniature off to the President, who always treasured this particular personal memento of his years in office. To Theodore it was an acknowledgment that, during his administration, the United States had truly come of age as a great power, for King Edward's gift was given with the familiar light intimacy that one monarch might use in addressing another. In his personal note to the President, he asked not only to be remembered to Mrs. Cowles but hoped "that Mrs. Roosevelt and the members of your family are in the best of health."

CHAPTER XXVII

"Dreadful Worst Time"

FOR Bamie the year 1904 was both the worst and the best in her life. March and April were the cruel months, for two serious mishaps at sea threatened to cut short the long and faithful naval career of her "dear Mr. Bearo." But Captain Cowles survived in heroic fashion, and in November there came the heartwarming nationwide endorsement of Theodore and his policies. This was the apex of her brother's political career and of his popularity and, for Bamie, the happy culmination of nearly half a century of devoted effort in his behalf. The part she had played in Theodore's triumph was implicit in the wording of the postelection telegram sent by her good friend, Lizzie Reid, not to the President but to Mrs. Cowles at the White House where all the family were gathered to hear the returns that gave Theodore his unprecedented landslide. Mrs. Reid's telegram to Mrs. Cowles read:

"Hearty congratulations not only on the wonderful victory but because the strain is over, and all is well."

Fergie, too, wrote Bamie, "And now all's well & happy?" How very different, he recalled, from those awful spring days in 1904 when they had sat together on the rocks overlooking the lake in Central Park worrying about the fate of Captain Cowles— "When you were having your dreadful worst time," Fergie said.

The strain of those early spring days, even more than the

excitement of the presidential campaign during the summer and fall, aged Bamie more than any previous ten-year span in her life.

The year had begun proudly for Captain and Mrs. Cowles. At the happy apex of his own career, Captain Cowles had been given command of the battleship, *Missouri,* one of the big new capital ships built under Theodore's farsighted naval policy. Early in February, Bamie joined her husband at Newport News, Virginia, to take part in the stirring shipboard ceremony as Captain Cowles assumed command of his huge, newly commissioned ironclad. She stayed on for a month at Newport News to be with the Captain and wave good-bye from the dock when the *Missouri* set off on her first cruise to join the North Atlantic fleet at Guantánamo Bay. Only a few days later, on routine maneuvers between Guantánamo and Pensacola with the fleet, which included four other battleships, Captain Cowles ran into frightful bad luck.

The *Missouri* was next to last of the five big ships of the line, with the *Illinois* following her at the standard ten knots and at the standard five-hundred-yard interval when the fleet admiral's flagship broke out the order—"Ships left half turn." As all the other ships smoothly and in unison moved majestically into the half turn to port, the *Missouri* veered sharply off to starboard. The steering mechanism on the brand-new ship had suddenly gone awry. First she answered the helm exactly contrariwise, and then the steering engines quit altogether. Captain Cowles quickly reversed his main engines to bring the *Missouri* to a standstill. Captain Bradford of the *Illinois* took rapid evasive action, but the *Illinois* was caught in the port quarter by the battering ram of the *Missouri.* Captain Cowles's prompt reversal of his engines minimized the impact but still the damage to the hull of the *Illinois* was considerable.

The Naval Court of Inquiry into this unhappy accident at sea sat for weeks during that sad spring. Captains Cowles and Bradford were temporarily detached from their commands to appear and testify at length before the Court. Testimony, often conflicting, was taken from dozens of other participants and witnesses during the seven sessions the Court of Inquiry held behind closed doors. During those long weeks of waiting for the findings of the Court to be reported, Bamie managed most of the time to keep up a confident front, particularly for Will Cowles. Behind the confident mask, she was altogether in despair. Here, for the first time in her life, was something she could do absolutely nothing about.

Bamie knew the navy inside out. She was well aware of the antagonism the navy line always felt towards any "civilian" interference, and this included not only the Secretary of the Navy and his assistants but the President himself, despite his title of commander in chief. It was hard, but she could understand her brother's decision not to send even a personal note of sympathy to Will or to communicate with him in any way until the navy's Court of Inquiry had a chance to ascertain all the facts connected with the accident. Theodore just had to bend over backwards. Already the anti-Roosevelt press was beginning to make election-year capital out of the incident at sea. There were rumors, quite contrary to fact, that the President had sent two telegrams to the Court of Inquiry on his brother-in-law's behalf. Such Washington gossip, sparked no doubt by the jealous wives of naval officers without White House connections, made the weeks of waiting for the naval Court's findings even more intolerable. Bamie had seen only too often how such petty jealousies, or rivalry among the highest ranking officers themselves, could destroy the most useful service career. But she also had tremendous admiration and respect for navy tradition. The Court of Inquiry would try to be objective and impartial, though its findings might be harsh. Whatever the Court's report, Bamie was resigned to the fact that she could personally make no appeal from it to the President as any other service wife would be quite free to do. Even if she were to consider such an appeal for Will's sake, she could not, for Theodore's.

The effect of the accident upon his campaign for election was certainly uppermost in Theodore's mind when he wrote his brother-in-law on April 1, the day the Court announced its findings:

"I have fully understood the anxiety and strain you have been under, but I did not think it was well for me to write you until the case was all over, because it was possible that I might have to pass on it. . . . It has been very hard for Anna too. Of course, the fact that you are my brother-in-law makes people on the alert to criticize anything you do. If you will let me suggest one thing, I should say that if you come either to New York or Norfolk I would stay pretty steadily with the ship and not come to Wash., and would so far as possible avoid giving any excuse for people saying that you were having overmuch social entertainment on board the ship. Until the election is over there will be in a lesser degree the same necessity for caution on your part as on mine."

The findings of the Court of Inquiry, published in the *Army & Navy Journal* on April 2, 1904, were somewhat equivocally phrased, but the initial blame for the accident was placed where it rightly belonged, on the builders of the new *Missouri*, for faulty construction of her steering mechanism. The first cause of the accident, the Court held, was the failure of the *Missouri*'s steering engines, for which its officers and crew were hardly responsible. But "the secondary cause," said the Court, was the *Missouri*'s failure to communicate fully, through *all* the proper signals, with the *Illinois*.

By quickly reversing his ship's engines, the Court said, "Captain Cowles acted promptly and decisively in the expedient he adopted to control his ship's headway. . . ." The Court also found that Captain Cowles had given prompt orders to his officer of the deck to hoist the breakdown flag and reverse the speed cones, which should have told the captain of the *Illinois*, then a good four hundred yards distant (1) that the *Missouri* was in distress and that he should give her wide berth, and (2) that the *Missouri*'s engines had been reversed in an attempt to bring her to a standstill. The point of conflict in the testimony was how soon the *Missouri*'s young officer of the deck had executed the orders Captain Cowles had given him. Officers and crew of the *Illinois* testified to a man that they had seen neither the breakdown flag nor the reversed cones in time to avert collision. The Court held that the *Missouri*'s officer of the deck had failed to execute Captain Cowles's orders promptly, and it further held that Captain Cowles himself should have ordered additional signals, indicating his "course to starboard by one blast of the whistle and of backing by three blasts. . . ." Had this been done, then perhaps the *Illinois* "could have maneuvered to avoid collision." The findings concluded with, "The Court recommends no further proceedings."

The Court's findings and recommendation that there be "no further proceedings" were concurred in by the Secretary of the Navy and by Admiral Dewey of the United States fleet, but gossip in and out of the service did not permit the matter to rest there. The worst offender was that scandalous sheet, *Town Topics*, whose attempt at wit this time was unusually heavy-handed:

"The recent bumping of the *Missouri* and *Illinois* has been a shock to social as well as naval circles, for Captain Cowles, the President's brother-in-law, is in command of the *Missouri*, the vessel supposed to be at fault. . . . The affair . . . has revived the ingenious suggestion made some time ago that official society ought to have a warship of its own, and that the *Missouri* be anchored off Mount Vernon and kept in commission permanently for dinners, dances or ocean cruises. There has always been more of the air of the drawing room than of carnage about the quarter-deck of the *Missouri*."

Events within the week were to make the editor of *Town Topics* wish he had eaten the words of that last sentence one by one. Meanwhile, the *Army & Navy Journal*, ever quick to imagine and resent possible civilian influence or interference in service affairs, made veiled reference in an editorial, on April 9, to the possibility that "favoritism" had played a part in the Court's findings. The editorial asked for full disclosure of all testimony before the Court of Inquiry "for the instruction of the Navy." Why, the *Journal* wanted to know, had not Captain

Cowles, when his steering mechanism failed, attempted to guide his ship by means of his twin-screw propellers? Or were they, too, involved in the *Missouri*'s mechanical failure? Why had Captain Bradford not been able to maneuver out of the way of the slowly drifting *Missouri*? Were our expensive battleships so cumbersome—at a time when the warships of Japan were proving surprisingly maneuverable against the Russian fleet—that *our* naval captains would apparently, in time of war and in the midst of attack, expect a kind enemy to oblige with all the signals prescribed by official United States navy regulations? Licking its grim chops, the line officer's journalistic bible then suggested that an open court-martial rather than a closed Court of Inquiry might "offer the only certain means of clearing the reputation of an officer and showing, where necessary, that he has not escaped through favoritism."

That last sentence in the *Journal*'s editorial was a dead giveaway that someone on the magazine was out after, not Captain Bradford, perhaps not only Captain Cowles, but the President himself. It was no surprise to Bamie, or to Theodore when she reported it to him, that Whitelaw Reid, who had his ways of finding out such things, had discovered the *Army & Navy Journal* editorial had been written by a close relative of the managing editor of the *New York Sun*, a Republican paper more opposed to Theodore's policies and his candidacy than any other in the land.

Still this was all part of the great game of politics as played in America, and Theodore was as helpless as Bamie to do anything about it. The *Town Topics* squib was too ridiculous to deserve comment. That frothy sheet could scarcely cast reflections on the solid career of a competent naval officer who came from a long line of dauntless New England sea captains dating back to the old clipper-ship trade with China. But the *Army & Navy Journal*'s questioning of the Court of Inquiry's findings and particularly its use of the word "favoritism" sent Theodore's blood pressure sky high. And this occurred at a time when he was having his own worst troubles with the publicity attendant on the behavior of his high-spirited daughter. Now, as Theodore's campaign for his nomination and election quickened, photographers from the *New York World* and the *New York Journal* dogged Alice's every step. They even caught her in the act of laying bets out at the Bennings' racetrack, and one photograph showed "Princess Alice" gleefully holding her skirt out as an apron to catch the day's winnings being poured into her lap by her escort, Congressman Nicholas Longworth. Somehow, perhaps through Whitelaw Reid, that photograph was suppressed, but the anti-Roosevelt press continued in full cry.

Poor Theodore, and poor family, for the presidential candidate in the White House could let off steam only to them or in his personal letters. One to Kermit, then away at Groton, indicated the temperature at which Theodore's blood boiled under such frustration.

"Dear Kermit," the President wrote the young man who was one of Auntie Bye's favorites, "Auntie Bye and Mr. Bob Fergie dined here tonight. . . . The *World* and *Journal* try to get pictures of poor sister when she is at the races; and the *Army & Navy Journal* which ought to be a reputable paper, has made as foul and dirty, and as false, an attack on Uncle Will as ever was made by any dog in human form. . . . It is awfully hard work to keep one's temper in public life. Such infamous lies are told."

Theodore's violent reaction to the *Army & Navy Journal*'s rather nasty insinuation that Captain Cowles might have been let off lightly by the Court because he was the President's brother-in-law was a gauge both of Theodore's touchiness at that time and of his respect for Will Cowles's nautical experience and competence. Captain Cowles's subsequent behavior, above and beyond the call of duty, in a second truly horrible, and completely inexplicable, accident at sea aboard the ill-fated *Missouri*—just two weeks after the Court of Inquiry's report on her collision with the *Illinois*—more than justified the President's faith in him. It gave the lie, with sad vengeance, to all of "Uncle Will's" gossiping detractors and sent shivers down the spine of anyone who recalled *Town Topics'* ghastly reference to the lack of an air of "carnage about the quarterdeck of the *Missouri.*"

On April 13, 1904, five officers and twenty-four men of the *Missouri* lay dead, and two more dying, on her decks as the result, during target practice with the North Atlantic fleet, of a twelve-inch gun explosion in one of her after turrets. There would have been hundreds of other casualties had it not been for Captain Cowles's lightning-quick response to one of the worst disasters ever suffered by the United States navy in peacetime. The newspapers played up the personal courage of a captain who dared dash into the fiery gun turret seconds after the explosion at the risk of his own life to bring out the dead and wounded, but even more than that it was Will Cowles's level-headed judgment in handling his ship during the disaster that saved the *Missouri* itself and its full complement from almost sure destruction. In the *Army & Navy Journal* for April 16, 1904, the full report of Will Cowles's heroism, and the *Journal's* now wholehearted acknowledgment of his nautical ability, covered three pages. Perhaps no other officer in United States naval history had ever had such complete vindication in so short a time at the hands of that august service publication.

In its lead editorial, "Tragedy on the *Missouri,*" the *Army & Navy Journal* said:

"The shock of horror which the frightful accident on the battleship *Missouri* sent to the heart of every patriotic American was immediately followed by a thrill of ineffable pride in the dauntless heroism which distinguished the conduct of the survivors of that appalling tragedy. Turning from the mute victims, whose lives were destroyed almost in an instant, to their more fortunate comrades, we find every man at his post, cool-headed, alert and eager to sacrifice himself to save others. It is doubtful, indeed, whether the recent naval experience of any nation, in peace or war, has presented a finer example of real heroism than the conduct of the *Missouri's* commander, Captain Cowles, in rushing into the turret of death and bearing out a dying member of the fated gun crew. . . ."

As to the possible cause of the explosion, the *Journal* doubted whether that would ever be ascertained, "As every man in the turret and all but two in the handling room below were killed" and "there is no one left to tell the story." But ". . . There is not the slightest evidence at hand that any of the usual precautions for firing big guns were lacking."

The *Journal* reminded its readers that "The accident on the *Missouri* is only one of a series which has attended the development of modern warships, modern ordnance and high explosives" and that such accidents "are among the penalties of naval greatness." The *Journal* also remarked that "on the day of the explosion of the *Missouri*, Russia lost a splendid battleship, the *Petropavlovsk* and her commander, Admiral Makaroff, together with Admiral Molas and upward of 700 officers and men, at Port Arthur. . . . Their passing was no more heroic nor any more worthy of honor than that of the splendid young officers and men who in the flame-scourged turret of the *Missouri* offered up the last supreme sacrifice of duty to the flag they loved."

In its news story about the *Missouri* tragedy, the *Journal* gave further details that completed the picture of Captain Cowles's cool and heroic actions in the face of certain death at sea. The Captain himself had declined to be interviewed, but another officer of the *Missouri* offered this eyewitness report:

"It was in the loading of the fourth shot when apparently the first half of the charge had been rammed home that while the second section was being rammed home the gases from the shot previously fired or particles of the cloth cover ignited the powder. That something was wrong was evident from a dull thud which was heard. Immediately after, without any loud report, flames burst from every part of the turret. Then another explosion occurred much worse than the first and louder in its report. The sixteen hundred pounds of powder in the handling room immediately below had become ignited. . . .

"Promptly fire quarters were sounded and the ship responded to a man. There was no disorder, every man did what he had been trained to do in just such an emergency. Captain Cowles at once gave orders for the flooding of the magazine, and in less than five seconds after the first explosion, it is said that several streams of water were playing on the burning turret and in the handling room. To Captain Cowles' call for volunteers every man aboard ship responded and pleaded to go into the burning turret to rescue the victims. Captain Cowles led the way before the fire was out and practically took his own life into his hands. Down into the handling room he plunged followed by Lieutenant Hammer, ordnance officer, and Lieut. Cleland Davis. In a few seconds the captain came up well nigh stunned by the smoke and gases, carrying a blue jacket in his arms. As he staggered to the deck with the dying blue jacket several officers rushed to him and prevented him from going below again. Several men who attempted to follow Captain Cowles into the awful hole of dead and dying humanity suffocated on the threshold.

"It all happened in a very few minutes. Officers and men were lifting out the dead and wounded before the flames in the turret had been extinguished. In a very few minutes surgeons from the *Texas* and the *Brooklyn* were assisting the surgeons of the *Missouri* in caring for the wounded. In the turret twenty-five men were found dead lying in a heap. On top of them lay the officer of the turret, Lieutenant Davidson, who had evidently, after the first explosion, ordered his men to leave the turret and was waiting for them to get out before going himself. So mutilated were the bodies that they could scarcely be recognized. The flesh fell from the bones in flakes at a touch. In the turret crew only one man was found breathing and he died as soon as he reached the deck."

Then said the *Journal*, "The reports of the accident agree in the statement that it was the good judgment and quick action of Captain Cowles in ordering the magazines flooded that alone saved the ship. The door was in all probability opened and the metal on the outside was shrivelled by the heat. Had the magazine exploded nothing more would have ever been heard from the ship or her men." The *Journal* also quoted a report in the

New York Herald that further confirmed Captain Cowles's excellent judgment:

". . . The *Missouri* was in danger of being run on shore as well as being blown to pieces by her magazine. . . . When the explosion of the powder charges in the after turret was followed by the more terrific eruption of the charges in the handling room, the officer of the watch thought that the magazine itself would be the next to go, and headed the ship for land, intending to beach the craft before the magazine went off.

"This was prevented by Captain Cowles, who had rushed to the scene of danger at the first alarm. Personally directing the men who had responded to the call for fire quarters, and leading the rescuing party, this cool-headed officer was made aware of the change of course and hurried an aide to the bridge with orders to shift the helm and stand off shore. The ship, it was said, was within 250 yards of the shore when the order was given and it was only by stopping the engines and backing them hard that the vessel was prevented from striking."

Captain Cowles's first act after the disaster was to notify immediately the families of the dead officers and men aboard his tragic ship as it limped into Pensacola harbor. Bamie's first act when she heard the awful news was to start a subscription fund for the relief of those families, and Theodore, who led off that fund with a contribution of $100, recommended to the Secretary of the Navy that a special commendation for bravery be given all surviving officers and men aboard the *Missouri*. Bamie's next move was to go to Will Cowles. Before she left, acting in the best tradition of brave navy wives, she asked her brother to urge the Secretary of the Navy to request fast action on repairs for the damaged *Missouri* so her husband and his ship could rejoin the fleet for duty at sea with all possible speed.

Modest Will Cowles, who remained aboard his ship in Pensacola harbor, did not even realize at first that he had become a hero. He feared to get in touch with anyone in the White House, or even with his wife. Instead he sent off a sad little note to Senator Lodge thanking him for his "cheering telegram" and telling Cabot that the *Missouri* itself was saved "thanks to fine work on the part of officers & men, dead & living. . . ." In a postscript, Captain Cowles added:

"Love to Nannie—Anna has been shivering with horror, I know, blessed person. My love to the Presidential family. I have not dared to write him, but now I believe I can thank him for his contribution—WSC."

CHAPTER XXVIII

Happy Honeymooners

WITH the election of 1904, happy days began for all the Roosevelts, including Eleanor and Franklin, since Franklin's mother at last became convinced it was useless to oppose their early marriage. From the start, Auntie Bye had championed this match, not for Eleanor's sake alone, but because she found Franklin attractive, debonair, and a young man of considerable promise. She had him down from Harvard often to visit at 1733 N Street while Eleanor was there, and she always took them with her to see "Uncle Ted," whom Franklin as well as Eleanor admired extravagantly—before Woodrow Wilson became his hero.

Since "Cousin Sallie" was very fond of Bamie and quite susceptible to her general advice, Sara Delano Roosevelt's opposition to her only son's desire to marry the President's niece finally collapsed in the fall of 1904. After their engagement was announced, they paid an ecstatic visit that brilliant autumn to Auntie Bye at Oldgate in company with a gay assorted group that included Bob and Hector Ferguson, young Congressman Fred Gillett, Cousin Rosy Roosevelt from Hyde Park, Mabel Boardman and Ruth Morgan, and Eleanor's cousin Alice, who showed no signs of wanting to settle down herself and get married. "Princess Alice" was hard to please. She even thought handsome

Franklin "80% Eleanor and 20% mush." The years did not change her opinion.

Once his election seemed assured, Theodore, too, reached a state of euphoria reminiscent of his early honeymoon days. He wrote Bamie that he and Edith were "having a really lovely time in Washington. The house is delightful. We breakfast on the portico, and then stroll through the garden; and at night we walk through the garden or on the terrace. Tomorrow we intend to cut church, and to ride out to Burnt Mills to spend the day walking through the gorge, and come back in the evening. I certainly do not know any one quite like Edith. She spent part of the hour before we left Oyster Bay reading Shakespeare's King John aloud with Ethel and Ted and taking one or more parts— both of the children being delighted when it fell to Mother to speak as the executioner."

When the election returns came in that November, Bamie and Alice, too, were both in the Red Room at the White House with all the members of the Cabinet and their wives whom Edith had invited, as Theodore laughingly told Bamie, "for a little feast which can be turned into a festival of rejoicing or into a wake, as circumstances warrant."

Theodore's last real political opposition had died with the Old Boss, Mark Hanna, in February of 1904, and he knew very well he was bound to win. It was, of course, a famous victory but in his continuing state of euphoria, Theodore made the political blunder of his life, before Edith or Bamie could do anything to stop him.

Alice would never forget her father standing in the doorway of the Red Room being interviewed by reporters on his triumph at the polls, or what he said then. On this occasion, in Edith's words, Theodore really "tied with his tongue" the biggest knot of all that he "could not undo with his teeth."

"On the 4th of March next," Theodore told the reporters, "I shall have served three and a half years and this three and a half years constitutes my first term. The wise custom which limits the President to two terms regards the substance and not the form. Under no circumstance will I be a candidate or accept another nomination."

This statement was to plague him sorely in two ways. As their time in the White House ran out, the Roosevelts, deep in their hearts, did not really want to leave Washington. Moreover, a president who announced to Congress in advance that he would not be around four years hence, automatically divested himself of some of the political power he needed both as Executive and as head of the party.

During his second term, as Theodore had insisted on calling it that evening in the Red Room, he was to meet with increasing opposition on the Hill, particularly from the entrenched Republican regulars in the Senate, but for a while all the Roosevelts were ecstatically happy straight through the most incredible Inauguration Day, on March 4, 1905, that Washington had ever seen. Corinne Roosevelt Robinson wrote her friend, Mrs. Parson, all about it.

They left New York "on the 3rd . . . a Rooseveltian multitude, in a special car with Emlen and Christine Roosevelt as our kind hosts. . . . Corinne, Eleanor and Franklin went to Bamie's house, Emlen, Christine, Douglas and myself to the White House and my boys to the Lodges. . . . At 10 o'clock we were all in the White House Hall, including Bamie's party and my boys to see him leave for the Capitol. . . ."

Theodore had a tremendous escort composed of the Inaugural Committee, the entire Cabinet, the Rough Riders, and Troup A. An hour later, the rest of the White House party followed, "Edith, Alice & Ted in the first carriage, then Mame * (looking not a day over sixty though she must be 80 I think!) with Kermit, Ethel, Archie and Quentin, then Douglas and myself in the White House brougham and then Bamie's party and Christine and Emlen."

As they drove to the Capitol, dark clouds threatened and the wind began to blow fiercely. They went first to the Senate Cham-

* Mame was the nurse Edith had had as a child, and nurse as well to "all the bunnies."

ber for the vice-presidential ceremony and then out to the inaugural platform where they "realized with joy" that Theodore was "standing on the platform in a blaze of sunshine and that every black cloud" had been "swept from the sky."

Corinne continued: "What a wonderful sight we look down upon! On the left—all the young cadets, on the right the middies from Annapolis and beyond as far as the eye can see a surging crowd, with every eye bent on Theodore, as old Chief Justice Fuller with his silky white hair floating in the wind administers the oath of office. . . . During part of his father's speech, dear little Quentin, who could not see very well, was 'boosted' on to the platform by two of the most reverend of the Chief Justices!"

At the White House luncheon following this ceremony on the East Portico of the Capitol, there were twenty proud guests, including Mrs. Cornelius Vanderbilt, but most of the company was either a Roosevelt or a Sewell, for Theodore's old guide and ranching partner had brought his children and grandchildren down with him from Maine, making nine Sewells in all. As Theodore dashed off to review the strangest inaugural parade in American history—which featured Bad Lands sheriffs and cowboys, Indian chiefs in feathers and warpaint, Grand Army of the Republic and Spanish-American War veterans, Filipino scouts and Puerto Rican militia and the anthracite coal miners marching with their banner, "WE HONOR THE MAN WHO SETTLED OUR STRIKE"—he was heard to boom out most politely, "I was *overjoyed* to see the Sewells, & very glad to see Mrs. Vanderbilt, too."

No doubt Mrs. Vanderbilt was there at the invitation either of Bamie or of "Princess Alice" for Theodore had an inherent dislike of the merely rich, and Edith, so Alice said, almost equated "fashionable" with "sinful." Theodore often complained that his daughter spent "most of her time," as he wrote Corinne, "associating with the Four Hundred—individuals with whom other members of the family have exceedingly few affiliations." He did not mean Bamie, for she liked some of the fashionable rich and did not cross them off her list for that reason alone.

Though Alice was seldom home, she would not have missed the 1905 inauguration for anything. She had made her own special preparations for enjoying it in her own way—having got ready a series of signs to put up on the homes of some of her friends in the Northwest part of town, for the amusement of herself and the tourists who flocked to Washington for the inauguration. That silver-tongued Irish orator, Congressman W. Bourke Cockran of New York, was to have received one reading, "Here Lives the Irish Ambassador. All He Needs Is an Embassy." For the Misses Patton who lived very near this eligible widower, there was another: "This Is the Irish Embassy. All It Needs Is an Ambassador." From putting up these slightly sadistic signs, Alice was dissuaded at the last moment only by one of her then current beaus, Bertie Goelet, who was stopping with the John R. McLeans during the inaugural festivities. But Bertie Goelet made no objection when, under cover of darkness on inauguration eve, Alice placed one of her signs under the broad library window of his archrival for her affections. After the parade on Inauguration Day, many tourists were convulsed to see a young man playing his violin quite unconscious of the sign beneath his library window that read: "I Live Here, Nicholas Longworth."

Such behavior did not endear Alice to Nick's devoted mother who lived with him in Washington when Congress was in session, but it certainly intrigued her son. In 1905, during an extended trip to the Orient, chaperoned by the William Howard Tafts, Alice and Nick became engaged. The exact date is not known, for when Mr. Taft said to Alice on shipboard, "I think I ought to know if you are engaged to Nick," she replied characteristically, "More or less. More or less."

Alice had not quite made up her mind even when the Taft party arrived in Japan, for during a ball in Tokyo honoring the distinguished American visitors, the following conversation took place between Alice and Lloyd Griscom, Bamie's young diplomatic friend who was then with the United States Embassy in Japan:

Alice: "Lloyd, do you see that old, bald-headed man scratching his ear over there?"

Lloyd: "Do you mean Nick Longworth?"

Alice: "Can you imagine any young girl marrying a fellow like that?"

Lloyd: "Why, Alice, you couldn't find anybody nicer."

Alice: "I know, I know. But this is a question of marriage."

Alice, who was twenty-two to her groom's thirty-six, married Nick Longworth in the East Room of the White House on February 17, 1906, before five hundred assembled friends and relations. Alice Roosevelt Longworth, tenth in the historic line of White House brides, wore white satin, ancestral lace, and a train five yards long. Her cousin, Franklin, whose wife was expecting her first child and could not be at the wedding, most gallantly arranged the bride's veil and train for the battery of photographers who took her wedding portrait. The bride also wore a diamond brooch from her father and a diamond necklace from the groom. All the other presents were equally staggering. As they began streaming into the White House, the President had found it necessary to announce it would not be proper for his daughter to receive official presents from other countries.

"So like him," said that sardonic friend, Cabot Lodge, "to come to that decision after the gifts were on the way."

"At least," said Bamie, delighted as always with presents that were real possessions and not just frittery—as well as with the marriage itself that she hoped would have a settling influence on her niece—"At least, Theodore didn't issue his awful ban before the string of pearls from Cuba arrived."

There was another wedding during those middle years in Washington, but about this one, Bamie was of two minds. It was another May and September match, between her devoted young friend and admirer, Fergie—who was the same age as Nick Longworth when he married Alice—and Isabella Selmes of Boone County, Kentucky who, at eighteen, was also the belle of New York and Washington. That wedding took place in

June of 1905—only three months after Eleanor and Franklin were married on St. Patrick's Day in New York, with Theodore, at Bamie's request, there to give the bride away. At the time of Eleanor's wedding, "Mr. Fergie" was too ill with a fever to attend, so the bride and groom stopped off at his apartment to see him before entraining for Hyde Park. But, two months later, resilient Fergie was sufficiently hale and hearty to pursue his Isabella all the way down to her home in Boone County.

Some members of the family thought Bamie never forgave the Kentucky beauty for capturing her favorite young man, but the letters at that time from Fergie to Bamie do not altogether support that opinion.

Fergie wrote Bamie from Kentucky in May of 1905 on the very day Isabella said she might marry him: "Anna, dearest, she does care, bless her and it's a rainy day & I'm awful happy & hope she may be half so much."

Bamie promptly had Isabella up to Oldgate early in June, and after that Fergie wrote again:

"Dearest Anna—You must have been very dear to the child for she came back as happy as could be. . . . It was so sad not to be able to come and see you, too, but perhaps she was far happier without me! (and you too!)

"We met at the train & took an electric hansom up to the park (which she says means a positive announcement in all cases) and sat on some rocks by the lake that we sat on in the spring when you were having your dreadful worst time—and now all's well & happy?

"Shall come up Friday this week if you will have me. . . . Love to Sheffield and tell him the radishes were delicious."

Fergie and Isabella were married very quietly in New York late in June and went directly to Oldgate for the first few weeks of their honeymoon. There Bamie's only other guest at the time was Cousin Sallie Roosevelt who very much missed her son, now on his own extended honeymoon abroad with Eleanor. After their visit to Oldgate, Bob Ferguson took his bride home to

Scotland to be welcomed by all the other Fergies, and there the two honeymooning couples met, as Fergie reported to Bamie:

"It's been so good having Eleanor & Franklin here for a day or two," and then he touched on *the* great event of the fall of 1905, the one that Theodore had brought about, quite off his own bat, "What a glorious business the peace affair was & is & will be & how cleverly & steadily managed & controlled. . . ."

To which Bamie said amen, for Theodore's triumph in bringing Russia and Japan peacefully together again—which brought him the Nobel Prize—took her mind completely off her own personal affairs. Bamie was now fifty and for the next four years she would devote her entire, undivided attention to her "dear Mr. Bearo," as well as to her "Dearest Mr. P."

From the very beginning of his so-called second term, however, Theodore did not rely quite so heavily on his sister as a sounding board and as purveyor of general advice, if that was the sort she offered him; at least, his visits alone to N Street were soon less frequent than they had once been. The First Lady herself was taking an increasingly active interest in the President's political problems and in his continual rumbles with Congress. Here Edith was at her best in helping Theodore realize where his own strengths and weaknesses lay and particularly in telling him whom he could trust and who his enemies were.

Curiously enough, Bamie bowed most gracefully to this slight but perceptible shift in their mutual relationships, and this came about for a number of reasons other than the very real fact that Edith had partially preempted, as was her right and duty, the role in Theodore's affairs that Bamie had so long played. For one, the height of Bamie's usefulness to her brother had been when she was helping him become president and during his first years in office when it was not at all sure he would be elected to a second term of his own. For another, Will Cowles was doing so well in his career that Bamie, from 1905 on, took an increasing interest in what her own husband was up to.

Will Cowles's naval career was not spectacular, but he made

a very real contribution, as chief of the Bureau of Equipment beginning in 1906, to Theodore's expanding "Big Navy" program. Contrariwise, Will Cowles's career was handicapped rather than helped by his having a brother-in-law in the White House, particularly one so sensitive as Theodore to the slightest hint that he might be playing favorites. As a result, though devoted to Will Cowles, Theodore always fell over backwards to appear absolutely objective on any matter touching the career of Bamie's husband. Not that Will Cowles needed his help, for he was made chief of the Bureau of Equipment, quite on his own merits, being particularly well liked on the Hill by the committee members who voted the necessary appropriations for the navy. Here, there was nothing to prevent the Captain's wife, if not his brother-in-law, from being most helpful, and Bamie, more than most navy wives, had a way with her as a hostess. Key people on the Hill, as well as the navy's top brass, thoroughly enjoyed Bamie's parties and at homes, and they were always as welcome as any of the "dips" or the many distinguished visitors to Washington who continued to gather at "The Little White House" on N Street.

Following his appointment as chief of the Bureau of Equipment, Will Cowles put in frequent appearances on Capitol Hill to testify, in convincing, straightforward fashion, on the increasing needs of the navy for capital ships and for heavier armament. These appearances also served to convince the public of the need for a bigger fleet with better firepower following Theodore's coup for peace, at Portsmouth.

So effective was Will Cowles, who was made admiral in 1908, that the navy would not let him go when he became eligible for retirement the following year. Much to Admiral Cowles's delight, he was asked to stay on as chief of the Bureau of Equipment, and he remained on active duty in that post until 1910, after the Roosevelts left Washington and well into the Taft administration.

In one of his final acts as president, Theodore did venture to recognize Will Cowles's very solid achievements by sending him in command of the United States squadron detailed to attend Quebec's tercentenary early in 1909. On that occasion, the proudest in Will Cowles's life, he had the pleasure of flying his admiral's flag, for a few brief weeks while on temporary detached duty from the Bureau of Equipment, on the handsome new battleship, *New Hampshire*. This was truly the high point of a long and faithful career, during the last four years of which Admiral William Sheffield Cowles undoubtedly did more for his brother-in-law than the President had ever had to do for him.

CHAPTER XXIX

Theodore vs. "The Plutocracy"

AS Theodore's turbulent "second term" began, Henry Adams wrote a friend in England, "Washington is now rather more amusing to me than other places, because I can laugh at all my friends who are running what they call a government. . . . This country is terribly interesting. It has no character but prodigious force."

Theodore had more than enough of both, but he had blundered in announcing prematurely, by three or four years, his departure from Washington. His troubles began immediately, even before the 1905 inauguration—with the lame-duck or do-nothing session of Congress. On hearing the President's election-eve statement, old Speaker Joseph G. Cannon rubbed his hands together and said, "Congress will pass the appropriation bills and mark time," and that was the beginning of the growing revolt on the Hill by most of the party regulars.

From the lame-duck session, Theodore got little more than two new battleships and this, he complained, put the navy only "a good second to France and about on a par with Germany." When that Congressional session ended, he wrote Bamie at Oldgate, ". . . I am then left to shoulder all the responsibility due to their failure . . . and have to spend an industrious summer engaged in the pleasant task of making diplomatic bricks without straw."

During the summer of 1905, Theodore did just that, and did it magnificently. He had no big navy, no big stick with which to force Japan and Russia to sit down together peacefully at Portsmouth, New Hampshire, in August of 1905, or to beat off any so-called honest broker among the great powers intent on carving themselves a slice of territory in Pacific waters out of the peace settlement. But he had the force and character to take a colossal chance; he acted as if he did have that power, as if America were already one of the great ones, capable of acting the honest broker without territorial ambitions of her own at the end of that disastrous Far Eastern conflict.

All during the summer of 1905, as John Hay lay dying, Theodore was his own secretary of state, and he completely bypassed the State Department itself. In June, he was writing his sister, "I want to see you and tell you about the Russian-Japanese matter." Preliminary overtures for peace were coming through to him from Commander Takahira, the Japanese ambassador in Washington. Theodore had decided to bypass the Russian ambassador, who now had good reason to have his "pink fits." The President dealt directly with the Czar in St. Petersburg, through the American ambassador, George Meyer, seconded and ably supported by Cecil Spring-Rice of the British Embassy there. Throughout July, only Bamie, Edith, and Cabot Lodge knew the secret channels of negotiation the President was using or the diplomatic methods he employed in his efforts to bring the Russo-Japanese war to an end. And "Springy," whom Bamie had helped wangle into his curious double-diplomatic post in St. Petersburg, was the keystone of all of Theodore's delicate behind-scenes maneuvers. It was Cecil Spring-Rice's utter trust in the President of the United States that brought in its train the confidence of the British Foreign Office and that, in turn, committed in support of the President's negotiations the might of a navy still second to none. Without that borrowed big naval stick, Theodore would never have been able, when the chips were down around the table at Portsmouth, to speak so softly, or so successfully.

On the domestic scene all during 1906 and 1907, there were rumors that the President might take back his spur-of-the-moment statement of November, 1904, made at the door of the Red Room. No doubt Theodore himself weighed carefully whether it would go down well with the American people if he said he had really meant he would not run for a second "elective" term and that 1904–1909 was, of course, the first of that particular sort. His daughter, Alice, would not give up hope that her father might be drafted for another term, in spite of his words, until the Republican convention of 1908 nominated Taft. But Theodore could not bring himself to say the weasel words; they went against the grain. Instead, thinking "with his hips," he used the rumors that he might retract and run again to overcome some of the opposition building up against him in Congress.

With these rumors, and a number of other political inducements—the carrot of presidential patronage, for example, that could be extended or withheld, and a very large stick threatening New England protectionists on the Hill with tariff reductions—Theodore managed to put through Congress in 1906 a bill that set an historic precedent for all government regulation of business, in the public interest, from that time on. Regulation of some sort, many had to admit, was long overdue. The need for it had been recognized a generation before by that astute observer of the American scene, Henry Adams, in an article for the *Edinburgh Review* in 1869: "The great corporations, whose wealth and power were now extending beyond the limits consistent with the public interest, found no difficulty in buying whatever legislation they wanted from State legislatures." By Theodore Roosevelt's time, the power of "the great corporations" extended much more subtly even into the United States Senate.

The Hepburn bill, for which the President fought tooth and nail, made possible for the first time effective regulation, in the public interest, of the country's railroads. Under this act, the Interstate Commerce Commission, on receipt of a complaint, could declare any particular railroad rate unreasonable and then set the maximum rate to be charged. This bill was the spearhead of Theodore's continuing attack on irresponsible business and, mild as it was, business then regarded it as giving license to Government to interfere in matters that were none of its concern.

Theodore's carrot-and-stick prodding of a Congress dominated by men friendly to the railroads and the great corporations was a masterpiece of political maneuver. By May of 1906, the dramatic last-ditch fight against the Hepburn bill put up by the Big Four in the Senate had collapsed and Theodore wrote his sister, who was then visiting Admiral Mahan and some of her wealthy friends on Long Island, "The rate bill went through in fine shape. It has been strengthened in the Senate and will now undoubtedly pass substantially in its present form. . . ."

Passage of the Hepburn bill and what it portended for all business did not escape that brilliant little financial wizard, Edward H. Harriman. He knew the Administration was out to pillory the railroads for being overcapitalized, and in August of 1906 he made a dramatic move that endeared him to all stockholders: He announced that the dividend on the stock of one of his large railroads had been upped from 6% to 10%. He explained to one of his directors, though not to the public, "The time has come when instead of putting most of our money back into the property, we should give a larger share to the shareholders. If we don't, the Government will take it away from us." Naturally, with this sizable increase in dividends—which Harriman's enemies called "stock-jobbery"—shares of Northern Pacific and Great Northern soared. Then, as well as before, Harriman sold. He took the $58 million he realized, between June of 1906 and March of 1907, on the sale of some of his Northern Pacific and Great Northern stock, and bought into ever more railroads that connected with and enhanced his main trunk lines. Even Mr. Harriman's friends, and they were few, had to admit that these purchases looked bad to the public.

By 1906 Edward H. Harriman had become, in Theodore's eyes, "an undesirable citizen," every bit as wicked as Jay Gould.

Now Mr. Harriman was Theodore's bête noire. It seemed to him that Harriman—who had pussyfooted over to see his sister at Camp Elsinore in the Adirondacks, whose money pulled the strings that made New York's Republican machine dance—was out to *get* him, even as Gould and Roscoe Conkling had once done for his father in the fight over the New York Collectorship back in the 1880s.

Edward H. Harriman's worst mistake, in fact his unpardonable sin, in the eyes of Theodore, and naturally of Bamie, was to let it become known that the President, so the railroad financier always maintained, had made a pre-election promise to him and then welshed on it. The President said flatly, that was a lie, and the whole sordid story broke out into the open on the front page of the *New York World* for April 2, 1907.

Harriman's side of the story was that just before the election of 1904 he had seen the President. At that meeting, Harriman said, he had promised to contribute to the President's campaign if, after election, the President would take care of wealthy old Senator Chauncey Depew of New York by sending him as ambassador to France. Harriman and friends did contribute to the 1904 Republican campaign—$250,000—the largest amount from any individual, group, or corporation.

The President said that he had indeed seen Mr. Harriman privately in October of 1904, but there had been no quid pro quo. He had encouraged the railroad man to support the Republican ticket in New York *State* that then seemed in danger of being defeated. He had not asked Mr. Harriman to support his own national campaign, and the name of Senator Depew had not been mentioned.

Privately, Theodore expressed himself as horrified even at the thought of sending such a decrepit old gentleman as Chauncey Depew as ambassador to France. Wealth was not enough. Hadn't he flatly turned down Cornelius Vanderbilt when he had asked for the same post? Besides, he wanted the diplomatic corps to be staffed with able, younger men. The United States, said Theodore, should be represented by men of the stripe of George Meyer in St. Petersburg and Henry White, United States ambassador to Italy, who had been Theodore's personal, nonpolitical appointments to their important posts. Of course, Bamie's friend, Whitelaw Reid, whom the President had appointed ambassador to Britain immediately following his 1905 inaugural, seemed not to be altogether of that stripe. He was wealthy, of course, and nearing seventy, but he was able.

No one will ever know what exactly was said at that private meeting in October of 1904 between the President and Mr. Harriman. But two things were certain: Theodore was not listening, which often happened when he did not wish to hear; and Harriman had failed to make himself understood, which happened even more frequently. One other thing was sure: from early 1907 on the President was out to get E. H. Harriman, who became a man sorely harassed by the entire Administration in Washington.

"The Harriman Extermination League," as it was called, was no secret enclave with a totally unidentifiable membership. Among the active members of the "League" were the many enemies, especially in the opposing Morgan camp, the little wizard of the big railroads had made in Wall Street on his way up. Equally active and identifiable, of course, was the President himself who, beginning in 1907, spoke openly, sneeringly and often of Mr. Harriman as "a member of the plutocracy" and of Mr. Harriman's Washington lobbyist as "the ambassador of plutocracy."

Much less readily identifiable was the antagonism to E. H. Harriman that was surely and steadily emanating from the President's sister, both before and after the unfortunate public feud over that $250,000 campaign contribution. But the very phrase, "member of the plutocracy," was Bamie's long before Theodore had begun to bandy it about, and she had used it quite early and specifically to describe that curious man, Mr. Harriman, who had tried unsuccessfully to give Sheffield that ridiculously expensive miniature train. The phrase was one of Bamie's spiciest, and it did more damage—as Theodore put it to use with a vengeance against Harriman, and every other member of what he considered "The Plutocracy"—than any of her other spicy remarks.

The phrase first appeared, after that unfortunate miniature train episode, in one of Bamie's letters to her brother from the Adirondacks, reporting, with some distaste, that Mr. Harriman, that "member of the plutocracy"—a class toward which, in general, Bamie did not feel at all spicy—was again back on the summer scene. She told her brother then, and even more firmly during the public feud, that the man could not be trusted. She had been annoyed at his presumption in trying to bestow on Sheffield such an expensive gift, on such short acquaintance, and she resented the implication, in the gift, that her favor and good-will could be bought. No more could Theodore, whom she idolized, have been guilty of making a political deal for $250,000 or for $250 million!

Yet even Bamie, who was basically much more of a conservative Republican than her brother, must have had qualms about the extent to which the President and the Administration hounded poor Mr. Harriman and "The Plutocracy." It was indeed while the anti-Harriman "League" was at its most active that the President's sister made her revealing remark to Colonel Archie Butt at the White House about how all the Roosevelts "think that they are just, but they are hard in a way." Her pensiveness following that comment may have been prompted less by her concern for her Southern mother and her difficulties with her Northern in-laws way back in Civil War days than by the sudden thought that perhaps she herself, when she felt Theodore was threatened in any way, could be more ruthless than any of them.

Despite the efforts of the "League," an Administration bent on his destruction was unable to discover a single thing that was illegal in the way Harriman had built up his railway empire. Admittedly, Harriman had sought power. He had even considered the possibility of running for the Senate himself in 1904. He was naturally bound to tangle with a president quite fond of power himself. No doubt Harriman had been unwise to buy up all those railroads. And of course, as even his friends said, he was utterly tactless and made a very bad witness, from the public's point of view, when called to testify before the Interstate Commerce Commission in 1907. Asked whether he would, if the law permitted, spread his railroad empire "not only over the Pacific Coast, but . . . over the Atlantic Coast," Harriman had answered in one arrogant word, "Yes."

After Harriman had contributed to the campaign of 1904, and told, Theodore flatly refused to receive him at the White House. During the Administration's investigation of the Harriman railroad empire, an old family friend of the Roosevelts, who was a friend to Harriman, too, asked the President to see Mr. Harriman and hear his side of the story. The President said coldly, he might do so, but only if a stenographer were present.

The meeting never came off. Beginning with a steady decline in railroad stocks the worst panic since 1893 hit Wall Street, and Harriman, interviewed by the *New York Times*, said sourly, "I would hate to tell you to whom I think you ought to go for an explanation of all this."

Wall Street and the country—once J. P. Morgan and friends had come to the rescue with quick financial support for a number of shaky institutions—recovered in time. But the argument about what had caused the panic of 1907 in the first place continued for years.

Theodore Rosevelt's supporters—as Franklin D. Roosevelt's were to do several decades later—held that he was no radical but a true conservative. Had the President not preserved the free-enterprise system by saving business from its own excesses? The panic of 1907, they said, was part of a worldwide depression. It had been set off in the United States by the overcapitalization of the entire railroad system and the stock manipulations of such financial wizards as E. H. Harriman, who always managed to ride out boom-and-bust to their own advantage.

On the causes of the panic of 1907, Wall Street went along with the interpretation of Otto H. Kahn of Kuhn, Loeb, who were Harriman's investment bankers. Mr. Kahn said the panic was "largely the result of President Roosevelt's attack on business combinations in general and Mr. Harriman's railroads in particular." One Wall Street economist estimated that during the six months following the passage of the Hepburn bill, railroad and other securities had depreciated in value by nearly $5 billion or "an amount in excess of the total cost of the Civil War."

No wonder the White House door had slammed shut on Edward H. Harriman, that "member of the plutocracy," whose health lasted only into 1909 when Theodore's second term had almost run its course. E. H. Harriman died in September of 1909 of a stomach ailment curiously alike in its symptoms to the cancer that had destroyed Theodore's and Bamie's father many years before.

The awful White House ban on Edward H. Harriman did not, oddly enough, extend to Mrs. J. Borden Harriman, who was the wife of the railroad financier's cousin. Mrs. Harriman was both witty and wealthy and remembered distinctly a White House luncheon she attended in February of 1909. As Mrs. Foraker had done before her, Mrs. Harriman could not help poking a little fun at the autocrat of the White House that Theodore seemed to have become during his last days there. Just before luncheon was served, Mrs. Harriman was startled to have Colonel Archie Butt come over to her twice and whisper anxiously in her ear, "The President will take you in to luncheon." Only then did Mrs. Harriman recall what Oliver Belmont had said after he had attended a White House function: "There is no place in the world where they put on such lugs except at the court of St. Petersburg. A woman has to cross the room to the Czar when he takes her into dinner, instead of his coming to her, and Theodore goes in for the same thing."

Mrs. Harriman crossed the room and took Theodore's arm.

When she asked the President in a voice loud enough for others to hear whether it bothered him to have a Harriman in the White House, Theodore obviously enjoyed her remark more than anyone. After luncheon Theodore further delighted and amused Mrs. Harriman by trying on for all his guests his new African safari suit that had arrived only that morning and asking how they liked it.

No matter how he behaved, one could not help liking the man. As the Irish policeman in Boston told Mrs. Larz Anderson, "He's a darlin' man. But he's so distressin'." And some grew even fonder of him with the years. Toward the end of February in 1909, the crotchety old Sage of Sixteenth Street was beginning to feel very lonely indeed. "Uncle Henry" sent over a chit to the White House asking if he might drop in to say good-bye. Then Henry Adams, who had seen so many presidents come and go, made one of his last trips across Lafayette Square. "After this spring," he told Theodore and Edith, "Andrew Jackson and I will be the solitary monuments of the Square."

One of Theodore's last proud acts in office was to review on Washington's Birthday in 1909 the United States fleet, now composed of sixteen sleek battleships, as it steamed into Hampton Roads, Virginia, at the end of its trip around the world. Theodore had made Admiral Mahan's dream, and his, too, come true. Here at last was a creditable United States navy for all the world to see. During its sixteen-month circumnavigation of the globe, Bamie had been receiving from Admiral Sperry, the Cowleses' best friend with the fleet, full reports of its reception in every important world port, and these confirmed Theodore in his belief that sending the fleet around the world had been "the most important service" he had "rendered to peace."

Mrs. Admiral Cowles, wife of the chief of the Bureau of Equipment, was no less proud of the fleet's performance and of the welcome it received abroad and at home. The review at

Hampton Roads, all the entertaining for fr
with the fleet, kept Bamie almost too busy to
dore's imminent departure from Washingto
the fleet review, she received a most sympa
standing letter from a dear old friend at La
Island.

"I fancy your life for the next ten days," A
wrote, "what with the coming of the fleet and th
administration, will be something of a whirlwind
member Cowles aright, that is the kind of quiet you
glad of the fleet's coming, but not of the administra
We shall miss the President."

Edith did not attend William Howard Taft's ina
March 4, 1909, at the Capitol. She went straight from t
House to Washington's Union Station. She did not s
William Howard Taft break all precedent, as Mrs. Taft
she must do over the objections of the Inaugural Commit
riding with her husband, the new president, up Pennsy
Avenue and home to the White House.

Bamie and Alice had already joined Edith in the preside
waiting room at the station by the time Theodore came—
rectly from the inaugural ceremony for his personally cho
successor. The only Roosevelt to watch the inaugural parade
1909 was young Quentin who would remain behind for a fe
months to finish school in Alexandria. He sat in the official re
viewing stand in front of the White House beside his friend,
Charlie Taft.

When Theodore arrived at the station, he found a crowd of
more than 3,000 well-wishers who had decided to forgo the Taft
inauguration parade. The family walked from the presidential
waiting room through two broad rows of people a dozen deep,
and not a few were in tears. As the train pulled out of Washington's Union Station, Theodore and Edith stood together on
the rear platform.

"Good-bye, Good-bye! Good luck!" he called over and over again. The crowd stayed on until they were two distant dots, for many thought they could still see that big, warm, toothy grin as Theodore continued to wave his shiny black topper high in the air.

CHAPTER XXX

Bubble and Hum at Oldgate

WHEN the Roosevelt family said good-bye to Washington and went back to Sagamore Hill, Bamie made Oldgate the center of her life. For more than twenty years after Theodore left the White House, she held court at Farmington in the rolling Connecticut hills in the most delightfully informal manner, drawing to her from two continents her friends and all the family. Nephews and nieces in particular, their friends and Sheffield's, enjoyed open house at Oldgate, spring, summer, and fall, perhaps even more than they had the freedom of 1733 N Street or, before that, of 689 Madison Avenue. For, despite increasingly painful ailments as she grew older, Bamie retained all the energetic gaiety that had made those other busy establishments so full of happy bubble and hum.

Bamie's guest book at Oldgate bulged with the signatures, the inscriptions, the light verse of its many distinguished visitors. All echoed the sentiment first expressed in its pages on Thanksgiving Day in 1906 by Corinne Roosevelt Robinson in this rhymed toast:

> To Admiral and Mrs. Cowles
> (Magnetic pair of sunlit souls!)
> We sing this hymn of loving praise
> For giving us the best of days.

Prominent among the names in the Oldgate guest book during the twenty-odd years that Bamie made Farmington her year-round residence were those of almost every important British diplomat and dignitary who came to the United States through every change of administration right up to the time of the Democratic Roosevelts—whose careers Bamie followed with keen, affectionate interest though she did not quite live to see them in the White House. Lord Bryce, Sir Cecil Spring-Rice, Sir Ronald Lindsay, the Esme Howards, and dozens of other distinguished Britishers all came to stay with Bamie and to relax at Oldgate in those tense days—before and during the time America fought in World War I—when such close friendships meant so much to the people of both nations. Bamie, too, sent a son to war, and happily lived to see Lieutenant W. Sheffield Cowles, Jr., of the United States Marines return to Oldgate healthy and intact. Assistant Secretary of the Navy Franklin D. Roosevelt virtually kidnapped his young cousin from his overseas division when the war was over and took Sheffield home with him on a navy cruiser to spare Bamie further anxiety.

The pages of the Oldgate guest book during the first three decades of the twentieth century also filled to overflowing with the names of America's own diplomats and statesmen. For Bamie made Farmington a *must* way station for many of the State Department friends who had grown accustomed in Washington to rendezvousing for luncheon or tea at 1733 N Street. Now they went out of their way, while traveling to and from their foreign assignments, to make a side trip to Farmington, if only to take tea with Bamie in the library at Oldgate.

Friends from the Washington years frequently stayed on for days or weeks. Visiting there one autumn on his return from his post as United States Consul General in Manchuria, Willard Straight rhymed his own reasons why in the famous guest book:

> I went away to Far Cathay
> An "open door" to find—
> A door of treaties, journalists—
> Of diplomatic minds.

For this old gate I've searched the East
And finding nary one
Have found a clue, and come to you—
"Oldgate" at Farmington.

It was as if that luxurious little Connecticut town, which had
always been the summer home of many comfortably entrenched
families from Boston, New Haven, and Hartford, had also
become a sort of unofficial State Department resort for diplomats
who could rest there from their arduous foreign duties and feel
at home again in a drawing room where the conversation was
more urbane and relaxed than any they were likely to find elsewhere on their return from abroad. Afternoon tea with Bamie
in the library at Oldgate became in time almost an institution,
an experience that some considered a necessary part of a young
diplomat's education. Friends from the Washington years often
brought promising younger State Department men along with
them to Oldgate or commended them to Bamie's attention. Gist
Blair wrote her from Cannes in 1926: "My young cousin, Percy
Blair, Secretary of our Embassy in London, is with us. He has
been making me a visit and I think him full of talent. One of
these days perhaps you will let me introduce him to you. He is
a studious Blair & keeps up the tradition for personal attractions
in society as well. . . ."

While younger diplomats may have regarded tea at Oldgate
with Mrs. Cowles as part of their training, everyone else simply
relaxed and had fun. Henry Marquand, a friend from the old
Madison Avenue days, often tried to capture in rhyme in
Bamie's guest book what it was that drew everyone there. He
had partial success with this early poem in 1903:

In dream one day I chanced to knock
At Peter's Gate—'twas five o'clock—
With merry twinkle in his eye
He bade me welcome to the sky,
And led me in. I turned and found
A multitude of tables round

With knots of two or three
Celestial gossips drinking tea,
Conversing softly as they sat—
The apotheosis of chat.

One group was larger than the rest,
An angel very simply dressed
Whose wings were scrupulously brushed
Began to speak—the murmuring hushed
One placed his wing behind his ear
And all at once pressed close to hear
And held their peace—did everyone
As Bamie's friends have always done.

Seeing her in those heavenly crowds
I thought I'd sink straight through the clouds.
She beckoned to me with her wing—
A cherub flew a stool to bring—
"Come sit a while," she said, "by me
And sip a cup of repartee."

In sweet discourse the moments passed
As time had never sped so fast,
For hers the gift vouchsafed to few
To find the best that lies in you.
I rose. She said, "What! Don't you know
In heaven it's never time to go!"
And then to make her meaning clear—
"It's always five o'clock up here.
In two hours more 'twill not be seven,
And that's the way we know it's heaven."

Henry Marquand's lines celebrating the daily gathering in the library were eclipsed only by others from the same pen in 1913. "A Bootless Quest" captured Oldgate's happy air of informality:

> At Farmington one summer day
> I land in time for dinner—
> My bag has strangely gone astray
> Oh, would that Cowles were thinner.

His waistcoat wraps me twice around
    But then it doesn't matter
I'll get the pants off Hopkinson
    Oh, would that he were fatter!

The coat I'll take from someone else,
    At least I think I oughter
My arms are most infernal long,—
    Oh, would that they were shorter.

I'll look to Sheffield for my pumps
    He's something of my figger
Although a most attractive lad
    I wish his feet were bigger.

The extraordinary thing about Oldgate's fascination for so many different people over so many years was that it came almost entirely from a hostess whose only means of locomotion was a wheelchair. Beginning in 1912, the very year Theodore came charging back, after his African safari, into the national political arena as a Bull Moose with a vengeance, rheumatoid arthritis had crippled Bamie so badly that it was almost impossible for her to walk. In her chair, the chief propelling force was her devoted small butler, Hopkinson, and, after "Mr. Bearo" installed a little elevator for her use, Bamie was, in her own home, almost as mobile and certainly as graciously ubiquitous as ever.

Even when, in later years, exhaustion from pain, of which she firmly refused to let anyone take notice, limited her daily appearance downstairs to an hour or two in the library at tea, this alone seemed to fill the house at Farmington to overflowing. Somehow the box acousticon, into which one had to speak so Bamie could hear, was simply a ridiculous object among the tea things on the table beside her, of which she made fun, and then one entirely forgot its presence. In the beginning and through all her years at Oldgate, Bamie dressed for this daily occasion with the care of a duchess going to a ball, always in the white tea gown, of which her little dressmaker in New York made at least two or three dozen exact copies.

With Hopkinson and the wheelchair, Bamie managed to travel now and then, down to New York to stay at the Belmont, her favorite hotel, or with the Reids or the Cuttings. Sometimes during the summer or fall, she went with the Admiral to Corinne's Henderson House in upstate New York or out to Sagamore Hill. And once she went all the way back again to Washington for a brief visit to Cabot Lodge, who was so very lonely after Nannie's death. But from 1912 on, Bamie's range —not quite so circumscribed as it had once been long before in her early childhood—was rather severely limited to the big white house set in its pleasant grounds and garden and surrounded by the high fence with the classic gate at the very end of Main Street in Farmington.

Bamie was, therefore, out of the picture during one of the most exciting national campaigns in American history. It was the first time in Theodore's career that she had not been standing in the wings when he took center stage, and it could be said that he would have benefited in those post-Presidential years from some of Bamie's on-the-spot "general advice." Physically, she was quite unable to help Theodore in 1912, and she grieved to the Admiral that "this campaign must be made without the close fellowship & work of some who stood close by him" in the last election. It was perhaps just as well for Bamie's peace of mind that her pain-wracked body kept her out of the Progressive campaign that split the Republican party in two.

Everything Theodore said and did as long as he lived had Bamie's complete support, still her basic convictions inclined rather more to the right of Theodore's Progressive party and towards the Republican regulars who supported William Howard Taft. That huge, genial, lovable man, with whom she had worked so satisfactorily when he had been president of the American Red Cross, was a close personal friend of hers, as dear to her still as he had once been to Theodore. She could not so easily forget him or the warm note he had sent when she congratulated him on his nomination in 1908 as Theodore's own personally chosen successor. "Dear, dear friend," Bill Taft wrote Bamie, "I can't send a formal letter like this dictated from me to you. I must put a little red blood into my expression of my affectionate regard and gratitude for your many kindnesses—W.H.T."

It was distressing to see Theodore so violently at odds with "W.H.T." and with Cabot and Elihu Root, the men who had "stood close by him," until he forced that unforgivable split in the party at the Republican convention of 1912. It was even more distressing to watch Theodore stand at Armageddon, against those close personal friends, and battle—for what? As it turned out, for the eventual benefit of the Democrats and Woodrow Wilson. Still, Bamie would have stood at Armageddon with Theodore had that been physically possible. After he was "definitely in the fight," she told the Admiral, "I long to take an active part, which sounds well from an anti-suffragist!"

By physical default, from 1912 on, Bamie's last waning influence on her brother's career, as politician and journalist, was incorporated into Edith's now prepotent reign over Theodore and Sagamore Hill. Bamie had to admit that, in his later years, the restraining influence of the mistress of Sagamore Hill had positive value, especially since Alice's aggressive championing of her father's interests in Washington's Republican enclaves encouraged him to dash off in directions that ran quite counter to Edith's wiser and more realistic plans for him.

In the Progressive campaign, Alice herself was split right down the middle—between father and husband. Speaker Nick Longworth of Ohio could not but choose to go along with the party regulars and his own Ohio's Taft, and this only increased the intensity of his wife's utter dedication to her father and his candidacy. "Blessed, brilliant Alice" often caused Bamie anxiety. She could not help following the Progressive years, at a distance, every painful step of the way, with her niece and with Theodore, from her wheelchair at Oldgate or while she was taking those awful mud baths at the sanitarium out in Michigan, to which she had first repaired in 1911 in the forlorn hope of curing her rheumatoid arthritis.

Bamie's physical ailments began to plague her in full force

about the time Theodore left the White House at the remarkably early age, for a Sage, of fifty. Bamie herself had just turned fifty-four in March of 1909—when William Howard Taft was inaugurated and the Great White Fleet Theodore had sent around the world came home, with much fanfare. Already attacks of inflammatory rheumatism, aggravated by a nagging skin irritation diagnosed as erysipelas, made walking difficult for her. Nevertheless, Mrs. Admiral Cowles, wife of the chief of the Bureau of Equipment, stayed on in Washington to do more than her share of entertaining for all the friends who had been with the fleet. Besides, it was a matter of pride with Bamie—and Alice, too—to attend all the official functions, the parties, dinners, and teas given in honor of the new President and the new First Lady.

This was a painful period in Bamie's life. Understanding and sympathy, which she never courted, came from an unexpected quarter.

"Do give my love to all the dear people," Edith wrote from Sagamore Hill only a few days after their return. "You seem to reap a little aftermath of farewells, which must be very trying." Edith said that Kermit and Theodore, who "seems just about 25 years old," were "desperately busy" packing for their African safari, and "they both remind me of 'Bye pack Bye's trunk' by their efforts." To this touching reference to the old Bamie saying that had become a family classic, Edith added some good, sound words of advice:

"I am sorry about your poor foot, but probably the time has come when its owner needs a little rest. . . . I meant to beg you to be careful about walking for a time, & only walk on a level & don't walk quickly as you do by nature. . . . Do see a doctor."

Bamie did not follow Edith's advice; there were still too many exciting things to do. While Theodore was off on his long safari with his son—and this caroming expedition left Edith to cope with all the fretful tag ends of their busy lives—Bamie began to take an interest in the promising careers of two young men who were on exactly opposite sides of the political fence. She followed the progress of Eleanor's husband, Franklin Roosevelt, with as much enthusiasm as she worked behind the scenes, through her Republican friends in Connecticut, for Joseph Alsop, that other "Jo-Bob," as Alice Longworth called him, who had married Bamie's other remarkable niece, Corinne, Jr., and lived in nearby Hartford and Avon. The month of July in 1910 found Bamie at Campobello Island and, from there, she wrote "Mr. Bearo," "I love being with Cousin Sallie & Eleanor. Franklin is off on a short cruise. Sheffield has had a fine time fishing . . . & I am enjoying the fish fresh from the water. Baby Cod, they are. . . ."

Since Theodore had—temporarily as it turned out—taken himself out of the political picture, it was almost as if, using Mrs. Senator Foraker's words, Bamie "would live it again." But, in 1911, her ankles became so swollen and painful that Auntie Bye simply had to give up being always on the go. It was then that she went out to the sanitarium at Mt. Clemens in Michigan to take those drastic treatments—deep massages, the strictest of diets, and black mud baths—in a desperate attempt to stay on her feet. From Mt. Clemens, during the winter of 1912, she wrote her "Mr. Bearo," breaking the news gently. The doctors said she might "walk fairly well some day," but when she returned to Oldgate in the spring, she would be in a wheelchair.

From the wheelchair that Hopkinson propelled around the house and grounds at Oldgate, there emanated some strong magnetic current that exercised, on family and friends out in the world of affairs, a strong, compelling attraction. Everyone visited Bamie regularly to report what was going on in Washington, London, Paris. Everyone wrote Auntie Bye—except Alice who communicated with everyone by phone at the weirdest hours— seeking advice or giving her all the latest political gossip. For three decades, the acousticon on the tea table in the library at Oldgate was an eager listening ear trained on the intimate affairs of the whole wide world, and what went into that little box remained discreetly locked in the breast of the mistress of Oldgate, who "never gave anyone away," so Hector, one of the Fergies, had said.

In the opinion of Cousin Susie Parish, who was Eleanor Roosevelt's godmother, "No one ever influenced more people," and speaking of Eleanor in particular, Mrs. Parish said, Auntie Bye's "influence over her was so great."

Eleanor remembered that Auntie Bye's advice about how to get along in Washington when she went there as the wife of President Wilson's Assistant secretary of the navy had been invaluable to her. And everyone, including old Henry Adams, was especially kind, Eleanor said, "because of Auntie Bye and Uncle Ted." During their first three years in Washington, Eleanor and Franklin rented what had once been "The Little White House" on N Street from Auntie Bye, and there, Eleanor also recalled, some very nice man came regularly to tend the flower garden. Busy with her children, her mother-in-law, and her Washington duties, it was some time before Eleanor realized this was not someone hired by Auntie Bye to keep the backyard at 1733 N Street in trim. He turned out to be the head gardener at 1600 Pennsylvania Avenue who came, at the end of his day's duties in the White House conservatories he supervised for Mrs. Woodrow Wilson, to tend Mrs. Cowles's Washington garden.

In 1917 Bamie's keen interest in Connecticut politics took a sudden spurt, for the Admiral pleased her immensely by getting himself elected to the State Legislature. But the bubble and hum at Oldgate and in Bamie's pleasant garden at Farmington began to subside thereafter as she grew less intense about immediate political events affecting the family and the Admiral and more interested in the general trend of world affairs. This was the all-important topic in the later letters she exchanged with Senator Lodge in Washington and with Sir Ronald Ferguson, who became Lord Novar and was active for many years in British politics. Now Farmington became a sanctuary for friends and family buffeted by their own private worlds, a quiet place of many memories for renewing spent energies.

Theodore paid his sister a visit in June of 1918. They sat together in the library at Oldgate and talked of many things: of the awful war that seemed to be drawing to a close;

of how Wilson would certainly make a mess of the peace, when it came; and how Republicans were sure to come back stronger than ever in 1920. Again, as in 1912, Bamie's brother, who was even then only fifty-nine and therefore quite eligible politically, loomed large on the horizon. But Theodore had spent his leonine strength and, as Bamie knew, he was far from well. He was "the same old darling," so Henry Adams wrote "Springy," but his "egotism has grown on him" and "so has his fat." Theodore and Bamie may also have spoken of Henry Adams, who had died only that spring in Washington. Of Theodore, who died in his sleep of a coronary attack at Sagamore Hill on January 6, 1919—less than a year after Henry Adams and six months following his last visit to Oldgate—the sardonic Sage of Washington had also written that all his faults "are but trifles like the warty growths on a magnificent oak tree."

Life went on at Oldgate—at a quickened pace, after Sheffield married a most delightful young woman named Margaret Krech, of whom Bamie thoroughly approved. They had a son, in March of 1923, and Cabot Lodge was one of the first to hear the news from Bamie, who wrote, "A small grandson appeared on the tapis yesterday, and we all four, parents and grandparents are perfectly enchanted." But death came, too, that very spring, on the first of May, in the form of a stroke, to Bamie's "Mr. Bearo." After the military funeral in Farmington for Admiral Cowles, Bamie refused to leave the library until everyone who had entered the old gate to pay their respects to Admiral Cowles had been received. She sat there for hours tightly corseted in her white tea gown and only Sheffield's wife, "Bobbie," knew the excrutiating pain such immobility caused. No, Bamie told Bobbie, she would *not* retire and go upstairs—"They have come to show their affection and I must be here to receive it for him."

Bamie carried on at Oldgate a number of years after the Admiral's death, though now she felt equal only to receiving such close friends as Elisabeth Reid and Olivia Cutting and her immediate family. Her sister, Corinne, Corinne, Jr., and her husband, Joe Alsop, were in and out all the time. Once a year regularly Edith would come to spend exactly one week at Old-gate and then off she would go—as restless in her widowhood as Bamie had once been—on her travels, to Latin America, the Orient, around the world, usually with one of her sons. And over and over again in the Oldgate guest book during spring, summer, and fall as late as 1930 there continued to appear the names of Alice and Nick Longworth, of Ethel and Richard Derby, and of Eleanor and Franklin Roosevelt. For it was to "Auntie Bye," as he called her, too, and to Oldgate, rather than any other home, that Franklin first chose to come in his wheelchair after he had decided, with Eleanor and Louis Howe, that polio would not blight his political career.

Franklin's mother, Cousin Sallie, was with Bamie at Oldgate only nine days before Bamie died, in August of 1931, at the age of seventy-six. Her pain was great, but she patted Cousin Sallie's hand and said firmly, to shut off the flow of sympathy, "Never mind, it's *all* right." These were the last words from Bamie any-one remembered before she went into a coma, out of which the doctors said she would never emerge, and then truly Oldgate was, for a time, a quiet place.

Corinne, Jr., could not bear watching Sheffield and Bobbie day after day at their bedside vigil, and one afternoon she man-aged to get them out of the house for a little exercise. They were on the second green at the Farmington Country Club when they saw running down the fairway Bamie's secretary-companion, Miss Helen Scarth, of whom she sometimes said in her "spicy" way, "dear, wonderful, sweet, lovely, *utterly* incompetent 'Scal.'"

"Hurry," Miss Scarth shouted as soon as she got within range, "Mrs. Cowles is coming down to tea!"

They managed to reach the library just as Hopkinson wheeled her in dressed as usual in her white tea gown. She opened her eyes and fixed each of them, for a moment, with a lucid, indomi-table look. Then, without a word, for she could not speak, she shut her eyes for good as Hopkinson wheeled her to the elevator and up to her room, and there she died that evening.

Remembering how she had lived and died at Oldgate, the old ladies of Farmington said, "Mrs. Admiral Cowles went down like a battleship with all flags flying," and there, said the St. Regis maître d'hôtel, who had once catered at the White House, went "the last of our great ladies." Among the hundreds of messages of condolence that came to Oldgate from all over the world in August of 1931, none offered more appropriate tribute than the words of Hector, one of her devoted Fergies, who cabled:

PEACE TO THE LION-HEARTED.

Bamie, People, and Books

THIS book about Bamie began in the blizzard of 1960. I was having tea with the most youthful person I had ever met—Alice Roosevelt Longworth—and that remarkable Washington personage, whom I had hoped to lure into letting me do *her* biography, suddenly fixed me with a cool, compelling blue eye and said, "Why not do Auntie Bye?" With an eye of my own on the February blizzard outside, which was rapidly enveloping my small two-seater parked on Massachusetts Avenue, I asked, "Who was Auntie Bye?" Mrs. Longworth's answer made me quite forget the weather and set me off on a quest that brought me more pleasure and delight in the people and books I met along the way than I can possibly describe.

It took me, for example, two years of intermittent but persistent search to find the personal memoir that Bamie had written for her son, William Sheffield Cowles, Jr. Wherever possible I enjoy letting people tell their own story, and so Bamie's own words and the words of all those she knew and loved are used frequently throughout this book. My eventual discovery of Bamie's delightful recollections—which were almost right under my nose but buried among the voluminous Roosevelt family letters at Theodore Roosevelt's Birthplace on Manhattan's East Twentieth Street—was more than worth two full years out of my life.

292

My difficulty in unearthing Mrs. Cowles's recollections was simply the usual one between people: lack of understanding. Carleton Putnam in his biography, *Theodore Roosevelt, The Formative Years* (Charles Scribner's Sons) had quoted a few lines from a document dictated by Anna Roosevelt Cowles, referring to it, correctly enough, as "typewritten memoirs." He thought the Theodore Roosevelt Collection in the Widener Library at Harvard might have a copy, but I searched there twice and could not find it. I asked everyone in the Roosevelt family whom I saw about those "memoirs," but no one had ever heard of them. The reason was that they thought of the "memoirs," again correctly, as "letters," for such they turned out to be, half a dozen long letters written at various intervals over the years by an old lady who wanted her son and his descendants to know what it had been like in the days of Theodore Roosevelt. The trouble was that everyone knew I had been given access to the Roosevelt family letters, in various libraries and in private hands, and everyone naturally assumed I had already seen those particular "letters"; they thought I was referring to some totally unknown and undiscovered "memoir" by Mrs. Cowles that they knew nothing about.

It took that competent curator of all the fascinating memorabilia and correspondence at Theodore Roosevelt's Birthplace, Miss Helen MacLachlan, exactly one minute to produce "some memoir Bamie might have written for her son," when I finally thought to put the question to her. After months of research on the premises reading the Roosevelt family correspondence, I realized one day that I had asked everyone but the one person most likely to know the answer, and suddenly Bamie's long-sought memoir was in my hand.

This is what comes of people-watching, which is my particular avocation. I can usually tell, so to speak, as Bamie would say, a duck from a gull but not always a wood thrush from a veery, and that makes it all the more interesting to me. But, busy as I am pursuing such fine distinctions in the surrounding two-legged fauna, I tend to overlook a perfectly obvious fact: that a *thing* like a sheaf of old typewritten pages can mean "letters" to some people and "memoirs" to another. Miss MacLachlan, who looks unaccountably like a younger version of the late Mrs. Theodore Roosevelt, Jr.—and knows all the Roosevelts, inside out, as if she had been—would never have been baffled by nomenclature as I was for so many months. And yet, this was all part of the fun of the quest for Bamie.

Mrs. Longworth warned me in the beginning that Auntie Bye was a complex character. She particularly feared that her first cousin, Eleanor Roosevelt, when I asked her about their mutual aunt, might give me the impression that Auntie Bye had been a totally "good" person, and this simply would not do. Auntie Bye, said Mrs. Longworth, had a terrific capacity for sheer enjoyment and "she shrugged at life, so to speak." If she had lived in medieval times, said Mrs. Longworth, *her* Auntie Bye might have been a St. Teresa, "not of Lisieux but a good jolly abbess like St. Teresa of Avila."

True enough, when I last saw Eleanor Roosevelt, the year before she died, I did get the impression that *her* Auntie Bye was both politically astute and "good"—along with some very valuable insight into Auntie Bye's behind-the-scenes influence on Uncle Ted, and Eleanor as well. Here again, people-watching away at tea with Eleanor Roosevelt in her Manhattan apartment, sandwiched in as I was between the visits of a Hindu photographer and his bride and the new Polish delegate to the United Nations, it suddenly occurred to me that Auntie Bye had no doubt "shrugged at life," though not quite so much as Alice Longworth had, and that Auntie Bye had also been good and wise, too, though not perhaps quite so "good" as Eleanor Roosevelt had been all her life.

I was, then, delighted to find at long last, with Miss Mac-Lachlan's help, Bamie's own memoir that confirmed the results of my people-watching. So, too, did all her other letters—in the Roosevelt family collection at Theodore Roosevelt's Birthplace; in the manuscript division of the Library of Congress (through which Miss Kate M. Stewart, manuscripts historian and specialist in the Theodore Roosevelt period, was my friendly and enthusiastic guide); in the Franklin D. Roosevelt Library at Hyde Park, and among the Lodge Papers at the Massachusetts Historical Society, as well as the letters in private hands, notably those of Mr. and Mrs. William Sheffield Cowles, Jr., of Farmington, Connecticut; of Mrs. Ogden Reid of New York City and Purchase, New York; of Auntie Bye's other remarkable niece, Mrs. Francis W. Cole (formerly Mrs. Joseph Alsop) of Hartford and Avon, Connecticut, and of Auntie Bye's great-niece, Mrs. Dean Sage of the Triangle-T Ranch, Sheridan, Wyoming.

I hope the use of this material so generously put at my disposal and my attempt to let Bamie tell her story in her own words have come as close as possible to the way such a woman might like best to be remembered.

The kind of woman Bamie was, especially in her middle years, was no doubt best caught, on canvas, by a little-known but extremely talented portraitist in oils, Ellen Emmett Rand of Farmington, Connecticut. Bamie sat for "Bay" Emmett during the fall of 1904 when she was forty-nine. This painting, photographed by E. Irving Blomstrann of New Britain, Connecticut, and reproduced on the jacket and in this book, still hangs in the dining room of Bamie's beloved Oldgate, the family home of the Cowleses at Farmington. It tells what one of America's great ladies was really like, at a glance—from her own strangely compelling, almost hypnotic blue eyes.

To round out my portrait of Bamie, I used not only her words and those of her friends and family but quite a number of interesting books that helped set the Washington and world stage on which she played her role with such gusto. Others interested in the period and its people might like to read:

Published Correspondence

The Letters of Henry Adams, edited by Worthington Chauncey Ford; Houghton Mifflin; 2 volumes; 1938. (Because, among American historians and Washington observers, he was the greatest, the most human, the most astute, and the most candidly outspoken of them all.)

Selected Letters of Henry Adams, edited by Newton Arvin; Farrar, Straus; 1951.

The Letters of Theodore Roosevelt, selected and edited by Elting E. Morison; Harvard University Press; 1951–54. (8 volumes in all, yet this definitive edition is but a handy, almost pocket-sized selection compared with the dazzling bulk of the twenty-sixth president's official and private correspondence.)

Letters from Theodore Roosevelt to Anna Roosevelt Cowles, edited by Anna Roosevelt Cowles; Charles Scribner's Sons; 1924. (This represents about a third of the letters Bamie received from her brother. She edited them for publication, seven years before she died at Oldgate, with a fine Victorian hand and an eye as acute as Theodore's for what would make posterity think well of him.)

Selections from the Correspondence of Theodore Roosevelt and Henry Cabot Lodge; Charles Scribner's Sons; 1925. (Senator Lodge edited these two volumes of letters for publication with, as he said in his preface, "the wise counsel and sympathetic aid of Mrs. Roosevelt." While in the course of this task, he wrote Bamie, at Oldgate, on April 3, 1924, how it was being done: "...I am at work on my correspondence with Theodore....I went over the first five years with Edith and I found that I was in entire agreement with her as to omissions. There are words resembling invectives, let us say, such as he did not print in his autobiography and which were not printed during his life, which I cordially agreed ought to be left out because they were so extreme, and I am sure that in cold blood, although he might have made the same criticism, he would not have made it in those precise words. That is only a question of a few words here and there. Of course, I left out all purely personal letters or family allusions, except where they come in natural connection with the general subject of his letter. Among my letters and, of course, still more among yours, there are some which are naturally extremely private, relating only to private affairs of his own family or of mine. Those go out. There was one which I happen to remember—a perfectly delightful description of Alfred Roosevelt, but I hardened my heart and took it out with Edith's full approval. It was very funny, but an ignorant public would not have understood it...."

Together, Senator Lodge and Edith used a firm Victorian hand on Theodore's correspondence, presumably for his own good. Corinne, Jr., always felt that much of the Roosevelt humor, particularly that of Uncle Ted and Auntie Bye, came from the kind of adjectives they used to describe people, and this she thought came from their Southern mother. In some of the unedited letters of Theodore Roosevelt, he occasionally speaks of so-and-so as an "18-in. calf from head to foot" or of someone else as a "circumcised skunk." A less conservative generation of Americans would, perhaps, have appreciated even more the robust flavor of Theodore if these spur-of-the-moment, Bunyan-esque characterizations had not been cut out of his letters to Lodge or, as in the case of his personal letters to Edith, lost to posterity in their entirety when, after his death, she burned the lot. The two-volume Lodge correspondence is, despite these few excisions and omissions, vastly entertaining.)

The Letters and Friendships of Sir Cecil Spring-Rice, A Record, edited by Stephen Gwynn; 2 volumes; Houghton Mifflin; 1929. (Through Nannie and Cabot Lodge, through Henry Adams and John Hay, as well as through Bamie and Theodore, "Spwing-Wice of the Bwitish Legation," as he called himself, was one of the best friends America ever had.)

The Letters of Archie Butt, Personal Aide to President Roosevelt; Doubleday, Page; 1924. (Colonel Butt was a most unusual combination: a military man with a distinct literary flair and certainly the best of the president-watchers.)

The Life and Letters of John Hay by William Roscow Thayer; Houghton Mifflin; 1915. (Two fine volumes to put beside the letters of his old friend, "Uncle Henry.")

Biography and Recollections

An Autobiography of Theodore Roosevelt; Charles Scribner's Sons; 1913. (A bowdlerized version, by himself.)

My Brother, Theodore Roosevelt by Corinne Roosevelt Robinson; Charles Scribner's Sons; 1921. (Bamie thought her sister's recollections too sentimental, but Mrs. J. Borden Harriman said, "All Roosevelts have a delightfully mad enthusiasm for each other and one can't help being fond of one of them without presently acquiring a contagious affection for all, and an amusing share in the family anecdotes." This book and the three that follow are full of them.)

All in the Family by Theodore Roosevelt, Jr.; G. P. Putnam's Sons; 1929.

Day Before Yesterday by Mrs. Theodore Roosevelt, Jr.; Doubleday; 1959.

Crowded Hours by Alice Roosevelt Longworth; Charles Scribner's Sons; 1933. (Great fun.)

The Roosevelt Family of Sagamore Hill by Hermann Hagedorn; Macmillan; 1954. (A charming group portrait by a veteran Roosevelt-watcher and poet. Mr. Hagedorn, who was good enough to put at my disposal many unpublished interviews that he and his daughter, Mary, had with members of the Roosevelt family, edited for Scribner's the definitive twenty-four-volume *Works of Theodore Roosevelt*. His *Roosevelt in the Bad Lands* and *Boy's Life of Theodore Roosevelt* are must reading for big and little boys both.)

Theodore Roosevelt, A Biography by Henry F. Pringle; Harcourt, Brace; 1931.

The Republican Roosevelt by John M. Blum; Harvard University Press; 1954.

Power and Responsibility, The Life and Times of Theodore Roosevelt by William Henry Harbaugh; Farrar, Straus and Cudahy; 1961.

Theodore Roosevelt, An Intimate Biography by William Roscow Thayer; Houghton Mifflin; 1919. (During her Oldgate days, Bamie recalled many episodes from the past for the benefit of this biographer.)

Roosevelt, The Story of a Friendship by Owen Wister; Macmillan; 1930. (He, too, visited Bamie at Oldgate in her later years and gave her advice on how to edit her letters from Theodore. She probably did not take it. Owen Wister wrote Bamie in 1925: "We've had 2 or 3 Presidents whose domestic policies equalled Theodore's; but didn't his foreign policy eclipse anyone's?" He thought that, even by the twenties, "The job has got beyond the size of any human being...."

Roosevelt and the Russo-Japanese War by Tyler Dennett; Peter Smith; 1958. (An astute historian on why, in certain respects, Theodore's foreign policy did "eclipse anyone's.")

Henry Adams by Elizabeth Stevenson; Macmillan; 1955.

In the Days of McKinley by Margaret Kernochan Leech; Harper; 1959.

Henry Cabot Lodge, A Biography by John A. Garraty; Knopf; 1953.

The Autobiography of Thomas Collier Platt; B. W. Dodge & Co.; 1910.

The Life of Whitelaw Reid by Royal Cortissoz; Scribner's; 2 volumes; 1921.

E. H. Harriman, A Biography by George Kennan; Houghton Mifflin; 2 volumes; 1922.

Diplomatically Speaking by Lloyd Griscom; Little, Brown; 1940.

Breaking New Ground by Gifford Pinchot; Harcourt, Brace; 1947.

Across the Busy Years by Nicholas Murray Butler; Scribner's; 2 volumes; 1939–40.

The Autobiography of William Allen White; Macmillan; 1946.

The Autobiography of Eleanor Roosevelt; Harper; 1961.

Mrs. R., The Life of Eleanor Roosevelt by Alfred Steinberg; Putnam; 1958.

Recollections of Full Years by Mrs. William Howard Taft; Dodd, Mead; 1914.

I Would Live It Again by Julia Foraker; Harper; 1932.

Never a Dull Moment by Marguerite Cassini; Harper; 1956. (The title is apt.)

Presidents & Pies by Isabel Anderson; Houghton Mifflin; 1920.

From Pinafores to Politics by Florence Jaffray (Mrs. J. Borden Harriman); Henry Holt; 1923.

Walks about Washington by Francis E. Leupp; Little, Brown; 1915.

Trolley Trips in & about Fascinating Washington by K. M. Abbott; Rand McNally & Co., pictorial guide; 1900.

White House Gossip by Edna M. Colman; Doubleday, Page; 1927.

Inside History of the White House by Gilson Willets; Christian Herald; 1908.

In & Out of the White House by Ona Griffin Jeffries; Wilfred Funk; 1960.

The Quest for Corvo by A. J. A. Symons; Michigan State University Press; 1955. (This has nothing at all to do with the Roosevelts but will delight anyone interested in the detective work of a beautifully obsessed biographer in pursuit of his character.)

Lilian Rixey
May 31, 1963

Index

307

Sherman, William T., 10
Southern Pacific Railroad, 205
Souvestre, Mlle., 13-14, 15-17, 18, 21, 26, 85, 90, 165, 197, 228, 234
Spanish-American War, 103, 104, 109, 111, 116, 118, 120-26, 152
Sperry, Admiral, 153, 276
Spooner, Senator, 162
Spring-Rice, Cecil, 63, 64, 66, 68, 69, 71, 78, 130, 143, 145, 236, 238-43, 268, 280, 289
State Department, 76, 124, 197, 201, 232, 233, 236, 268, 280, 281
State of Texas (relief ship), 124, 125
Steffens, Lincoln, 200
Sternburg, Baron Hermann Speck von, 179, 222, 232, 237
Sternberg, Baroness Hermann Speck von, 232
Stevenson, Adlai E., 159
Stewart, Kate M., 294
Stillman, Mr., 215, 217
Storer, Bellamy, 161
Straight, Willard, 280
"Summer White House," 213, 215, 219
Swinderen, Jonkheer R. de Marees van, 225-26
Sylph (presidential yacht), 219

Taft, Charlie, 277
Taft, William Howard, 107, 261, 269, 277, 284-86
Taft, Mrs. William Howard, 277
Takahira, Kogoro, 231, 268
Tammany, 98
Tarkington, Booth, 220
Taylor, Dr. Charles F., 5, 9
Texas (battleship), 254

Thayer, Nathaniel, 20-21
Tiffany, Willie, 126
Togo, Admiral, 236
Topeka (cruiser), 121
Town Topics, 187, 188, 231, 249, 250, 252
Townsend, Mrs., 140-41
"Tranquillity," 31, 44
Trimble, William, 34
Tweed Ring, 29
Tweedmouth, Lord, 198

Union Pacific Railroad, 205, 214-15
United States Steel Corporation, 211

Vanderbilt, Cornelius, 271
Vanderbilt, Mrs. Cornelius, 260
Venezuela, 91-94, 97, 103
Victoria, Queen, 195

Walsh, Thomas J., 141
Weld family, 26
Westbrook, Theodore, 38-41
Wetmore, George Peabody, 186, 187
White, Daisy, 102
White, Henry, 98, 99, 238, 242, 272
White, Stanford, 141
White, William Allen, 174-75, 220
White House, 177-82, 183-90, 191, 193-95, 220-21, 222-26, 230, 231-33, 240, 245, 259, 262, 275
Wilhelm, Kaiser, 199, 200, 237
Wilson, Woodrow, 257, 285, 289
Wilson, Mrs. Woodrow, 288
Winslow, Cameron, 227
Wister, Owen, 220
Wood, Leonard, 116, 151, 152
Wyndham, Percy, 187

Yale University, 112, 127